Dissonance (if you are interested)

Dissonance
(if you are interested)

Rosmarie Waldrop

THE UNIVERSITY OF ALABAMA PRESS

Tuscaloosa

Copyright © 2005
The University of Alabama Press
Tuscaloosa, Alabama 35487-0380
All rights reserved
Manufactured in the United States of America

Typeface: New Baskerville

∞
The paper on which this book is printed meets the minimum requirements of
American National Standard for Information Sciences—Permanence of Paper
for Printed Library Materials, ANSI Z39.48-1984.

Library of Congress Cataloging-in-Publication Data

Waldrop, Rosmarie.
    Dissonance (if you are interested) / Rosmarie Waldrop.
        p. cm. — (Modern and contemporary poetics)
    Includes bibliographical references and index.
    ISBN 0-8173-1469-5 (cloth : alk. paper) — ISBN 0-8173-5197-3 (pbk. : alk.
paper)
        1. Waldrop, Rosmarie—Authorship. 2. Poetry—Authorship. 3. Poetics. I. Title.
II. Series.
    PS3573.A4234D57 2005
    811'.54—dc22
                                                                        2005000111

Dissonance
(if you are interested)
leads to discovery
—William Carlos Williams

Contents

III. POETICS

Acknowledgments

"Monsieur Teste and Der Ptolemäer: Abstraction in the Fiction of Valéry and Benn," *East-West Review* 1, No. 3 (winter 1965), 317–27.

"Helmut Heissenbüttel, Poet of Contexts," *Germanic Review* (March 1969), 132–42.

"Marat/Sade: A Ritual of the Intellect," *Bucknell Review* 18, No. 2 (fall 1970), 52–69.

"A Basis of Concrete Poetry," in *Twentieth-Century Poetry, Fiction, Theory,* ed. H. R. Garvin (Lewisburg, PA: Bucknell UP, 1977), 141–52.

"Charles Olson: Process and Relationship," *Twentieth-Century Literature* 23, No. 4 (December 1977), 467–87.

"Mirrors and Paradoxes," *Kentucky Romance Quarterly* 26, No. 2 (1979), 143–55.

"Calling All Ants," in *New York Times Book Review* (December 1, 1985). This is the original title and publication information for the essay titled "Palmer's *First Figure.*"

"Chinese Windmills Turn Horizontally: On Lyn Hejinian," in *Temblor* 10 (fall 1989), 219–23. A longer version of this talk was presented at the conference on "Radical Poetries/Critical Address" at SUNY Buffalo, in April 1988.

"Shall We Escape Analogy?" *Studies in 20th-Century Literature* 13, No. 1 (winter 1989), 113–29.

Schwindel. Gefühle, W. G. Sebald. A peer review report of *Vertigo* [literally *Vertigo. Feelings*] (Frankfurt: Eichborn, 1990) for New Directions, April 1995.

"*Rocks on a Platter* and *Miniatures.*" This chapter is a combination of two peer reviews written for Wesleyan University Press in 1997 and 2001, respectively.

"From White Page to Natural Gaits: Notes on Recent French Poetry," *American Poet* (spring 1998), 31–38.

"Scalapino's *New Time.*" This chapter was originally a 1998 reader's report to Wesleyan University Press.

"Zukofsky's *Le Style Apollinaire.*" This chapter was originally a 1998 reader's report to Wesleyan University Press.

"The Joy of the Demiurge," *Translation: Linguistic, Literary, and Philosophical Perspectives*, ed. William Frawley (Newark: U of Delaware P, 1984), 41–49.

"Silence, the Devil, and Jabès," in *The Art of Translation: Voices from the Field*, ed. Rosanna Warren (Boston: Northeastern UP, 1989), 225–37.

"Alarms and Excursions," in *The Politics of Poetic Form* (New York: Roof Books, 1990), 45–73.

"Split Infinite," *Denver Quarterly* 27, No. 4 (spring 1993), 102–06.

"A Key into the Key," *A Key into the Language of America* (New York: New Directions, 1994), xiii–xxiv.

"Form and Discontent," *Diacritics* 26, No. 3/4 (fall–winter 1996), 54–63.

"Thinking of Follows," in *Onward: Contemporary Poetry and Poetics*, ed. Peter Baker (New York: Peter Lang, 1996), 73–83.

"The Ground Is the Only Figure: Notebook Spring 1996," (Providence, RI: Impercipient Lecture Series 1, No. 3, 1997).

"Between, Always," *The Hanky of Pippin's Daughter* and *A Form/Of Taking/It All* (Evanston, IL: Northwestern UP, 2001), vii–xix.

"Nothing to Say and Saying It," *American Letters & Commentary* 14 (2002), 24–28.

ILLUSTRATIONS IN "A BASIS OF CONCRETE POETRY":

Décio Pignatari, "beba coca cola," *Artes Hispanicas* 1, No. 3/4 (winter–spring 1968), guest ed. Mary Ellen Solt.

Gerhard Rühm, "bleiben," *Gesammelte Gedichte und visuelle Texte* (Hamburg: Rowohlt, 1970), 270.

Uwe Bremer, "rendering the legible illebigle" and Heinz Gappmaier, "ich," *Anthology of Concrete Poetry*, ed. Emmet Williams (New York: Something Else Press, 1967)

Introductory Note

Every word implies a world of expression that precedes it, that is both permission and obstacle. And a poet depends on a community (both present and past) sharing a language. This came home to me on a personal level when I immigrated into the United States. After a while I found it impossible to write poetry in German while "living in English." It is true, many expatriate writers have been able to do just that. I suspect they had fully developed their working relation with their language, whereas I was a fumbling beginner, without any basis to build on. At this stage, the company of German books was not sufficient. I would have needed a physically present community that shared my language.

It followed, I thought, that the only way I could work with poetry would be translating (into German) and teaching. It was only gradually that I mustered the courage to attempt poems in English and to translate into English. It came with the realization that the discrepancies between my two languages need not be an obstacle, but could, on the contrary, become a generative force.

Looking back at the early essays in the section "Apprenticeship and Affinities," it seems that my choice of subjects was motivated by two questions of form that became important to me as a writer (and to many other writers). One is the question of genre and of countering the expectations of genre: how Valéry and Benn undermine narrative ("The Urge to Abstraction"), how the Concrete poets make syntax spatial rather than grammatical ("A Basis of Concrete Poetry"), how Peter Weiss combines two dramatic modes that seem mutually exclusive ("Marat/Sade: A Ritual of the Intellect"). The other question is the move away from metaphor in poetry and toward an emphasis on contiguity: metonymy, the horizontal relations of combination and syntax, the reference to the context ("Helmut Heissenbüttel," "Charles Olson," "Shall We Escape Analogy").

Of course, reading and writing is a two-way traffic. Reading is experience. It shapes our thinking as much as it is determined by our thoughts and predilections. T. S. Eliot is right to say: "A thought to Donne was an experience; it modified his sensibility. When a poet's mind is perfectly equipped for its work, it is constantly *amalgamating disparate experience*." But Eliot is preposterous in reserving this amalgamating function of the brain for poets and postulating the "ordinary man's" experience as "chaotic, irregular, fragmentary."[1]

The three essays on translation struggle with the process and with the problem of where to position the translation in regard to the conflicting claims of source and target language. Over the years, I have moved closer to the pole of "foreignness," allowing more of the strangeness of the foreign language into the English. But as Wilhelm von Humboldt put it: "Translation should indeed have a foreign flavor to it, but only to a certain degree. . . . As long as one does not feel the foreignness (*Fremdheit*) yet does feel the foreign (*das Fremde*), a translation has reached its highest goal; but where foreignness appears as such, and more than likely even obscures the foreign, the translator betrays his inadequacy."[2] Just how and where to draw this line is not easy to know and must be decided for each individual case.

Within each section of this book, the essays are presented in chronological order.

Dissonance (if you are interested)

I

APPRENTICESHIP AND AFFINITIES

The limits of one's writing are the limits of one's reading.
—Norma Cole

The mind has no edge, but the folds of the brain afford both the maximum surface for touch and the possibility to fall between them inexorably like the sequence of seasons.
—Friederike Mayröcker

The Urge to Abstraction

When I began graduate studies at the University of Michigan in 1959 New Criticism was in full swing. For me it was an exciting change from the biographical criticism that had been the dominant mode at the Universities of Würzburg and Freiburg (although a few *Anglisten* had begun to talk of the new trend under the solemn name of *werkimmanente Interpretation*). New Criticism and the Russian Formalists to whom it introduced me taught me the invaluable skill—maybe I should say art—of close reading, close attention to texts, to details. As we know, God (or the devil!) is in the detail, no matter how thrilling the large sweep of recent theory.

I had the good fortune to study with Austin Warren, one of the subtlest and most erudite among the New Critics. Only the poor practitioners did what all of New Criticism has been bashed for: disregard context and history. For Austin Warren it was unthinkable not to put the work in its context of history, other arts, philosophy, and religion, though the currently privileged areas of sociological and political thought were less present. He taught me that we must always take *everything* into account, though there is freedom and variety in where we place our emphasis. I am amused to find that in recent theory, detail has been devalued as a "women's concern." If it is indeed necessary to assign gender roles, I propose to amend the phrase to "*valued* as a women's concern" and to welcome men like Aby Warburg and Walter Benjamin as honorary women.

My first published essay was originally titled "*Monsieur Teste* and *Der Ptolemäer:* Abstractness in the Fiction of Valéry and Benn" and appeared in *The East-West Review* 1, No. 3 (winter 1965). It now seems strange to me that I wanted to compare two works so different, written in different countries and in times that were separated by two World Wars. The oldest part of *Monsieur Teste*, "The Evening with M. Teste," goes back to 1895 (though the last fragments were added to the volume as late as 1946). Benn's novella was written in 1947.

It is true that the two works illuminate each other, but I was mostly interested in the way that both go against the grain of narration, against the norms of genre. I now think I was also fascinated, at least subliminally, by the way they illustrate the essential relation with death inherent in writing, art, knowledge. As Hélène Cixous says in her discussion of Poe's "Oval Portrait," "Life cannot be on both sides. Double bind: either you do not render life or you take it. Everything is a failure, *everything is crime.*"[1]

The following text is somewhat revised.

The Urge to Abstraction stands at the beginning of every art.
—Wilhelm Worringer

Islamic art is the textbook example for abstract art. The religion's taboo on representation explains it to some extent, but not sufficiently. André Malraux does better. He sees abstraction as a rejection of the human in favor of cosmos, fate, God. Islamic art is abstract because "Islam—all of Asia maybe—was interested in God, but never in man."[2] This is a "better" explanation because it also applies when there is no taboo on representation. The method, then, is to isolate things from their human context and place them in a sacred one. This is the principle of ritual and therefore, in literature, closest to drama. Even without considering the origins of drama, we can find plenty of examples for a tendency toward ritual in contemporary plays—most striking in those of Jean Genet. *Les Bonnes,* for example, consists entirely in the rehearsing and enacting of a murder in which it does not matter who is killed.

In seeming opposition to Malraux, Wilhelm Worringer defines abstraction as man's rejection of nature, as the result of a "conflict between man and the natural object which he sought to wrest from its temporality and unclarity" by giving it "a value of necessity and a value of regularity."[3] Really, the difference is slight. It is one of emphasis— and of secularization.

Testimonies to this nonacceptance of nature abound in literature, at least since the second half of the nineteenth century, from Arthur Rimbaud's "dérèglement de tous les sens" to Malraux's "Our art seems to me a correcting of the world" (*Noyers* 90). Though the alternative is not necessarily abstraction. In poetry, attempts at abstraction have gone as far as destroying the relation of the words and their denotation, which, in the extreme, leads to the isolation of syllables and even of letters, as in the "lettriste" experiments of Isidore Isou and his followers.

Among literary genres, fiction seems the most remote from abstraction, for it usually depends on the presentation of a series of events happening either in the physical sphere (as in the adventure novel) or on a psychological level. Even novels that are primarily concerned with intellectual problems are usually careful to provide a physical balance: the dialogues of Malraux's characters are embedded in action; the treatise on the disintegration of values in Hermann Broch's *The Sleepwalkers* is cut into pieces and interleaved with narration.

The abstractness of *Monsieur Teste* and *Der Ptolemäer* (*The Ptolemean*) lies not so much in the subject, which is thought or, rather, thinking, but in Paul Valéry's and Gottfried Benn's refusal to give it this balance with action.[4] As for its emphasis, it is not Malraux's abstraction, not a rejection of the human, at least not of the human mind, and certainly not in favor of the sacred (even though Benn's protagonist briefly flirts with mysticism). Both seem closer to Worringer's definition, although neither novel phrases its rejection in terms of nature, but rather of the material world generally, of so-called reality.

In both novels external events are reduced to a minimum. In *Monsieur Teste* we are given an evening with a visit to a theater, some conversation fragments, and M. Teste's going to bed; two letters with hardly any events; and a logbook of thoughts. This is hardly enough for the reader to get caught up in his life, hardly enough activity to energize a narrative. In *The Ptolemean* we see the ruins of World War II, a change of seasons, and the business of a beauty shop, but these are either static background or a cipher for something else.

We do get some physical description of Teste, but it is mostly given in abstract terms or in connection with them: "This skull that made acquaintance with the angles of the capital" (21) or "When he talked he never lifted an arm or a finger: he had *killed the marionette*" (17). The same may be said for the physical details in the "panopticon" of the Ptolemean's mind: "The Occident! Born out of the Western Mediterranean, then some terrestrious gains—a prow in Amalfi, a kiln in the Ardennes—amphibious: scales, but at the same time feet—: a dragon! Continental gravity and urge towards the sea" (216).

These quotations also show the difference in style. Valéry works by restriction to essentials and achieves a somewhat dry, skeletal effect.[5] Benn, although he elaborates, makes his language abstract by extensive use of scientific terms. We could almost think of the difference in terms of neoclassical and Baroque styles if Benn's "Baroque" were not overlaid with the hard-edged abruptness of Expressionism.

The main characters themselves reject materiality. The difference here is that Teste has already completed his rejection, whereas the Ptolemean's is in process. It is this process that takes up most of the novella. Both reject action, which, as expenditure of energy, is most closely connected to life and nature. It is mentioned only in the subjunctive: "If he had turned the steady power of his mind against the world" (*Teste* 19). "Of course, one could bring it to the attention of the public" (*Ptolemäer* 207). For everything else, their manner of negation is different and in proportion to the degree of rejection completed. In Monsieur Teste's world the negated things are simply annihilated. In this respect he is the heir of Stéphane Mallarmé's "bibelot aboli," even though Valéry denied any connection with Mallarmé and claimed the character was closer to his idea of Edgar Degas as "a person reduced to the rigor of a hard drawing, a Spartan, Stoic, Jansenist artist."[6]

In *Monsieur Teste* the historical situation is ignored. Teste exists in a vacuum, in timelessness. There is no mention of a detail that could be used as chronological indication, not even the toilettes of the ladies at the opera. And while one of M. Teste's great subjects of research is "the delicate art of duration, time, its distribution and reign" (17), it is the abstract notion of time, not the historical one. We would look in vain for traces of the Dreyfus Affair or, in the later parts of the story, of World War I.

The same holds for society. Contact with people cannot be altogether excluded from the novel, because Valéry needs a narrator of sorts, a person to tell about Monsieur Teste. But Teste himself ignores people to a large extent—"He did not smile, said neither good morning nor good evening; he did not seem to hear the 'How do you do?'" (17)—unless he uses them as objects for observation, as he does with the crowd at the opera. His attitude makes the narrator feel "confounded with things: one felt pushed back, a part of the houses, of the hugeness of space, of the bustling colors in the street" (18).

Monsieur Teste's voluntary isolation seems to stem from immoderate pride: "What, this block ME finds parts outside itself!" (41). Even though his logbook admits that his solitude—"the lack over the years of friends known long and deeply"—costs him dearly (45), his solipsism seems absolute: "what do I care about others . . . I am *chez MOI*, I speak my language," which is later called "the language Self" (42). The "monster of isolation" (33) is aware of the limitations of such a retreat into himself: "I know myself by heart. The heart too" (24), but it seems to be the necessary laboratory condition for his mental operations.

It is in his intellect that M. Teste concentrates all of his energy, paying little attention to the body ("he ate as one would take a purge" [17]), or to the emotions, which he has disciplined to a point where he can play with them ("He became passionate at will and in order to attain a definite goal" [18]). His goal is to explore all the possibilities of consciousness by way of precise logical thinking—without realizing that this is a contradiction in terms, that his commitment to logic will be an obstacle and limitation rather than an aid to exploring *all the possibilities*. The preferred procedure of his "intellectual gymnastic" (17) is classification, expressed in his motto, "To die learnedly . . . *Transiit classificando*. These views [capable of generalization] kill the others which cannot be extended to the general" (39). He finds his beauty in clarity, in the general, in abstract laws—as if to illustrate Worringer's urge to abstraction, which tries "to wrest the natural object out of its natural context, out of the unending flux of being, to purify it of all its dependence upon life, i.e. of everything about it that was arbitrary, to render it necessary and irrefragable to approximate it to its absolute value."[7]

In all of his operations, M. Teste is extremely careful not to attach himself. He detaches himself even from all he knows. Only unsolved problems interest him, and of those, only "the *ease* or the *difficulty* of knowing them" (19). He finally draws back from even the "supreme thought" that he had prayed for, "because no other can follow it" (37).

He wants to stay "always upright on the cape Thought" (39), independent from any condition outside his intellect, independent especially from contingency and change. By bringing everything under the control of his will, he becomes free to experiment with ideas as with chemicals, now "manipulating and mixing, changing, putting in communication" (19), now treating them with repetition: "he watered them with numbers" (17). Finally, he lives not just "in the midst" but "*by means of* rare states, in a perpetual supposition of purely ideal experiences; continually using borderline conditions" (43, my italics).

In this "personal game" (44), things outside his thoughts have no function except to provide material for experimental transformation. Hence his close observation: "he did not lose an atom of all that became perceptible" (21). Even his wife—how amazing that he has one —does not know whether he loves her, or whether he studies her, or whether "he studies through" her (31).

In the course of the experiment, the material is destroyed by the intellect, the object his eyes are fixed on is "the object that his mind wants to reduce to nothing" (26). His wife thinks that this destruction is unconscious, that he does not know what he petrifies. But Teste's words "I obliterate the quick" (17) seem to indicate the contrary. In any case, this destruction is a quality inherent in intellectual power in Valéry's sense. As he says in "Introduction à la méthode de Léonard de Vinci," "The character of man is consciousness, and that of consciousness a perpetual exhausting, a detaching without rest or exception of all that appears, whatever it may be."[8]

In Benn's novella the case is different. The negation of reality is not yet complete. The historical situation, winter 1947, "a winter during the occupation time" (205), impinges with its postwar confusion and chaos, its ruins, heaps of rubble, frozen bodies lying in the streets —and the corpses of recent history in the minds. It makes all too understandable a striving for abstraction as the only possibility of repose, as the means to get out of contingency into a realm of clarity and necessity. At the beginning of the story, the Ptolemean, our first-person narrator, felt the material and social world so unbearable that he tried to annihilate it by force: "Finally alone! At last even the ringing and knocking at the door began to annoy me; I aimed a machine gun at the street of approach and shot down all suspects" (205). This entails, naturally, a discussion of morality or, rather, its absence. Monsieur Teste, too, is detached from any moral issue (an Abbé tells his wife that "he abstracts himself terribly from good, but luckily he abstracts himself from evil also" [33]), but it is a personal, individual detachment. In the Ptolemean's world, such an attitude is part of the historical situation:

> Today the moral evaluation of deaths—whether so-called normal or induced—was completely irrelevant, as out of date as weeping women and stand-up collars[9] . . . If there had once been a specifically moral aura to mankind—and reading of old writings makes it appear likely—by our time it had waned altogether. (206)

After the two World Wars, it is romanticism to imagine an individual corpse.

The Ptolemean's act of violence seems completely out of character. He emphatically does not want to act. Even on a symbolic level, action would involve him in his society, in all he wants to get away from. We quickly come to suspect his alleged taking to the machine gun as rhetoric, a device to introduce the comment on morality. It is also a metaphor for what he does in the course of the novella: looking at the physical ruins around him, he makes all of Western culture pass in review and proceeds to reject and "destroy" it in his mind.

His profession of beautician is part of the general ironical relativization. Although Benn takes some pains to reconcile the Ptolemean's profession and his intellectualism by making him an autodidact, we are not to take this seriously. The protagonists of Benn's earlier prose writings are almost always physicians, so the hairdresser seems to signal withdrawal from meaningful action. It seems a self-irony of the physician Gottfried Benn—perhaps also of the writer Benn, who for a while tried to put "a good face" on the Nazi state. But it is definitely emblematic of the Ptolemean's view of the world: he sees it as a sham surface on something no longer curable but, rather, ready to be destroyed:

> To give advice concerning a broken fingernail, to evaluate combs, to recommend Birkenbalsam Hair Restorer, while in my mind

thinking destroyed and destroying things: this paradox I had developed to the point of virtuosity. (225)

What respect he might have left for accepted values and institutions —the state, for instance—crumbles when a close look shows it to be empty behind a facade of excess administration: "It [the state] tracked down rabbits and had tooth-fillings registered. . . . In concert halls and lecture series it processed the beautiful, made it fall into line: the bow of Philoctetes and the 'Parzenlied' well behind the *Weisse Flieder* and the *Caprifishers*" (213), the latter two titles being popular songs. Likewise, he attacks the idea of progress, demonstrating that history is a series of contingencies, and ironizes science by relating it to cosmetics. More seriously, he sees our defining reality in terms of the empirical sciences as "the definitive obstacle to the constituting of a new cultural consciousness" (215).

Monsieur Teste does not question the intellect. The Ptolemean does not stop his demolition here. Not that he denies intellect as such, but he scorns its present historical stage, where he claims cerebralization has reached a point—the Monsieur Teste point—where its only relation to things is to define and turn them into concepts.

When he calls the intellect lethal and bionegative, we may be tempted to think he is on the side of life, a Bergsonian.[10] But we find he sneers at life even more:

Life—this spittoon they all spat into, the cows, the worms, the whores—life that they all devoured down to its last idiocy, its lowest physiological forms of digestion, sperm and reflex—and then they serve it up garnished with eternal purposes. . . . Life shows procreation to be the center of its attention, and that is easy enough to manage as experience has shown. (214–15)

Yet there is this difference: life is devalued in general, the mind only in its present European manifestation.[11] "Modern European life has ganged up on the spirit, tried to tame and disinfect it, subject it to disciplines and methods, has made it scientific, i.e. not suspect, and covered up its lethal bionegative traits" (216). For this variety of mind there is no future. No shift of worldview will be able to change this. The dogma of homo sapiens has had its day. The Ptolemean speculates that the coming era might tolerate only two types of men: those who want to get on and act, and those who are silent and wait, criminals and monks. In this era he envisages a Monsieur Teste: "The only others would be a few remnants of lonely souls, a very conscious, deeply melancholic spirit experiencing itself in silence" (219).

Unlike Teste, the Ptolemean questions the Occidental, analytical way of thinking while feeling trapped in it. It is not enough to isolate himself in skeptical solipsism, in the Ptolemean region, where nothing turns except around itself. It is not enough, for it is no way to escape his stage of cerebralization. Hence the repeated cry: "Is thinking compulsory?"

Throughout the novella, but especially in the first chapter, "Lotus Land," Western thought stands in tension with the desire for a more "immediate union with the world of things" (240), for the anorganic, the horizontal, the amorphous, the Asiatic: "regaining former states of existence: becoming water, going to the lowest level which all avoid —an altogether anti-European tendency, near the Tao" (240). This opposing tendency is summed up in the cipher of the Lotus Land, where nothing happens, where everything stands still, where there will be a "non-evolving consciousness, introverted among squalls from Nirvana" (251 K/W). It is a surprise that this hard-boiled skeptic should fall for such well-worn nostalgia and irrationalism. However, "Lotus Land" is also the name of the protagonist's beauty shop, which rather undercuts the turn to the East from the start. Looking at both Occidental and Oriental forms of thinking, the Ptolemean finds that he is not capable, nor willing, to adopt either one of them. He lives between the two.

This disillusion with Western rationalism, this temptation of irrationalism seems to describe Benn's own state of mind in 1933 that drove him—temporarily—to "declare for the new [Nazi] state because it is my people that is trying to make its way here. Who am I to exclude myself?"[12] He did not resign from the literary academy when writers like Heinrich Mann were kicked out. Though by 1935 the romance was over; Benn retreated into the position of an army doctor, and the Nazis banned his writings.

The imaginary Lotus Land is likened both to Meister Eckhart's concept of the "silent desert of the godhead" and to similar concepts of Indian mysticism, just as the lake where the Ptolemean wants to live borders both Jordan and Ganges. Does this mean that all this elimination and relativization leads to mysticism, in either Western or Eastern form? This view seems supported by the fact that the Ptolemean claims at times to hear the "voice of the infinite."

In *Monsieur Teste,* too, there are suggestions of mysticism. One is Teste's remark that "there are moments when my body becomes luminous" (24), which is one of the physical phenomena of mysticism. His wife calls him "a mystic without God" (34), and his logbook contains paradoxes that resemble those of Saint Teresa: "What I see makes me blind. What I hear deafens me" (38).

As for the physical phenomena, the Ptolemean's "voice" speaks neither in symbols nor rhythmically, which Baron von Hügel considers the chief criterion of genuine mystical voices. On the contrary, it is colloquial in tone and rational rather than symbolic:

> Do you think that Kepler or Galilei were great light over the sea?—they were nothing but old biddies, really. It was their knitting that the earth turns around the sun. . . . Now watch this hypothesis shrink! Today everything turns around everything, and when everything turns around everything nothing turns except around itself. (207)

Further, according to Evelyn Underhill, a genuine mystical message has to convey material that is absolutely new to the recipient; if not, the voice is an activity of the dream imagination. Neither the contents nor the manner of the message differ from the Ptolemean's own way of speaking. The case for M. Teste's luminous body is ruined by his knowing about it and uses it to analyze the "geometry of my suffering" (24).

If we accept Underhill's definition of mysticism as "union with the absolute . . . purely from an instinct of love,"[13] it is even less possible to speak of mysticism in either case. For if anything is absent in both of them, it is love. Both oscillate between the spheres of the intellect and the physical, skipping anything in between. M. Teste, when his consciousness "has just lost its ideal object, . . . falls back on" (30) his wife as if on "the earth itself," in order to be *"animals together"* (33).

Both Teste and the Ptolemean are self-seeking in their pursuit and would, if anything, rather be classified as inclined to magic, to the use of the supernatural for obtaining something, for example, knowledge. Neither is seriously interested in an absolute in the religious sense. Even if Monsieur Teste would identify "the supreme thought" with the absolute, we have seen he wants no union with and not even possession of it. Rather, he wants to know what the human mind is capable of. "What can man do?" is his central question.

And the Ptolemean? What seemed to be a mystical inclination turns out to be just another rather desperate device for opposing rationalism and perhaps breaking out of his solipsism. It is quickly made relative, not to say belied by his mental habits. He, too, is preoccupied with what *man* can do. But he does not look to push the limits of thought ever further. Instead, he turns to art. For all his seemingly absolute relativism, in the middle chapter, "The Glass Blower," we find the credo of an artist. It is pronounced by a certain Herr von Ascot, who may very well be as much a projection of the Ptolemean himself as is his "voice of the infinite." Ascot's first two maxims sum up what the Ptolemean has been doing:

(1) "Recognize the situation"—which includes knowing about the surface nature and relativity of everything.

(2) "Start with what you have"—which parallels the reatreat into the self, into Ptolemaism.

Maxim 3 then states the core of the credo, the transformation of the world into art, in the figure of the "glass-blower":

Don't perfect your personality, but each single work. Blow the world as glass, as a breath from a tube: the stroke that severs everything: vases, urns, lecythi—that stroke is yours and decisive. (232)

Art is the only absolute postulated in the Ptolemean's later words: "It is a gift to have something in you, it is moral to express it, it is talent to find an interesting way of expressing it—*I know of no other cosmic conditions*" (247, my italics). It is the only value that survives in the otherwise nihilistic retreat into the Ptolemean self. And it is a purely formal value.

Where Teste is engaged in the quest for the ultimate possibilities of man's will and consciousness, the Ptolemean has been searching for a utopia, a state that is not so much a synthesis of spirit or mind and body—for synthesis presupposes brokenness—but a union of the two, where no disintegration has ever taken place. He finds it only in the act of creating, which combines the "certainty of the body" with the "ghostliness of the mind in its variable materializations" (252).

The Ptolemean is not just talking about art. He has created a work of art, the one we have been reading. And his comment on his method in writing *Der Ptolemäer* shows that in art even the dichotomy of surface and whatever lies behind it disappears. Art does not have to aim at essences behind appearance, because in art the surface itself becomes valid:

> I am a prismaticist, I work with lenses. As regards, for instance, my way of writing, anyone can see that it is prismatic infantilism. It doubtless stirs everyone's memories of childhood games; we ran round with little pocket-mirrors, caught the sunlight in them, and flashed it on shopkeepers standing outside their shops across the street. . . . All we got out into the light was, of course, just skin, stucco, patches, moles on the surface of things, warts on the Olympus of appearances. (255 K/W)

Two things keep such abstract fiction from ceasing to be fiction at all, from turning into essay, into argumentative prose: the first is the presence of the protagonist. Neither *Monsieur Teste* nor *Der Ptolemäer* tries primarily to convey ideas. Instead, both present an individual. An essay may use an individual to illustrate a point but does not present that person for its own sake; whereas in a novel the thought system is of importance only as far as it is consistent with the mind portrayed. The thought system is fiction, an "as if," and at a considerable distance from the author, as the ironical presentation of Teste and the Ptolemean brings home. Perhaps there is even a direct ratio—the more abstract a novel becomes, the more ironical it has to be in order to remain a novel.

And, second, while in an essay the stress is on reasoning or convincing an audience, in fiction it is on language. Of course, we find care for language in an essay too, but as it is subordinate to the ideas, it will mostly be rhetoric, whereas in fiction it is representational. It is the surface that matters.

Helmut Heissenbüttel, Poet of Contexts

This essay came out of my thesis, *Against Language?* (The Hague: Mouton, 1971). Heissenbüttel was my main example for the poetic use of the difficulty with naming that Roman Jakobson calls "similarity disorder." If the thesis had not been limited to French and German literature, I would have chosen Gertrude Stein as my example. Much of what I say here applies to her work as well. She is the major influence on Heissenbüttel, who began publishing in the 1950s and quickly became one of the most important avant-garde poets of Germany. His originality lies at least partly in the way he gives a political focus to Stein's method.

"It seems we have forgotten, nowadays, that literature does not consist of representation, images, feelings, opinions, theses, objects of controversy, 'mental utensils' [*geistige Gebrauchsgegenstände*], etc., but of language, that it has to do with nothing but language."[1] Helmut Heissenbüttel, who complains here, has certainly not forgotten it. His entire work as a poet has been given to exploring the structure of language and its limits. It is one of his recurrent themes—sometimes stated as directly as this:

to say what can be said
to experience what can be experienced
to decide what can be decided
to reach what can be reached

to repeat what can be repeated
to finish what can be finished

what cannot be said
what cannot be experienced
what cannot be decided
what cannot be reached
what cannot be repeated
what cannot be finished

not to finish what cannot be finished[2]

But does not every poet explore language? Is it not nearly a definition of creation to say the unsayable or, rather, to say what up to this point had not been sayable? Yes. But Heissenbüttel's most original work plays with the basic rules of the language to the point where it seems a word heap if looked at superficially. Consider the first section of *Einsätze:*

überall : immer und überall : je und je : morgens mittags und abends sogar im Büro : ein dies dies ist ein : wasfürein : wie am wenn auf oder in das heisst als was andersartiger als : und das was wenn nichts als dies und so fort : Fixierung fixiert : in der Lage ich man leit in genau ins man : chanisch chanisiert pfern : meta fern : domizil mizivil zivil : ein Zel mir griffig mir greifend mir Kiel (*Textbücher 1–6,* 35)

everywhere : always and everywhere : ever and ever : morning noon and night even in the office : a this this is a : whatkindofa : as at if on or in that is as what other than : and that which if nothing but this and so on : fixation fixes : in the position I one lead to precisely into one : chanical chanized phfor : meta far : domicile micivil civil : sin gle graspable grasping a keel

The extreme quality of his work may account for the fact that most criticism so far has been partisan, either an absolute yes or an absolute no. P. K. Kurz is an exception.[3] He goes beyond the common amplification of Heissenbüttel's own programmatic statements and does a very thorough close reading of early texts (especially of "Topographien," which is still closer to the manner of Ezra Pound or T. S.

Eliot than the lines quoted above). But he too leaves us with isolated observations and the irrelevant conclusion that Heissenbüttel's world is without grace of "positive orientation." I will come back to an analysis of the text I quoted. First, a few less difficult examples of Heissenbüttel's attack on our basic grammatical pattern of subject-predicate-object. For this is how he describes his aim: "Sentence subjects, sentence objects, sentence predicates are omitted because the experience talked about stands outside the clear-cut [*eindeutig*] subject-object relation. Only a formulation that leaves open one of the elements of the old basic model can say anything about it."[4]

A relatively simple way of leaving grammatical parts "open" or indeterminate is used in Heissenbüttel's poem "black currants."[5] The first line reads: "somebody goes there and does something" [*jemand geht hin und macht was*]. Although it is a grammatically complete sentence, it is one that leaves us quite unsatisfied. We expect the following sentences to tell us who this "someone" is. All we learn is that he is male (he is referred to as "he") and that he is not just anybody ("just as little as somebody is anybody" [*genausowenig wie jemand irgendjemand ist*]). Again, our subject fulfills its function in the sentence but frustrates our expectation of identification. This would perhaps not disturb us if we at least found out what it is that he does (or makes). But instead of qualifications or definitions, the next stanza/paragraph gives us a series of subordinate clauses:

somebody goes there and does that because where he goes he
finds something that can be done and he finds it because what
can be done and what he does is something that is there where
he goes and does something[6]

These clauses tell us nothing new. They affirm the possibility of the first sentence, which, however, was implicit in the statement of that sentence.

There are two interesting phenomena in this text, which continues in this manner. One is that it works with sentences that are grammatically correct but have only very vague meaning because they have no nouns, no specific names. There are some nouns later on, but not for either subject or object. The verbs that name the activity are the vaguest to be found in the language. The other point of interest is what we find instead of nouns. We find either pronouns—which have an implicit reference to a context that is, however, not stated. Or we find subordinate clauses: "where he goes" instead of a place-name, "what can be done and what he does" instead of the object. In other words, this text replaces names by either a context or a reference to a context.

Having located this interest in context and combination rather than in single words, let us consider a poem that at first glance seems to go in a different direction. The material of this poem is a very small number of words repeated several times. The title of the group to which the poem belongs is *Sprech-Wörter*, "Words for Saying" (with an untranslatable pun on *Sprichwörter*, "proverbs"), which seems to point to the importance of single words rather than sentences. However, it quickly becomes clear that the single words (*always, again, go, I, back*) in this text are much less important than the typographical arrangement:

immer	wieder	geh	ich	zu	rück
		geh	ich		
immer				zu	
				zu	
immer		geh	ich		
	wieder			zu	
			ich		
		geh		zu	
immer	wieder				
immer				zu	
		geh	ich		
	wieder			zu	rück[7]
[always	again	go	I	on/to	back]

It is the latter that articulates the poem. It combines the *zu* of *zurück* with other words so that we find *geh ich zu*, "I go on" (or if we want to assume an incomplete statement, "I go to"), and *immerzu*, which reinforces the "always" of *immer* with a sense of motion. The arrangement gives us new phrases that, however, do not add any new meanings or even overtones; both *immerzu* and *ich geh zu* only underline the repetitive and continuous character of the basic sentence: *immer wieder geh ich zurück*, "again and again I go back." The repetition of the words in varying order (if we read line by line) serves the same function. Or if we read the text like an orchestral score, it is again the spacing that produces the wave effect or perhaps contraction-expansion effect, which goes only too well with the words.

There is a temptation not to stop here, with the look at the pattern and the savoring of the various combinations. There is a temptation to interpret this "again and again going back," to make it a metaphor. Does it perhaps refer to frustration and starting over? Or to writing always starting over from zero? Does it talk about the daily routines we have to go through? Is it about the difficulty of making a decision, or about the relation between two people? None of these suggestions are convincing. We are given too little beyond what the words actually say, beyond the sheer repetitiveness of always going back. It is impossible to make this text symbolic, to see it with Hegel's "relation to the inner world of consciousness," which Heissenbüttel disdains.

This is not just a matter of writing poems that do not *use* metaphors. Bertold Brecht's famous "Radwechsel" (Tire Change) does not use a single one:

I sit on the shoulder.
The driver changes the tire.
I don't like to be where I come from.
I don't like to be where I'm going to.
Why do I watch the changing
With impatience?[8]

It does not use metaphors, but the poem as a whole becomes a metaphor. The situation between two disliked places allows a precise analogy on the symbolic level—for instance, a human being between two kinds of nonexistence, before conception and after death, or, on a more specific scale, the expatriate between two countries. Heissenbüttel's text gives only a structure. The structure can be applied to a number or relations, but not by analogy. It is more like a geometric shape: the shape of a circle can be seen in many different circles, but the shape of one circle is not *similar* to another. The shape is identical. Thus the structure of "always going back" is identical in the examples of interpretation I attempted and could be seen in a great many more examples. Brecht's structure of "being between," on the other hand, is qualified enough not to fit just any "in between."

Heissenbüttel's poem seems to move right along the borderline of symbolic significance. It seems to demand an interpretation and yet refuses it. It attracts our attention to what it does *not* do, just as "black currants" kept the reader conscious of the undefined subject and object. If we remember that in both cases contexts or arrangements were given, whereas key nouns and metaphors were omitted, we notice that this borderline is also that between the two references of every linguistic symbol: the reference to the code of the language and that to its particular context. In Roman Jakobson's words, "the given utterance (message) is a *combination* of constituent parts (sentences, words, phonemes, etc.) *selected* from the repository of all possible constituent parts (code). The constituents of a context are in a status of *contiguity*, while in a substitution set signs are linked by various degrees of *similarity*."[9]

It is similarity—also the basis of metaphor—that Heissenbüttel refuses. While any symbolic process involves both selection and combination, both similarity and contiguity, Jakobson shows that cases of aphasia can be divided according to an atrophy in one or the other of these two functions. His study thus seems very relevant to my problem. For the sake of contrast and greater clarity, let us first consider the atrophy that is the opposite of the one Heissenbüttel uses:

This contexture-deficient aphasia, which could be termed *contiguity disorder,* diminishes the extent and variety of sentences. The syntactical rules organizing words into a higher unit are lost; this loss, called *agrammatism,* causes the degeneration of the sentence into a mere "word heap." . . . As might be expected, words endowed with purely grammatical function, like conjunctions, prepositions, pronouns and articles disappear first, giving rise to the so-called "telegraphic style" (71).

The "telegraphic style" that Jakobson describes is one of the most common features of twentieth-century verse. In the wider sense, any poet who juxtaposes images instead of connecting them with a discursive statement makes use of this syndrome—and that means practically all Expressionists and Imagists. But let me take an extreme example, the Expressionist August Stramm's "Angststurm:"[10]

Grausen

Ich und Ich und Ich und Ich
Grausen Brausen Rauschen Grausen
Träumen Splittern Branden Blenden

Sterneblenden Brausen Grausen
Rauschen
Grausen
Ich.

[Literally, without taking the sound into account:

Storm of Fear

dreading
I and I and I and I
dreading roaring rushing dreading
dreaming splintering surf blinding
star-blinding roaring dreading
rushing
dreading
I.]

Except for the second line with its connecting "and," this poem is indeed a heap of single words, of one-word sentences. The line arrangement, though it combines up to four nouns in one line, does not provide any relation between these—other than rhythmical. The longer lines make the reader speed up. Yet in spite of its agrammatical nature, this poem is not nearly as disturbing as Heissenbüttel's *Einsätze*.

There is nothing specific about Stramm's "Angststurm." The first word, *Grausen,* fixes the emotional state of dread and is repeated every few words as if this one name, if only said often enough, would communicate what it stands for without further explanation. It is the procedure of magical conjuring. One other word is repeated this often: *Ich,* "I." Indeed the words *Ich* and *Grausen* make up half of the body of the poem. There is a strong sense of "I am alone" in the "I and I and I and I" of the second line, just as the impact of the poem as a whole is that of an "I" alone with his fear in an uncanny but vague world. What are we told about this world? What causes the dread? We can infer that it is dark, because there are some blinding flashes of light (*Blenden*). And there are sounds. But they are presented by gerunds, abstracted from their agents, from anything definite. The first associations are those of wind (*Brausen,* "roaring"), water or trees

(*Rauschen*, "rushing," "rustling"), the sea (*Branden*, "surf") and breaking (*Splittern*, "splintering"). But except for the last, all the words might be used for something else. We could be in a forest, at a coast, or on a battlefield. The very vagueness of the circumstances makes it a poem about fear as such, about a basic emotional state. It is true that this state of fear includes a dramatic climax (after all, it is a *storm* of fear), which is achieved by careful arrangement. The word that seems to indicate a relaxation of the fear (*Träumen*, "dreaming") is followed by those verbs that indicate suddenness and blinding brightness, perhaps an explosion, and that also have a brighter vowel sound than the *au* of *Grausen, Brausen, Rauschen* that the poem then settles back into. But this does not distract from the effect of momentary insight into a quasi-archetypal state.

This kind of epiphany and single expressive word is clearly not what Heissenbüttel aims at. For him, as for Gertrude Stein, who is the most important influence on him, composition is explanation. In a world where all the elements are known and constant—there is nothing new under the sun—all new knowledge is that of new combinations. But let us see how Jakobson describes this type of aphasia, "similarity disorder," where the context dominates over the capacity of naming:

> The more a word is dependent on the other words of the same sentence and the more it refers to the syntactical context, the less it is affected by the speech disturbance. Therefore words syntactically subordinated by grammatical agreement or government are more tenacious, whereas the main subordinating agent of the sentence, namely the subject, tends to be omitted. . . . Words with an inherent reference to the context, like pronouns and pronominal adverbs, and words serving merely to construct the context, such as connectives and auxiliaries, are particularly prone to survive (*Fundamentals*, 64–65).

Now we are ready for an examination of *Einsätze*, which I quoted at the beginning. The text begins with a series of adverbial qualifications. First, *überall*, "everywhere," followed by a cliché phrase that contains the same word: *immer und überall*, "always and everywhere." Then variations: *je und je : morgens mittags und abends sogar im Büro*, "ever and ever: morning noon and night even in the office." The subject can hardly be delayed any longer. *What* is always and everywhere?

The subject is even announced by an indefinite article that, however, is not followed by the expected name but by a pronoun: *ein dies,* "a this." Clearly, "this" is unsatisfactory. The text tries to define: *dies ist ein,* "this is a"—again stopping short of the noun as it does in the following question: *wasfürein,* "whatkindofa." The attempt at naming and defining has failed. Now begins a groping for a circumlocution, for something similar to the unnamed subject. To make the structure clearer, I am inserting ellipses between the elements of the phrase: *wie am . . . wenn auf . . . oder in . . . das heisst . . . als was . . . andersartiger als,* "as when . . . if on . . . or in . . . that is . . . as what . . . other than." Again failure. Each attempt is rejected even before it is completed. The whole idea of looking for a description seems summarily dismissed with "and so on," which ends the next phrase: *und das was wenn nichts als dies und so fort,* "and that which if nothing but this and so on."

"Fixation fixes." We have reached a new stage. Here is a complete sentence, even though it is tautological. It seems to give us the reason for the failure of naming. What Heissenbüttel is trying to say defies being "fixed." Not that it is something esoteric; after all, the text affirms at length that it is always and everywhere. Thus the difficulty of naming and defining is declared an everyday problem. Or is this the statement we have been waiting for: that "fixation fixes," that any pinning down, any formulation establishes a rut and leads to ossification? Is it the process of "fixation" that is taking place always and everywhere? In that case, the difficulty of naming extends even to the name of the process that makes naming possible.

The rest of the paragraph tells more about this process of "fixing." It fixes *in der Lage ich man.* Does Heissenbüttel mean to say that it fixes us in the tradition position of subject ("I") versus an impersonal object (represented by the impersonal pronoun "one")? Or does definition, fixation, put us in a position where the "I" becomes identified with the impersonal collective *man,* "one," where everything personal is lost in favor of the larger, cruder mold that fits everyone and is therefore communicable? The second half of the phrase seems to support the latter interpretation. I read *leit in genau ins man,* "lead into precisely into the one," as still referring to "fixation" and meaning that "fixation leads to precisely the impersonal 'one.'" This is to say that I take *leit* as the truncated form of *leitet,* "leads." *Leit* could of course be an imperative, but the context and the fact that from here on words appear in obviously atrophied form make a mangled third-person singular more likely. The impersonal character of man, "one," is not all that goes with fixing. It is also mechanical or mechanized. These words appear truncated as *chanisch chanisiert,* "chanical, chanized." Note that here it is part of the stem of the word that is atrophied, not an ending. It is the part that carries meaning that is also suppressed in the next word, *pfern.* I do not know what word was mangled into this form. It might have been the dative plural of any number of words such as *Hüpfer* ("jump") or *Tupfer* ("dab," "swab," "tap"). It might very likely be a combination of *Metapher,* "metaphor," and *tapfer,* "brave." Or the form *pfern* might also have come about through combination of *Pferdestärke* ("horse power," an association of "mechanical") and the *fern,* "far," which follows. That would mean that the surroundings determined which part of the word survives. At any rate, the difficulty with naming persists. First we were given "contiguity words," which mainly build context. Now, when we finally find words with more meaning, the words are atrophied.

Next comes the word "metaphors," but as a pun: *meta fern,* "meta far." Metaphors are farther than far away, are beyond far, definitely out of reach. Elsewhere, Heissenbüttel speaks of never using images or metaphors, because they are unambiguous and identifiable—"part of that language which is precisely unavailable."[11] And we have seen how he skirts the metaphor while avoiding it in *immer wieder geh ich zu rück.* Instead of proceeding through metaphors, the last two lines connect one word with another by overlapping syllables (*domizil mizivil zivil*) or by giving different derivations from the same root (*griffig mir greifend*). Both are procedures that use contiguity rather than similarity. The words seem to refer to metaphor, or still to "fixing." Both notions are related in Heissenbüttel's description of metaphor. All the following words suggest the idea of security or singleness, which can also be easily reconciled with this description. I have already quoted the sequence that involves "domicile" and "civilian." The pair *ein Zel* suggests both *einzel,* "single," and *eine Zelle,* "a cell," *mir griffig mir greifend,* the notion of being reachable, handy and gripping or grasping, which is reinforced by *mir Kiel* if we take *Kiel* as the keel of a boat that you might be able to hold on to. *Kiel,* however, also has the possibility of meaning *Federkiel,* "quill," "writing."

Writing and naming are closely connected. Thus we have come full circle thematically. This text tries to write while rejecting the easy, secure, unambiguous name, metaphor, or definition. I have yet another idea about the end. The words *Domizil, Kiel,* and the pseudo-word *Zel* seem to approach an unmentioned word from different angles of sound: *Ziel,* "goal." Is "goal" the unnamable notion the whole text turned around? Or is metaphor actually the aim? Is it to become available again at some later point, on a different plane, made less determined and "fixed" by having gone through much work with the indeterminate? Or is the goal the successful solution of Heissenbüttel's problem, the separation of writing and naming? In other words, is the goal to make sayable what as yet refuses to be named and can only be approached and intimated like the word *Ziel* itself?

"The aphasic defect in the 'capacity of naming' is properly a loss of metalanguage," says Jakobson (67). Some of Heissenbüttel's refusals of metalanguage seem to parallel the Logical Positivists' refusal of metaphysics. Especially, of course, when the topic is appropriate, as in the poem *Mittwochsgespräch,* "Wednesday's Conversation," or better, "Wednesday's Colloquium," which is partly a lecture on the topic "What Is Reality?"[12] As in *Einsätze,* the lecturer starts to give a definition and stops short: "Lecture: What is reality? Reality is something that." Note the period. Rainer Maria Rilke would at least have put an ellipsis at the end and thus opened the door to an infinite number of suggestions. But Heissenbüttel's sentence is complete. It is supposed to attract attention to the impossibility of defining "reality." When the lecturer seems to complete the statement in the next sentence, he again bars the reference by first offering a tautology (*Etwas das wirklich ist,* "Something that is real") and then launching into exploring derivations of the root of the word *Wirklichkeit,* "reality:" *wirken,* a word related to the English "work," produce, have effect, and *wirksam,* "effective": *Etwas das wirklich ist wirksam ist. Etwas das wirkt wirksam wirkt auf mich einwirkt* ("Something that is real, is effective. Something that works works effectively has an effect on me").

The lecture is interlarded with a listener's train of thought that stays very much with sense impressions and concrete observations (*schlechtes Licht es zieht durch die Fenster schlecht geheizt . . . ,* "bad light, there's a draught from the windows, badly heated"). This counterpoint, which gives us some of the reality the speaker cannot define, is free of "similarity disorder." But we are not surprised that the lecture after a while disintegrates into heaps of contiguity words like: *Etwas worüber man nicht reden kann. Etwas das etwas wovon etwas worüber,*

"Something about which one cannot speak. Something which something of which something about which." Here, as in *Einsätze* I, Heissenbüttel comes close to what Jakobson quotes as a typical utterance of similarity disorder:

> Ich bin doch hier unten, na wenn ich gewesen bin ich wees nicht, we das, nu wenn ich, ob das nun doch, noch, ja. Was Sie her, wenn ich, och ich wees nicht, we das hier war ja (*Fundamentals* 65)

> I'm down here, well if I was I don't know, how this, well if I, if this after all, still, yes. What you here, if I, oh I don't know, how that was, yes

It is true that in its pure state this kind of speech indicates illness. But we must admit that a good part of everyday speech consists of similar stammering or of talking in tautologies and with references to unstated antecedents—above all, when the subject of conversation is difficult or embarrassing.

This is what Heissenbüttel exploits in his *Textbuch 5* (1965). He uses the technique of similarity disorder for social and political comment. The unstated words assume the aura of the taboo; and the relative clauses, the "it" or "that which," imply hedging. This can be very funny—for instance, when the taboo is sexual as in "Shortstory" (194), which begins like this:

> he did it with her she did it with him
> What did he do with her what did she do with him
> he did it also with this one she also did it with that one
> what did he also do with this one what did she also do with
> that one
> he did it with her and also with this one

By the time all the changes are rung, everybody has done "it" (or, as the German says, "had it") with everybody else, including himself. On the other hand, the poem *Endlösung*, "Final Solution" (171) is one of the most powerful poetic statements about Germany's *unbewältigte Vergangenheit*, the past that it has not yet come to terms with. Here Hitler's "final solution" for the Jews is talked about without being mentioned, except in the title. Likewise, the Nazis are referred to as "those who just simply thought of that." The prose poem is too long to quote in full, but here is a sample paragraph from about the middle (after most of the elements have been established in shorter sentences):

> they thought it up and they hit on it when they wanted to start something but what they hit on wasn't something you could be for but you could be against or better yet something you could get most people to be against because when you can get most people to be against something you don't have to be very specific about what you can be for and the fact that you don't have to be very specific about this has its advantages because as long as they can let off steam most people don't care what they are for

The power lies exactly in the fact that the text does not state what it was "they" thought up, what it was they could get people to be against. Nothing but this circling around an unnamed middle could convey so much ambivalence. It seems to range through a whole scale of reactions—from shying away from the horrible and grappling with something that seems incomprehensible to pushing away responsibility. Paradoxically, the refusal to name is more expressive (in this case) than naming could be. And the length of the poem is a factor too, building up to sheer relentlessness.

Since Heissenbüttel is to some extent using speech patterns, his work fits both of his own categories of new contemporary techniques. The first is "reproduction," which he divides into "overt" reproduction, the montage of preexisting passages or the quoting of "socially definable speech areas" (his examples are William Carlos Williams, Bertold Brecht, Raymond Queneau), and "covert" reproduction, the reference to whole contexts as practiced most obviously by Pound and Eliot.[13] This is a far cry from mimesis of "objective reality" or ideas or subjective states of mind. It is a mimesis of contexts. He might have added himself as an example of "overt reproduction," except that his speech patterns do not belong to a particular social class, but rather to certain psychological states (e.g., the hedging of "Final Solution") or to the empty talk of so much of the media. His second category, internal linguistic change or "free syntax," again seems to describe his own work. "It means that language is removed from the area of grammatically definite statement by destruction and reduction of syntax and even vocabulary, by alogical couplings, by new syntagmatic procedures, by use of phonetic indeterminacy and typographical etc. supplements." It is these changes that I have tried to examine in this essay.

One could also say that Heissenbüttel's texts cut across the similarity-contiguity distinction. There are instances where indeed the *context* is atrophied. The form *leit* in "Einsätze," for example, leaves off the grammatical ending that would have established its context, but keeps the stem that carries meaning. Or the counterpoint voice in "Wednesday's Conversation" works with sentence fragments. This is not really surprising. After all, Heissenbüttel is not an aphasic and does not use these patterns out of compulsion, but freely and willfully. However, the emphasis on context and arrangement is unmistakable.

The literary significance of this emphasis becomes clear when we read definitions of poetry like "immediate expression of inner processes in the poet's soul" (Gero von Wilpert), or when Jakobson declares that metaphor is the basis of poetry. These definitions, while claiming to define poetry as such, fit poetry only since the pre-Romantics or the German *Sturm und Drang*, and nearly none that was written earlier. In other words, Romantic poetry is taken as the norm of all poetry, "organic form" as the norm of all poetic form. This view is still widely held or, rather, it is not so much a view as an unquestioned assumption underlying much critical comment on poetry. Romantic poetry, with its emphasis on content as determining the form of expression, tends to stress the function of selection, of similarity and metaphor over the factors of arrangement or combination. We have seen an extreme development of this tendency in the Expressionist August Stramm. Heissenbüttel overemphasizes the opposite dimension, that of combination, the one that had so long been neglected in poetry. He is not alone. The same stress on arrangement can also be seen in the work of Stein; in Pound's *Cantos*, with their musical arrangement; in the spatial, typographical arrangements of Concrete poetry; and in the theory of Max Bense and other aestheticians with a bias toward linguistics and information theory, that aesthetic information consists of an arrangement of signs in which the signs are treated not as meaning but only as parts of an order.[14]

It is at least a corrective, a restoring of the balance, in the long run. It might also indicate that the pendulum of taste is swinging back to a kind of formalism and neoclassicism. This is of course an open question. It is even a question whether taste and aesthetic trends behave like a pendulum and whether the dichotomy of selection and combination, or similarity and contiguity, basic as it is, exhausts the directions in which the pendulum could swing. As far as Heissenbüttel himself is concerned, it is consistent with his bias that he quotes with respect Johann Christoph Gottsched, the arch-neoclassicist who has been the black sheep of German literary history since Gotthold Ephraim Lessing.

Marat/Sade

A Ritual of the Intellect

If I were writing this essay today, I would add this epigraph from Claude Lévi-Strauss:

> Forgetting as a category of mythic thinking expresses a lack of communication with oneself and makes a system with misunderstanding (lack of communication with another) and indiscretion (excess of communication with another). Every time we encounter in a myth this "lack of communication" it leads to the foundation of ritual practices that reaffirm the continuity of life which forgetting had broken.[1]

Peter Brook's production of *Marat/Sade* by Peter Weiss was a milestone for the theater. The combination of Brechtian *Verfremdung* with Artaud-style ritual would seem to be a recipe for disaster, pulling the audience now toward empathy, now toward emotional distance and analysis. The production proved the paradoxical mix a success, and it has had a noticeable effect on the more experimental theater groups in this country.[2] It is most obvious in the work of La Mama Troupe and its director, Tom O'Horgan (e.g., his production of *Tom Paine* by Paul Foster). There is no question that this mixture of opposed methods works theatrically.

But there remains the question whether or not there is an intrinsic necessity in the text for the contradictory techniques and how they function for the play as a whole. This is the question I would like to examine. It will to some extent involve the question: can the implications of Bertold Brecht's and Antonin Artaud's styles be reconciled?[3] Can we have a presentation of social actuality with a demand for change and, at the same time, a celebration of an eternal metaphysical entity, life? Can we appeal to the intellect at the same time that we appeal to the body and the subconscious? Weiss deals with the polarity by polarizing his two main characters, Marat and the Marquis de Sade. Their relation will therefore be central for this essay. But there still remains the basic question of the total effect of the two techniques: can we, the spectators, be at the same time detached, critical (as Brecht would have us), and totally involved (as Artaud would make us)? How can a play succeed in providing distance and involvement at the same time? And what kind of a play does it have to be in order to do that?

To answer this question we have to go through the play examining the admixture and its effects. The general design is Brechtian enough. One of the characters in the play, the Marquis de Sade, writes a play about a historical event and has it shown to an audience represented in the play. Neither the Napoleonic audience nor we, the actual audience, are given the illusion of being present at the event itself. This might be compared to Brecht's *The Caucasian Chalk Circle,* with its frame on the collective farm. Also, the storyteller of this play may well have been the godfather of Weiss's Herald. But the audiences are different: one comes to be amused, the other to learn. And the action of Sade's play is not a parable. The comparison does not work very far.

Let us instead consider actors and setting. The distance between actor and role is assured as much as Brecht could wish. Their illnesses and physical tics do not allow the actors to identify with their parts. Audience identification with the characters is likewise made impossible. We are never unaware of the person of the actor, since his illness again and again intrudes into the action. Except for Marat. In his case, the patient's paranoia fuses perfectly with his role.

The madhouse setting already allows for some Artaud elements. It is true that the asylum first of all makes plausible the freedom of protest in the play. The fool is traditionally permitted to say the truth. Sade takes special advantage of this in the scenes where it remains ambiguous whether the action is a spontaneous reaction of the patients or whether Sade wrote the text. Beyond the obvious symbolism of the world as madhouse, the fact that a person confined in a madhouse is absolutely powerless is symbolic in a more important way, since the possibility of action is a central theme. It makes for an ironic counterpart that Marat, the representative of action who wants to change the world, is played by an inmate who lacks all freedom—an irony that Brecht would probably have disliked, since he shared Marat's socialist beliefs, but an irony that author Sade relishes. The inmates, being victims of society, are emotionally set to identify with Marat and their roles even though their bodies' syndromes interfere.

But all of these effects seem subordinate to the emotional impact of the setting. Weiss said in a *New York Times* interview (December 26, 1965): "I think just because those people are mad everything gets so much stronger when they express it." Weiss does not explain why this should be so. But Artaud would recognize a situation similar to what for him is the archetype of the theater, the plague. The ordinary conventions of society do not control life in the asylum (though they are of course responsible for the institution's existence and administration). Patients will act gratuitously, without purpose or profit. There is constantly the possibility of anarchy, which is not countered by arguments but by straitjackets. Here communication does without the conventions of language and normal behavior; it is on the level of the body, of force, of impulse, of cruelty. In other words, life in the asylum is much more primitive than what we usually encounter, less sublimated or, as Artaud would say, less diluted. It is in keeping with this setting that the action presented is death—death winning out over action, over mind, over civilization.

Sade taunts Marat:

what are all your pamphlets and speeches
against her
who stands there and will get to you (120)[4]

The author throughout the play converses with his character. Sometimes it seems as if Sade wrote the play just to be able to talk to Marat. The relation of these two figures seems to me the key to the play. Their relation has been seen too much as an antithesis: as the confrontation of the individualist with the socialist, the pessimist with the optimist, the sensualist with the man of principle, the contemplative man with the man of action.[5] These antitheses are there. But we must not forget that the relation is weighted in favor of Sade. He is the author of the play within the play. Why does he choose Marat as his subject? Why does he argue with him? Why does he seem to feel he has to convince Marat? He obviously considers him an opponent worth fighting with. Indeed, Weiss's Sade admires Marat, and his play is on one level a celebration of Marat.[6] I have already mentioned that Marat is the one major loophole in the Brechtian scheme. Sade (or at least Weiss) does not give this role the distance he gives the others. Does he perhaps want us to be able to empathize with Marat?

On the other hand, Sade's play is a defense of his own inability to follow his hero's example. For Sade is too much of an intellectual not to have doubts—which no man of action can afford. Sade is skeptical about the use of action, because he sees life on a cosmic scale where life stays constant. Social change for him is a change of personnel. There will always be death and there will always be poverty. Sade's cosmic scope of vision also keeps him from getting absorbed in a limited goal in the way that Marat does. Marat can see violence as nothing but the necessary means to an end; Sade cannot help considering violence in a more complex way. Marat fights for equal distribution of goods; Sade cannot help seeing side effects and implications like the totalitarian state (with the benefit of Weiss's hindsight).

Thus Sade has an ambivalent attitude toward his subject. He admires him, but with reservations. Sade is the doubting Thomas of Marat's revolutionary religion. It is Sade's ambivalence that is the actual subject of Weiss's play. The state of mind that sees more possibilities than the simple "he that is not with me is against me" and that therefore finds it difficult to decide on a course of action or to consider action at all has been a successful subject of novels—for instance, by André Gide and Robert Musil. It is Weiss's achievement and his difficulty to treat this mental state in a medium that depends on action. It becomes possible as Sade is cast as an author who projects some of the contradictions of his mind into his play. His action stays on the level of the imagination and therefore allows him to leave the questions open. But the ambivalence requires the fusing of opposed theater techniques in order to be translated into stage terms.

Let us now consider Sade's play in more detail, especially from the angle of his relationship to Marat as it is reflected in the two styles. This will neglect the didactic-satiric side of Sade that dominates his relation to his audience(s). But I hope to make amends at the end.

The play begins with four short scenes ("Assembly," "Prologue,"

"Tableau," and "Presentation") that establish Brechtian distance and the play within the play. The assembling of the actors on stage and their forming a heroic tableau attract attention to the performance by purely visual means. The "Presentation" gives us the figure of the "Herald," who introduces the characters in *Moritat* style and fixes the historical frame: the performance takes place on July 13, 1808, fifteen years after Marat's assassination, five years after Sade's being committed to the asylum. The Herald is perhaps the most consistent "epic" factor in the play, narrating (often ironically), providing transition between scenes, addressing (and prompting) the actors, and pacifying the director of the asylum, Coulmier, whose many interruptions are another epic element.

Coulmier's "Prologue" is more complex. It stresses the performance quality when he, as director, welcomes the audience to Sade's play. He divides the two Horatian functions of art neatly between the two groups. He assigns only entertainment to the audience and thus immediately tries to put the play at an even greater distance: that of something not to be taken seriously. On the other hand, he expects the play to be useful for the patients as therapy and for himself as publicity. To describe the therapeutic value he expects from the play, he chooses a word from the religious and moral spheres: *Erbauung,* "edification." It is a word that he keeps coming back to when he interrupts the play, a word that he later defines more closely by contrasting it with excitement (scene 11). This shows us that he hopes the play, like the religious services he knows, will be a kind of spiritual sedative that helps everybody accept the status quo. Thus, amid all the stress on play-acting, he is the first to associate the performance with religion, if not directly with ritual.

In scene 5, Sade's play proper begins—not in the manner we might expect in a historical drama, not by giving the background or going right into the action. No, Sade's play starts with a *Huldigung,* an "homage" to Marat. Four singers, who seem to be doubling the function of the Herald, start with a narrative rhymed doggerel that fixes the historical moment: *Vier Jahre waren damals vergangen / seit unsere Revolution angefangen* (18), "Four years had passed since our revolution had begun." When the chorus then breaks into the present tense with revolutionary slogans, we feel we have indeed arrived in the year 1793 and are set for the presentation of the historical events. But the next recitativo of the quartet shows that we cannot expect a linear chronological progression. We are not allowed to forget the time of the presentation. The year 1808 is brought in as a counterpoint to the year 1793: *Und wie wir heute gedenken des Krieges / gedachte jener des ersten grossen Sieges* (18), "And as we today think of the war / he thought of the first great victory." As the present tense has now been used for both 1808 and 1793, there is some uncertainty where to locate the crowning of Marat and the cheers of *Hoch Marat / . . . du bist der einzige dem wir vertrauen* (20), "Long live Marat / . . . you are the only one we trust." We can still take it as historical. But then the chorus says at the end of the scene:

> *Marat was ist aus unserer Revolution geworden*
> *Marat wir wolln nicht mehr warten bis morgen*
> *Marat wir sind immer noch arme Leute*
> *und die versprochenen Änderungen wollen wir heute*
> (21)

> Marat what's become of our revolution by now
> Marat we don't want to wait for tomorrow
> Marat we are still the poor
> and want the promised changes now

There is no doubt that they are talking about the situation of 1808, yet they address themselves to Marat. He is treated as if he were still alive, or being brought back to life. Or, rather, he is taken out of his historical moment and given the timeless status of a god or saint who can be invoked at any time. And this is what the singers are doing. Through a slight equivocation in the use of tenses, they have changed from narrators into worshippers.

With such a first scene there is little hope left for historical drama. We are in for a ritual, which properly started with an invocation of its saint. The next scene (6: "Stifled Unrest"), whether it is spontaneous or not, functions as a kind of *De profundis* of the "congregation." There is much to be miserable about in 1808, especially if you are locked up in an asylum. There is much reason to invoke a savior of the Fourth Estate. Coulmier cuts the invocation short by pretending that the patients' gripes are old grievances, no longer relevant, and therefore to be seen in a "transfiguring light." Again he uses a religious term in a sentimental way, betraying his view of religion as palliative. The scene ends with nuns singing a litany. This Christian ritual element has exactly the effect Coulmier expects: it calms the patients. Sade's ritual, however, a ritual of the revolution, will have the opposite effect all through the play and will again and again be pitched against Christian elements.

The next group of scenes (7 through 11) deals with the confrontation of the protagonists, Marat and Charlotte Corday. After the emotional surge of the two previous scenes, distance is reestablished as the Herald addresses the audience directly, "You see Marat . . . " (23). Also, the patient playing Corday has gone to sleep and misses her cue. But while this makes us very conscious of the scene being acted, the very delay is used for a mild ritualistic effect as a whispering of "Corday Corday" spreads among the cast. Even the Herald, in order to fill in the delay, falls into repetition:

> *Und niemand von uns*
> *und niemand von uns*
> *und niemand von uns kann was dafür*
> (24)

> and none of us
> and none of us
> and none of us are to blame.

The effect of such repetition is inevitably incantatory. At this point the stage directions become explicit: Corday's being put in position is likened to a ritual act. After this preparation, we are not surprised that she addresses her introduction to Marat even though the action has not yet come to her meeting him for the first time. Her speech hinges on her "Marat / I've come" and anticipates the actual meeting. This is only the first instance of a pattern of anticipations and repetitions that give the potential of ritual to otherwise neutral or not represented scenes—for instance, her first visit, where she does not even succeed in seeing Marat.

Before we come to this first visit, though, Marat (like Corday) is allowed to introduce himself; for in the "homage" scene he had remained quite passive. Marat introduces himself as "I am the revolution" (27). He assumes a stature larger than life for himself, the stature of a symbolic figure (Sade, of course, writes the text). Therefore his death can stand for the death of the revolution and become an act that allows all victims to identify with him in a ritual reenactment. The identification began in the "homage" scene with the line: "Marat what has become of *our* revolution." To keep up the pattern of repetitions, Marat is already the victim; he is already shedding his blood by scratching his skin. Simonne points out that his bath water is all red. Marat replies: "What is a tub full of blood / against the blood that will flow" (26). Here dramatic irony reinforces Marat's explicit identification with the revolution; for it is his own blood that is presently to be shed and to mingle with all the other blood the revolution caused or will cause to flow.

This double triumph of death we now see enacted—first, the private death of Marat, which Corday obsessively anticipates in her first visit. Refused entrance by Simonne, she says:

Was ich ihm zu sagen habe kann ich nicht schreiben
I will vor ihm stehn und ihn ansehn

. . .

In beide Hände werde ich den Dolch nehmen
und ihn in seine Haut schlagen
und dann will ich hören
was er mir zu antworten hat.

(28)

What I have to say to him I cannot write
I want to stand before him and look at him

. . .

With both hands I'll take the dagger
and drive it into his skin
and then I want to hear
what answer he has.

She stands by the tub ready to strike so that Sade has to stop her: "Not yet Corday / Three times you'll come to his door" (28).

Symbolically, she has already murdered Marat. She will murder him three times during the play. Only after she has visited Marat are we shown her arrival in Paris in a "Song and Pantomime of Corday's

Arrival in Paris." Why the disregard of chronology? Ritual puts first things first—first the essential act, then there is time to fill in some of the details. Just as we progress from Marat the individual to Marat the symbol of the revolution, so Corday is shown to proceed from the imaginary experience of killing Marat to the experience of collective death. For Paris is the city of death. It is the city to buy the dagger in. It is a city steaming with slaughter. It is a city "where naked flesh lies in the streets" (31). And if we are given Corday's arrival with all the distance that narration on stage can give, it is just a moment's respite before another openly ritualistic scene, before her questioning horror brings forth the pantomime of executions, the "Triumph of Death." This pantomime again causes a general uproar among the patients. Even though there are no explicit references to 1808, Coulmier gets uncomfortable with the patients' gusto as well as with Marat's "What's happening now cannot be stopped" (32). The pattern of "Stifled Unrest" is repeated, but this time it is the Herald who provides the historic distance.

Perhaps I should mention the moment toward the end of this scene 11 when Corday, watching the guillotine, anticipates and imagines her own execution. This completes the ritual triumph of death. The roles are reversible: the killer is killed and joins the victim—just as Marat killed through the revolution, and the revolution killed through him and is finally killed with him. At least this is the way that Weiss/Sade presents it.

At this point we suspect that the distancing through play-acting and history has been only a strategy to ensure freedom to proceed with the ritual that will ultimately undo all distance. But now that all the elements of the ritual have been presented, Sade the worshipper gives way to Sade the doubter. Sade now interrupts the ritual he has set up. He cuts off the growing empathy with Marat in order to argue his own position against Marat's. In this conversation, which dominates scenes 12 through 21, there are a number of points that touch on the subject of ritual and drama. However directly these views may be derived from the historical Marquis's writings, they are also very close to Artaud's dramatic theory.

Sade makes two basic points. The first is that all life is based on death and that therefore life, and all appetite for life, is cruelty (to use Artaud's term). The second point is that death (and with it cruelty) only exists in the human mind, in consciousness. Nature is completely impassive. Here is the junction with Artaud's claim that the theater can produce a purification by putting violence on a virtual, disinterested plane. A ritual of violence can satisfy the appetite because it shows life in a much purer form than we live it, unencumbered by the pettiness of the everyday. And if the appetite for cruelty is thus satisfied in the imagination, it need not be satisfied in actuality.

Sade suggests something very similar when he contrasts the impersonal manner of revolutionary execution with the ancien régime execution of the would-be regicide Damiens. Sade describes his torture in detail and clearly considers this spectacle as fulfilling the function of a ritual of cruelty. True, it was not on a virtual level, but one man's pain became a festival for thousands, whereas the mechanized guillotining of thousands provides fun for no one.

Marat has no use for this kind of catharsis nor for the metaphysical consolation of ritual. Consolation weakens the revolutionary spirit. He counters Sade's argument with mocking ritual (scene 13: "Marat's Liturgy"). It is a parodistic chant showing how the Church has always used ritualistic technique to ensure the status quo: "one . . . believes / what one hears again and again" (40). Ironically, the sincere litanies of the nuns halfway through join Marat's chanting and illustrate his view (which is also Coulmier's). Mocking as Marat's liturgy is, it nevertheless sparks off a blasphemous version of the "Our Father" (scene 14) that testifies to the power of ritual since it causes a strong emotional response even when the stimulus is faked. Or if we assume Sade has written this "Regrettable Incident" into the script, he at least attributes such power to it.

Sade as author has the advantage over Marat. To convince his adversary of the futility of action, he chooses a moment when experience in the form of constant itching and pain makes it difficult for Marat to continue his work, when reality, far from being affected by his ideas, has limited him severely and is rapidly moving out of his control. Even when scene 16, "The Reaction of the People," repeats the verses of the initial "Homage," the words are no longer simply prayerful, but take on ironic overtones from the context of the argument. What indeed has become of Marat's revolution? It must be said for Marat that all of his optimism and conviction of being right do not blind him to the actual state of achievement. He knows that even those who work for the revolution are full of private ambitions and have their eye on private property—a far cry from Marat's socialist ideal:

während wir weiter als je
von unserem Ziel entfernt sind
ist in den Augen der andern [he points across the auditorium]
die Revolution schon gewonnen.

(49)

while we are farther than ever
from our goal
in the eyes of the others
the revolution's been won.

The words may have been spoken in 1793, but the actor's gesture explicitly includes the audience of 1808. Again Marat does what he did with "I am the revolution": he puts himself beyond his historical moment. He turns himself into a revolutionary force that reverberates past 1808 up to 1965 or today and is proper material for myth and ritual.

It is worth noting these little reminders—sometimes a whole scene, sometimes just a few words (often put in Marat's own mouth)—because they keep the ritual in our minds, even while we have the effective *Verfremdung* of the author interrupting the show to argue with his character, even while discourse and formulation dominate over suggestiveness and emotion.

The argument between Sade and Marat continues in this manner. Sade always makes use of the interruptions as examples for reducing principles to their psychological and physical roots: patriotism to a taste for blood, revolutionary ideas to self-interest. The next scene (scene 17) inserts "The First Conversation Between Corday and Duperret" into the argument, which it parallels to some degree. Here, too, we see one person interested in examining experience and sensations, while the other wants to affect reality directly. Like Sade, Duperret counsels to give up, go home, and let things work themselves out. Of course Corday is not Marat, nor is Duperret Sade. But Sade had Corday unite herself with Marat in death and through the sexual tinge of her crime. And why did Sade/Weiss add sensualist and erotomaniac traits to Duperret's historical role if not to bring him closer to Sade and thus show that the great argument is one between two basic types of people[7]—an argument that will be held by many different people in many different places, an argument that itself has ritual possibilities.

The next interruption brings us back to religion and ritual more directly. Jacques Roux's two "Agitations" (scenes 19 and 20) are described by the Herald as the sermons of the revolutionary religion:

> *Sie hören den Priester Jacques Roux*
> *der erkennt eine neue Religion im Nu . . .*
> *So macht er sich erstmal zum Propheten*
> *angesichts dieser geschundenen Proleten*
> *und stellt ihnen Marat als Heiligen hin*
> *denn das verspricht schon einen Gewinn*
> *weil dieser wie ein Gekreuzigter ist*
> *und daran erbaut sich jeder Christ*
>
> (62)

> You are hearing the priest Jacques Roux
> who knows a good new religion when he sees it . . .
> So he turns himself into a prophet
> facing the ground down proletariat
> to present Marat as a saint
> this promises good profit
> because he's like the one crucified
> so every Christian is edified

Here we have it: a direct identification of Marat and Christ. And now we come to the culmination of the whole argument section. Sade makes his last long speech on the revolution, working out the set of oppositions mentioned earlier. But he begins with an address to Marat the sacrificial victim, Marat the sufferer for mankind: "Marat / They need you today, you're to suffer for them" (68). While he speaks, he has Corday whip him. He joins Marat in suffering. He identifies through pain with the saint of his ritual. True, this identification is not in the spirit of Marat, who would certainly prefer a convert to his ideas. Yet in Sade's own terms, in terms of experience, it is an identification. Peter Brook's otherwise magnificent production destroyed this high point of Sade's celebration, his communion with Marat, as it were, by transforming it into sheer erotic pleasure: he had Sade being stroked with Corday's hair. Not that there is no eroticism in the whipping as presented in Weiss's text (or in the relation between Corday and Marat). But to take all pain out of Sade's whipping is like having Corday go to bed with Marat instead of stabbing him. (I must admit, though, that it was a beautiful and memorable scene.)

It is interesting that this surrender of Sade comes neither at the moment of assassination nor in the early ritual part but at the end of their argument. It is now clear why Weiss was so careful not to drop the ritual strain altogether. He wanted to maintain a continuity between the ritual beginning and this ritual identification. But Sade is not finished yet. He hardly speaks again for the remaining scenes of act I. He lets Marat argue against Corday's and Duperret's operatic vision of an ideal society of the future. He has Corday come for her second visit. But everything leads to Sade's triumph (his revenge?), namely, "Marat's Visions" (scene 26). At one further remove yet, Marat's subconscious becomes the stage as the actors act out his nightmares. We see his life as a series of rejections and humiliations repeated over and over. It sounds very plausible when the actors finally accuse him:

Und er ging zu den Unterdrückten über
Und nannte sich Freund des Volkes
Doch er dachte nicht an das Volk
Sondern nur an seine eigene Unterdrücktheit
(94)

And he went over to the oppressed
And called himself friend of the people
But he did not think of the people
But only of his own oppression

Sade is triumphant. He has reduced Marat's principles to his painful personal experiences. Although he allows Jacques Roux to defend Marat, that plea remains lame and without effect. Marat has been assassinated psychologically.

This is the end of act I. It is the one point where the Herald, who has throughout insisted on play-acting and historical distance, sneaks an oblique claim to truth into his announcement of the intermission:

So schalten wir in die schnell abrollende Zeit
in der der Schluss schon nicht mehr weit
zur Erleichterung eine andere Zeitspanne ein
ganz als würde *hier alles zum Schein*
nur vorgetragen und gespielt
und als könnte *das Ende auf das alles zielt*
nach eigenem Wunsch und nach eigenem Verlangen
geändert werden und aufgefangen

(96/97)

So into the quick flow of time
with the end already in sight
we insert, for relief, a different scale of time
as if everything here *were* only play
were only reciting and acting
as if the end we're moving toward *might*
still be changed and redeemed
according to our own wish and desire

On one level the Herald simply refers to the historical fact of the assassination, though with a strong hint that "we" (which refers more likely to the author and cast than to the audience) would rather see Marat live. On the other hand, he also claims a truth deeper than play-acting for "everything here," for the actual resurrection of Marat in the imagination and for his message to the present time.

To look back briefly: the first act, after four introductory scenes, has taken us through three major stages. The first (scenes 5 through 11) is strongly ritualistic: "Homage," presentation of the two agonists in their ritual functions, Corday's first visit with anticipation of the murder, Paris as the great death ritual. In the second stage, which is the longest (scenes 12 through 21), the conversation between Sade and Marat breaks the ritual but is interwoven with scenes that are at least potentially or ironically ritualistic. Finally, argument and ritual fuse in Sade's identification with Marat the sufferer. The third stage (scenes 22 through 26) centers on Marat's nightmare, which assumes a doubly ritualistic quality. Not only does his life seem almost a ritual of humiliation, but Sade has it reenacted. It is Sade the author who stabs Marat's ego in order to prove his point—and perhaps to take revenge for Marat's making him want to identify. But this cutting down does not ruin Marat for his role. The assassination ritual absorbs this virtual assassination. And as Marat's humiliation had turned him toward his revolutionary career, his death (in all its forms) makes him the martyr whose appeal to Sade's imagination resurrects him and lets him continue to preach his message.

Now what is left for the short second act? Exactly this preaching. For Sade now gives Marat a chance to deliver an imaginary speech to the National Assembly, which is actually heard by the audience. Two fairly short scenes serve as a transition to the actual killing. They also summarize and pointedly play with the levels of time. The singers (in scene 28) juxtapose:

Armer Marat in deiner Wanne
Von Zeit hast du nur noch ne kurze Spanne
(108)

Poor old Marat in your tub
Your time on earth is almost up.

with

Armer Marat in deinem belagerten Haus
du bist uns um ein Jahrhundert voraus
(112)

Poor old Marat besieged in your house
you're a century ahead of us

The final assassination is presented with a heavy dose of ritualistic elements. It begins with a polyphonic wake-up call:

Herald	Corday
	wake up
Chorus	Corday Corday
	Wake up
	Wake up

> Wake up Corday
> Corday wake up
> (113)

Corday again envisions her own death and repeats part of her horror of Paris as the city of death. Sade presents Corday to Marat with a copulation pantomime. She is the personification of reality, physical reality, the reality of life and death, which are one for Sade. Corday herself chants her list of names in a kind of litany.

The last theatrical coup is the "Interruptus." Corday already has her dagger poised as in her first visit when Sade, again, stops her and inserts a summary of political events from 1793 to 1808. My first reaction is delight with Sade's Brechtian playfulness—to interrupt the action at this of all moments! But the interruption serves Sade's double purpose. It serves as Sade's last argument against Marat. He has appealed to Marat's subconscious; he has appealed to the reality of Marat's life and death; now he appeals to history. History, too, proves Sade right. Marat's work has been futile. The people are still watching with empty stomachs and the blessing of the priest while the politicians (now Napoleon) play their game. On the other hand, Sade's ritual has again and again blurred the line between past and present, between 1793 and 1808. Now he fills the gap with a continuity of events. He brings Marat literally up to date and has him die when his theatrical time has openly reached 1808. He has him die in the present. He uses chronology in order to defeat chronology and establish timelessness.

One problem remains: how does one end a play in which death is no end because it is repeatable and timeless, a play that also deals with opposites that are irreconcilable? Weiss does not try to round things off. The questions remain open and the stage goes into chaos. Sade laughs triumphantly as life and impulse defeat the attempts at establishing order.

While we must of course not identify Weiss with any of his characters, Sade's relation to Marat seems to me quite parallel to Weiss's own. When Weiss declares that he is wholly on the side of Marat but that he understands Sade (*New York Times*, December 26, 1965), the statement is ambiguous only on the surface. As I have shown, Sade shares Weiss's admiration of Marat and has perhaps even a suspicion that Marat is right. And Sade, like Weiss, is a writer who can follow the activist only on his own terms, in terms of words and the imagination.

I have stressed Sade's point of view and the way the two theatrical modes translate his ambivalence: the ritual builds up Marat, the Brechtian manipulation permits Sade to get his doubts in. But we also need to consider Sade's relation to his audience. A purely didactic play is out of the question with these people. They come to be amused, not taught. The ritual is able to involve them, to get empathy for Marat. But a purely ritualistic play would limit attention to the person of Marat and his suffering, whereas the main interference with the ritual, the conversation with Sade, gives the stage to Marat's ideas. Though Sade has reservations for himself, he clearly thinks Marat's views are very good medicine for his audience—as Weiss thinks they are for us. And while Sade is didactic and appeals to the intellect, he nevertheless cuts off the defenses of the intellect—detachment—by keeping up the ritual involvement. Marat is well served by Sade's play, as well as Sade himself. And Peter Weiss may have written the first ritual that is not just a ritual of life but also a ritual of the intellect.

A Basis of Concrete Poetry

In the 1950s Concrete poetry caught the imagination in places as distant from one another as Austria, Scotland, and Brazil, but failed to arouse much interest in the United States. I myself have written very few visual poems (some are collected, together with Keith Waldrop's, in the chapbook *Letters;* others, based on systematic printing errors, in *Camp Printing,* both published by Burning Deck Press in 1970), but I remain fascinated by the spatial constellations.

———————

Familiar shapes in familiar surroundings are invisible. We do not usually *see* words, we *read* them, which is to say we look through them at their significance, their contents. Concrete poetry is first of all a revolt against this transparency of the word—as is all poetry. I hardly need to quote "A poem should not mean but be" and all the similar statements. But there is a difference. While poetry has always used the material aspects of the word as functional in the "poetic information" process in poems *about* whatever subject ("The sound must seem an echo to the sense"), Concrete poetry makes the sound and shape of words its explicit field of investigation. Concrete poetry is *about* words. Further, it stresses the visual side, which is neglected even in the "sound and sense" awareness of ordinary poetry (as well as in the oral bias of most linguists).

This does not mean that Concrete poets want to divorce the physical aspects of the word from its meaning, which would be a most difficult thing to do. Words are not colors or lines: their semantic dimension is an integral part of them. In order to destroy meaning, you would also have to destroy the word as a physical object: you would have to atomize it into letters, fragments—or go to a language you do not understand. To judge by the name "Noigandres," which the Brazilians Augusto and Haroldo de Campos and Décio Pignatari chose for their group, they seemed to intend exactly that. The name is taken from Pound's "Canto XX," where the old Provençal scholar Lévy says:

> "Noigandres! NOIgandres!
> "You know for seex mon's of my life
> "Effery night when I go to bett, I say to myself:
> "Noigandres, eh, *noi*gandres,
> "Now what the DEFFIL can that mean!'"

But the name is more polemical than the Noigandres manifesto, which makes very clear that these poets intend to work consciously with all three dimensions of the word, with its "verbivocovisual" nature.[1] What they are against is not meaning, but representation. Lest this seem a gratuitous difference, let me quote Willard Van Orman Quine's example of the analogous difference between *meaning* and *naming*:

> The phrase "Evening Star" names a certain large physical object of spherical form, which is hurtling through space some scores of millions of miles from here. The phrase "Morning Star" names the same thing, as was probably first established by some observant Babylonian. But the two phrases cannot be regarded as having the same meaning; otherwise that Babylonian could have dispensed with his observations and contented himself with reflecting on the meanings of his words.[2]

Concrete poets using either of these phrases would be interested in the meaning (plus sound plus shape) of the words, but not in the "large physical object" referred to ("named"). Their intention is antimimetic. Eugen Gomringer calls each of his "constellations" "a reality in itself, not a poem *about*."[3] It is a structure that explores elements of language itself rather than one that uses language to explore something else. The parallel to the nonrepresentational painters like Mondrian and Kandinsky is explicit. Structure is contents: "structure-contents," says the Noigandres "Pilot Plan."[4] This is not, Mary Ellen

Solt to the contrary, a reversible statement.[5] It is the clear opposite of the Romantic notion of organic form, where content is structure—in other words, where content determines the structure, the form. With the Concrete poets it is the structure that determines the content. The emphasis is formalist rather than expressive.

If the real Concrete text represents only itself and is identical with what it shows, we can immediately rule out shaped poems that illustrate a content—for example, George Herbert's "Easter Wings" or Guillaume Apollinaire's "calligrammes." Let us also, for the moment, rule out those works that go below the word unit, that become visual works using alphabet elements.

Within these limits, the most obvious feature of Concrete poetry is reduction—a few words at a time, or maybe just one. Our reading habits tend to construct contents even out of fragmentary texts. Therefore the Concrete poet reduces his material to a point where even the inattentive reader is forced to pay attention to the word as word, as a meaning and a "body." Siegfried Schmidt has pointed out this function of reduction,[6] which is much more plausible than Gomringer's explanation that language in general is becoming simpler in the service of fast communication.[7] To put it in more linguistic terms: the reduction functions as a foregrounding. It says "this is a word" (in the singular), much as the convention of the line, which ends before the margin of the page, says "this is a poem."

Since Concrete poetry investigates language elements, it seems natural to turn to linguistics for a method of interpretation and analysis. Jakobson has defined the poetic function in terms of the two basic linguistic operations: selection and combination. He has defined it specifically as taking equivalence in the axis of selection and projecting it into the axis of combination.[8] If we look at Concrete poems in terms of this definition, we find that as long as there is more than one word, there is certainly equivalence in the axis of selection. The words will almost always be chosen from the same semantic field or will share phonemes. There is nothing unusual about selecting the words "wind wave bow star" (Ian Hamilton Finlay) for a poem, or "guerra terra serra" (Carlo Belloli). It is in the axis of combination that we must look for the difference.

Here I would like to draw attention to Mary Ellen Solt's reading of Robert Creeley's "le Fou," wherein she isolates the repeated key words and shows them to be something like a Concrete poem—while being fully aware that this is only one element of the poem in counterpoint with "the too-slow movement of the old grammar and syntax."[9] It is tempting to think of a Concrete poem at the core of every traditional poem, to think of their relation as one of building up or of dismantling. But this idea is inexact, for the sequences I quoted or that we might isolate from a tradition poem are not Concrete poems but only their potential material. So we are still where we were at the end of the last paragraph, with the finding that both kinds of poems tend to have chosen a certain number of words (or key words) that are in a relation of equivalence, usually semantic or phonetic.

In ordinary poetry these words are embedded in sentences as well as in a structure of poetic conventions—and in such a way that it stresses their equivalence. This is what makes for unity. Samuel R. Levin has shown that this way tends to be a coupling of the "natural" equivalences (semantic or phonetic) with linguistic or conventional equivalences—that is, the same position in the sentence or the same position in the line (or with regard to meter, rhyme, etc., though with rhyme this is rather tautological).[10]

In Concrete poetry both poetic conventions and sentences are replaced by spatial arrangement. I will not try to classify the varieties of spatial articulation (Franz Mon has made steps toward this[11]), but will instead look at a few examples for couplings analogous to the ones Levin talks about.

wind
wind

wave
wave

bough
bow

star
star

In the original of this poem by Ian Hamilton Finlay the word "bough" is green, all others are blue.[12] As I have said, the blue words (wind, wave, bow, star) are part of one semantic field. The spacing in one column reinforces the unity of field, while the equidistant pairs seem to indicate equal importance of the elements. The repetition (wind

/ wind, wave / wave) seems to point to a slow identification of the elements of the field, one at a time. But when we get to the point of divergence (bough / bow), the identical sound is coupled in a pairing that, on the model of the preceding pairs, demands identical words. But they are not, and the different color underlines the semantic distance of "bough," distance both from its phonetic "twin" and from the whole field. A tree intrudes into the seascape. On the level of reference, the bough is above the perceiver and therefore leads naturally to looking up and noticing the star. Stephen Bann transfers the tree image to stars as the foliage of the mast.[13] Further, the combination of "bough" and the one man-made object in the text, "bow," might make us think about the closeness of man to trees in contrast to wind, wave, and star. But the core of the poem is the linguistic tension of different meanings for identical sound; and it is evident that the effect is indeed due to a coupling of semantic/phonetic groupings with equivalent position on the page, notably, the pairing of identical words.

In Décio Pignatari's "beba coca cola" the words are not related semantically but phonetically.[14] Again, we have columns, with a wider space between "beba" and "coca cola" than between the two words of the product name. Even though the three words are set up in three separate columns, evidently to be treated separately, their relation is not equal. The product is set off against the imperative to the potential consumer. The second line introduces Pignatari's main procedure: transposition. The syllables "be" and "ba" are switched around, which changes "drink" to "drool." The two are claimed to be the same thing through their position in the column and the identity of their letters. The same method turns coke into "shard" (bits of broken bottles for future archelogists? or figurative shards of an already dead, or at least doomed, civilization?) and finally "cloaca." The first new words had been unpleasant and viscous ("drool," "glue"). Now the viscosity is openly identified as excremental. There is no mistaking the message of this anti-advertisement, the identities postulated through position and through identity of letters that need only to be switched around (or not even that: a secondary procedure of simply isolating "coca" and "cola" sets free their meanings as Portuguese words). But there is one more switch: of columns. Right before the cesspool punch line, "caco" and "cola" appear in the "beba" column, negating the spatial separation that seemed to separate product from consumer. The sides are interchangeable; those who drink are no better than those who manipulate them into drinking. The two sides are but different transpositions of one pattern: socially as well as linguistically. And this last point is made by coupling transposition inside the word with transposition in the spatial arrangement.

A single-word poem, such as the following one by Gerhard Rühm, would seem to go beyond the possibilities Jakobson and Levin thought of:[15]

leib leib leib leib
leib leib leib leib
leib leib leib leib
leib leib leib leib
leib leib leibleib

Reading the reiterated word *leib*, "body," sets free another: *bleib*, "remain" (imperative). In case we do not trust the reading gesture, the last line's running together, *leibleib,* makes clear that the second word is indeed wanted. Here the axis of combination generates rather than just underlines a series with close phonetic similarity and whose semantic tension (the near paradox of the transitory "body" and the idea of "remaining," "lasting") brings up a host of possible associations. First there is the idiomatic connection of *bleib mir vom Leib* ("don't bug me"). Then we might take it as an injunction to stay on the level of the body, addressed to either man or to the poem; after all, that is the intention of the Concrete poem. We could read it as addressed to the body, an anti–death wish: remain, my body. The repetition would go with this, making it a magic charm that by extending the duration of the word would lengthen the duration of the body. If we consider that the word *bleib* is actually the product of the word *leib* repeated and think of the geometric, unorganic shape of the poem, we might say it is about the conservation of matter: body remains, though its state will change. But though it may set all these speculations in motion, the poem is *about* the physical closeness of the words *leib* and *bleib.*

Rühm has done another even more strictly one-word poem with the word *bleiben.*[16]

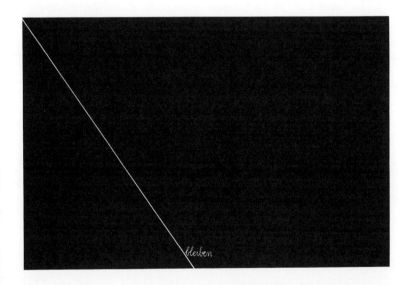

Here the poem is made entirely through positioning. The diagonal that comes sliding down from the upper-left corner introduces an element of movement into the even black rectangle. Thus the spatial arrangement puts the word *bleiben,* "to remain," in tension with its conceptual opposite. The visual aspect creates semantic complexity. We could again construct readings, like coming to rest after movement, a wish for stability, stability as a result of running down, and so forth.

In all of these cases a spatial arrangement couples with or even generates equivalences on the level of sound or meaning. It must be added that all of these examples use semantically rich words and use them evocatively, much as traditional poetry does, though with a different syntax. It is therefore not very surprising that it is possible to apply (with some adjustment) methods of interpretation derived from traditional poetry. Renate Beyer makes a good case against the claim of radical innovation by pointing out such "poetical," evocative uses of language, as well as many techniques that depend on a traditional understanding of language and poetic genres (parodies, line structure, punch lines, poetic genres as in Solt's "Moon Shot Sonnet," etc.).[17] Not that this invalidates Concrete poetry, as Beyer seems to think. It only shows that the manifestos are overstated (which is hardly surprising: it is the nature of the genre).

But Jakobson's axiom is general enough in its formulation that it is not limited to instances of what Levin calls the "natural" equivalences of words. Take this poem by Ernst Jandl:[18]

```
                    e
                   e e
                  e e e
        ooooooooooöööööoooooooo
        oooooooooööööööoooooooo
        ooooooooöööööööoooooooo
        oooooooöööööööööoooooo
        ooooooöööööööööööoooooo
        oooooööööööööööööoooooo
        ooooöööööööööööööoooooo
        oooöööööööööööööööoooooo
        ooöööööööööööööööööoooooo
        öööööööööööööööööoooooo
        eöööööööööööööööoooooooo
        eeöööööööööööööööööoooooooo
        eeeeeeeeeeeeeeeee
```

This visual genesis of the German "ö" through a meeting of e's and o's couples with the fact that the "ö" is articulated phonetically between the German "o" and "e" and that the same sound is sometimes spelled "oe." There are no emotional associations conjured up, only linguistic fact. Yet the visual arrangement of these vowels definitely underlines the nature of their preexisting phonetic and conventional (spelling) closeness.

The following is one last example, by Claus Bremer, for whom selection is often determined by what can be shown on the page:[19]

rendering the legible illegible
rendering the illegible
rendätlegibthe
réhdegiblg

We can no longer really speak of equivalences within the axis of selection or of combination. We rather have a total equivalence of the two axes themselves: the visual arrangement does what the phrase says. Such isomorphism is an extreme case of the effect of coupling equivalences, namely, unity.

Lack of unity would hardly seem a danger in poems that work with so few words at a time. This brings us to the question of complexity and to my concluding question: what is the advantage of such a spatial syntax? The advantage seems precisely that its complexity is potential. It needs the reader to activate it. The absence of context and the non-linear combination leave words in their full lexical meaning, with none of its possibilities ruled out. The reader is free to construct his own contexts. He is given a stimulus rather than a product: he has to become a coproducer of the work. This is even more the case when a strewing effect allows one to take the words in many different sequences.

A great number of interpretations are possible. But beyond a purely linguistic one there is no way of claiming that one reading is right to the exclusion of all others. In this perspectivism Schmidt sees the social importance of Concrete poetry, its political and revolutionary potential: it presents a text (and thereby "reality") not as something given, fixed, to be accepted, but as a structure that can be seen differently from different perspectives and can therefore be changed.[20] Schmidt claims that Concrete poetry puts into practice Robert Musil's *Möglichkeitssinn,* or sense of possibility. Whether we share this revolutionary optimism or not, Concrete poetry fulfills in an exemplary way the function of all art—namely, to save us from ossifying in habits, in clichés, which would eventually keep us from seeing and feeling.

We also must keep in mind that I have isolated out of the spectrum of Concrete poetry only the segment where the word dominates and where the spatial syntax is rather simple. There is much work to be done to develop a vocabulary for the interaction of the word with a visual syntax for its letters, as in Heinz Gappmayr's "ich poem."[21]

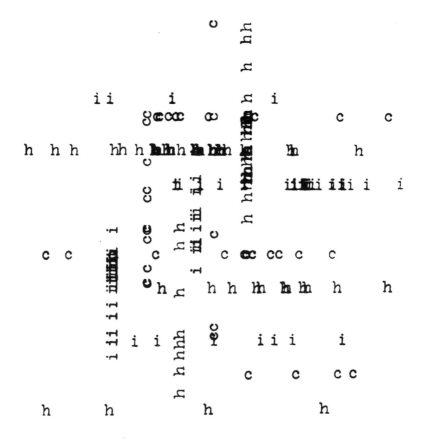

Likewise, we must explore those visual structures that treat the word as a shape or use the shape of letters, of word fragments, and that seem to explore the borderline between shape and sign, the possibility and beginning of sign, meaning, and communication.

Charles Olson

Process and Relationship

For most American poets, Charles Olson's essay "Projective Verse" is *the* manifesto of open form, of composition by field.[1] Its mere influence makes it an important document. But it is more than a call for a kind of versification: it is a manifesto of an attitude toward reality.

Olson's essay, however, is written in an elliptical manner that has made it appear slight to hurried readers. I am not even referring to those who have reduced it to a single idea in order to be able to ridicule it: the notion that the rigid spacing of the typewriter gives the poets a kind of musical stave and allows them to indicate the precise length of silence between words. This is a valid notion, I think, though hardly as precise a notation as Olson would have it. But even readers with good faith are likely to underrate the scope of this essay unless we read it in the context of Olson's other works, both his theoretical writings and his poems.

For instance, I used to take Robert Creeley's phrase "FORM IS NEVER MORE THAN AN EXTENSION OF CONTENT" as nothing but a reiteration of the concept of organic form, only more direct than Goethe's analogies between the idea of the work and the seed of a tree. Likewise, Olson's stress on breath did not seem very original to me. It is a commonplace that rhythm has a physical basis: breath, pulse.[2] And when Olson opposes the "possibilities of the breath" to "'closed' verse, that verse which print bred" (*HU* 51), he not only seems to say nothing new to the age of Marshall McLuhan, but even appears unjust. Olson's own "composition by field" depends at least partly on the spatial articulation of the printed page. Also, it is doubtful that Olson would consider the more intricate troubadour poetry as "open" even though it came before print could breed anything. (I don't even want to pun on *trobar clus,* because it means "closed" in a different sense, hermetic, difficult to understand.)

But these objections come from taking Olson's opposition in isolation (and, which comes to the same thing, giving it a context different from its own, proper one). If we read just a bit further, we begin to understand that by "the 'closed' verse that print bred" Olson means an emphasis on the result, the text on the page, the finished product, the art object; whereas he wants to show what verse "involves in its *act of composition*" (*HU* 51). His emphasis, like that of the surrealists, is on process, activity, hence on breath, which gives birth to rhythm and to the poem. Breath stands for the process of the poem's coming into being.

It follows naturally from this stress on process that Olson wants composition by field rather than by stanzas. For the field is a kinetic concept. In physics it designates the region under the influence of an electromagnetic force. Kurt Lewin transferred the notion to psychology, a kinetic model of mental states as balances of forces and vectors. It is very likely that Olson came to the concept through Gestalt psychology, but Don Byrd traces approximations to the concept already in Pound and Williams:

> The analogy of the field has begun to appear as suggestive for twentieth-century poets as the analogy of the organism was for the Romantics. As early as 1913, Pound writes, "We might come to believe that the thing that matters in art is a sort of energy, a force transfusing, welding and unifying." In his essay on Cavalcanti, he says, "We appear to have lost the radiant world where one thought cuts through another with a clean edge, a world of moving energies . . . magnetisms that take form, that are seen, or that border the visible." And William Carlos Williams speaks of "the poem as a field of action."[3]

I am less happy when Don Byrd goes on to explain how the field concept applies to poetry: "Applied to poetry, of course, the assumption is that consciousness defines a field under the influence of the imagination or the force of emerging self-hood." I cannot see what "emerging self-hood" has to do with the writing of a poem, and besides we still know too little about the creative process to establish one-to-one equivalents to the terms of the electromagnetic field. But this is not important. It is important that, for Olson, the poem is written out of a field of forces and that it remains a field even when finished. Even the poem on the page is not a static object but remains open to its process, remains a "high energy-construct": "A poem is energy transferred from where the poet got it . . . by way of the poem itself to, all the way over to, the reader. Okay. Then the poem itself must, at all points, be a high energy-construct and, at all points, an energy-discharge" (*HU* 52). He spells out that he does not regard this energy as some mystical entity but, strictly in terms of electromagnetic energy, as a relation between terms (here syllables, words, lines): "We now enter, actually, the large area of the whole poem, into the FIELD, if you like, where all the syllables and all the lines must be managed in their relation to each other" (*HU* 55).

Relation is central to Olson's view of the universe, not just of poetry. Repeatedly, in nearly identical phrases, he insists: "At root (or stump) what *is*, is no longer THINGS but what happens BETWEEN things, these are the terms of the reality contemporary to us—and the terms of what we are" (*HU* 123). Or he adds: "what happens BETWEEN things, in other words: COMMUNICATION" (*HU* 18).

We know the importance of Alfred North Whitehead for Olson, which is evident in these quotations. For as Robert von Hallberg puts it: "Action and motion, in Whitehead's philosophy, supplant the Aristotelian concept of matter as substance. At the center of the object is no nucleus of tangibility but instead a system of relationships: 'This means that the essence of being is to be implicated in causal action on other beings.'"[4] Von Hallberg goes on to quote this passage, which is underlined in Olson's copy of *Process and Reality:*

> Thus the actual world is built up of actual occasions; and by the ontological principle whatever things there are in any sense of 'existence,' are derived by abstraction from actual occasions. I shall use the term 'event' in the more general sense of a nexus of actual occasions, interrelated in some determinate fashion in one extensive quantum. An actual occasion is the limiting type of an event with only one member.[5]

Olson also underlined this passage in Ernest Fenollosa's *Notes on the Chinese Written Character*, which presents a linguistic parallel to Whitehead's occasions and nexus: "A true noun, an isolated thing, does not exist in nature. Things are only terminal points, or rather the meeting points, of actions, cross-sections cut through actions, snap-shots. Neither can a pure verb, an abstract motion, be possible in nature. . . . thing and action cannot be separated."[6] The "true noun" would be the equivalent of a "thing" in an Aristotelian universe. Both Fenollosa and Olson invoke "nature" and "truth" against that universe of things and classes of things. What matters is what happens *between* things, *between* words. You cannot separate things and actions, you cannot separate an occasion into its discrete components.

I have quoted these passages at some length to show that the field concept is not just a poetic technique but a model of the world for Olson—and not only for Olson. Just as the concept of organic form was not limited to art (consider the theory of evolution, for instance), the field concept is proving useful in the most varied disciplines.

But back to "Projective Verse," to the poem itself or, rather, to the process, the activity that "terminates" in that balance of forces that we call a poem:

Now (3) the *process* of the thing, how the principle can be made so to shape the energies that the form is accomplished. And I think it can be boiled down to one statement (first pounded into my head by Edward Dahlberg): ONE PERCEPTION MUST IMMEDIATELY AND DIRECTLY **LEAD TO A FURTHER PERCEPTION.** (*HU* 52)

"ONE PERCEPTION MUST IMMEDIATELY AND DIRECTLY LEAD TO A FURTHER PERCEPTION" has nothing to do with association of ideas, even less with *Ideenflucht*. For one thing, the direction is outward and physical, toward perceptions rather than ideas. Secondly, the passage describes, rather, a moving within the total interconnectedness, within the tension and flow of energy between things or perceptions: it is a matter, as Olson says, of "keep moving, keep in, speed, the nerves, their speed, the perceptions, theirs, the acts, the split second acts, the whole business, keep it moving as fast as you can." And again: "fast, there's the dogma." It is clear that such a movement has no "organic" closure, that it could go on forever, that it is definitely "open." Even the balance of forces that tells writer and reader that the poem is finished is temporary. On contact with, in the neighborhood of, another poem the balance proves to have vectors toward yet further perceptions. The occasions form a nexus of occasions, an event. The single poems form a cycle, *The Maximus Poems,* which becomes the one absorbing, total enterprise that goes on forever or until an outside force, death, puts a stop to it.[7]

We must turn to the essay "Human Universe" to realize how radical Olson's claim on totality and unity is (which is only hinted at in the poetic theory). He declares unsatisfactory any act "of living and of writing" that has arrived at its form "by selecting from the full content some face of it, or plane, some part." Such selecting—which may seem unavoidable to most of us and may even be a definition of form—he sees as mere demonstration or classification and therefore as false. Because

> this is not what I know is the going-on (and of which going-on I, as well as they, want some illumination, and so, some pleasure). . . . For any of us, at any instant, are juxtaposed to any experience, even an overwhelming single one, on several more planes than the arbitrary and discursive which we inherit can declare. (*HU* 5)

But, we want to say, how can he object to selecting some facet out of the fullness? Even if experience impinges on all sides, we can live only by separating out, by choosing. What does Olson want? Some primitive preconscious unity? Chaos? But Olson is not naïve:

> What weeds
> as an explanation
> leaves out, is
> that chaos
> is not our condition.
> Not that relaxation.
> —(*Maximus* 96)

Even if he sees the fullness of "unselectedness" as our original condition, he also knows that "selectiveness" is our original impulse. It is not selection as such that puts him off, but the "arbitrary and discursive" ways of selecting "which we inherit."

The attack seems again directed against the Aristotelian universe of discrete substances, discrete things, discrete beings, with a language of discrete words combinable into discourse and hierarchies. He marshals philosophers and mathematicians in support of alternatives: Whitehead, as we have seen; Bernhard Riemann, with his two kinds of manifolds, the discrete and "what he took to be more true, the continuous" (*HU* 117). Olson anticipates or parallels much of what we have more recently become aware of through the efforts of semiologists, communication theorists, and environmentalists when he stresses again and again what happens *between things* and when he labels it communication. We must take communication in the wide sense, not just as what happens between two persons who are a sender and a receiver in the narrow sense. Olson says "things" and definitely regards environmental interactions in this light as well as what happens between words—a grammar of sentences rather than of the single word and its paradigm.

Again, Olson is not alone among poets with his call for a more continuous, ecological way of ordering our world. Robert Duncan, in discussing the critical reception of Donald Allen's anthology *The New American Poets*, seizes on the example of Carl Linnaeus, who classified plants according to certain qualities he selected as significant. He thereby isolated his specimens, removed them from "the field in which they had their living significance." Duncan quotes with approval Ernst Cassirer's verdict on the failure of such classification to give us a picture of the organization and structure of the world:

> Such a picture is possible only by a reversal of his procedure. We must apply the principle of connection rather than that of analytical differentiation; instead of assigning living creatures to sharply distinguished species, we must study them in relation to their kinship, their transition from one type to another, their evolution and transformations. For these are the things which constitute life as we find it in nature.[8]

I might object that this was not Linnaeus's aim and that his way of looking at plants has its use as well as the ecological perspective. Perhaps the latter is more useful to us at this point simply because it is new and thus shows us neglected aspects in our picture of the world.

At any rate, Aristotle's classifications are as arbitrary to Olson as those of Linnaeus. And they have the same shortcomings, the most serious of which is to isolate man as the only being with an "inner" life, with mind and soul among things that, to this mind, are only material to be sublimated. We need to be in touch with what Olson calls our two phenomenal universes, our organism and our environment. As Whitehead said, "the essence of being is to be implicated in causal action on other beings." How Olson overcomes the separation of the so-called inner things from the so-called outside reality is crucial.

As said earlier, he sees man placed in a paradoxical position between "unselectedness," his original condition, and "selectiveness," his original impulse, and concludes:

> one is forced, is one not, to look for some instrumentation in man's given which makes selection possible. And it has gone so far, that is, science has, as to wonder if the fingertips are not very knowing knots in their own rights, little brains (little photoelectric cells, I think they now call the skin) which, immediately, in responding to external stimuli, make decisions! (*HU* 9)

He goes on to outline the consequences of this idea. Either it declares the "soul" to be mechanical or it considers external reality to be more than merely a substance to be taken in by man:

> By making the threshold of reception so important . . . you have gone so far as to imply that the skin itself, the meeting edge of man and external reality, is where all that matters does happen, that man and external reality are so involved with one another that, for man's purposes, they had better be taken as one. (*HU* 9)

Skin versus soul. Or, rather, the soul placed in the skin, this "meeting edge," the organ that articulates the contiguity of man and his environment—the syntax, as it were, of Olson's "Human Universe." There is no fusion, though, no *participation mystique*. The skin separates as well as it links. But it is by its very nature "in touch," unlike the traditional soul, which was, whatever the particular place it was given, always deep inside, well insulated by muscles or cranium from the outside, toward which it had, moreover, not the slightest inclination. Its vectors were upward, transcending the organism inward, rather than outward as those of the skin. Olson battles against this soul, this "peculiar presumption by which western man has interposed himself between what he is as a creature of nature . . . and those other creations of nature which we may, with no derogation, call objects." And the same passage praises the objectivist poets for getting rid of "the lyrical interference of the individual ego, of the 'subject' and his soul" (*HU* 59–60).

Most important of all, he associates this traditional soul and its tendency to transcend the organism with "the suck of symbol." This peculiar phrase occurs again in the context of the interconnection of all things. It means also that the so-called inner things are not separable from the objects and events around them, "despite the suck of symbol which has increased and increased since the great Greeks first promoted the idea of a transcendent world of forms" (*HU* 10). The symbol—and Olson takes it in the widest sense: the relation by analogy, which includes metaphor, allegory, simile, and most images—is bedeviled because of its vertical transcendence, its association with the soul.

Since Olson's attacks are usually directed against Aristotelian notions, I find it interesting that Aristotle's classic definition of metaphor limits it strictly to the transfer of a name from one thing to another. This means, as Paul Ricoeur points out in *La métaphore vive*, that metaphor is for Aristotle on the level of the single, discrete word rather than on the level of utterances.[9] This fits with Olson's stance against the discrete and for the continuous. And while we might object that Aristotle treats metonymy in the same way, the very definition of contiguity, the spatial element inherent in it, makes us think less of "things" than of adjacent areas, fields. However, I have not found any evidence that Olson was consciously thinking of Aristotle when he rejected metaphor.

We might lament a lack of logic in Olson's rejection of symbol and analogy because of an association (surely metaphorical) with the soul. But this kind of pairing of tropes with theological terms is common. Gérard Genette calls it a "temptation," which, I take it, we ought to resist: "*Dans le couple métaphore-métonymie, il est tentant de retrouver l'opposition entre l'esprit de transcendance religieuse et l'esprit terre à terre, voué à l'immanence d'ici-bas.*"[10] But rather than lament Olson's falling into this temptation, let us ask: what does a writer do once he rejects relation by similarity? What can he do but emphasize the opposite kind of relation, relation by contiguity, that is, all the forms of metonymy. Olson certainly associates contiguity with his "Figure of Outward," his horizontal stance toward reality, his skin in touch with the environment, the Whitehead universe of process and interconnections. In terms of language it means attention to sentence and sequence. And sure enough, Olson thinks in these terms. He writes to Elaine Feinstein, opposing sentence to image, contiguity to analogy: "As we had a sterile grammar (an insufficient 'sentence') we had analogy only . . . the Image is all we had" (*HU* 96).

So under the somewhat incoherent and groping surface of Olson's prose (again, he is after the process of thinking rather than well-formulated thought) there is a remarkable consistency whether he is concerned with poems or with the universe. Moreover, this passion for contiguity and against analogy between discrete entities seems to me a key to his poetry and also the crucial difference between him and Pound. (This is important because Olson is often put down as a mere imitator of Pound.) The difference is not just that Pound abounds in images and metaphors, whereas in Olson's poems there are relatively few (so that, *if* you identify poetry with images, Olson's work may seem arid). It is a structural difference between *The Cantos* and *The Maximus Poems,* which also leads us back to the problem of open and closed form.

The Cantos is often regarded as the open work par excellence, though Pound himself seems to have thought of it as a closed work, a mosaic that, once the hundredth canto was written, would have a clear and evident structure. But he was, in his own estimate, unable to close it. This does not mean that he "botched it," though. It is very likely that *The Cantos* evolved into a more open structure than Pound's critical understanding could deal with—in other words, that Pound the poet was more innovative than Pound the critic. One portion of *The Cantos* was, however, from the beginning conceived in an open, even casual, way. W. B. Yeats, in *A Vision,* reports a conversation where Pound showed him the model for the structure of *The Cantos.*[11] It was a painting by Cosimo Tura, a "decoration in three compartments, in the upper the Triumph of Love and the Triumph of Chastity, in the middle Zodiacal signs, and in the lower certain events in Cosimo Tura's day." Pound parallels this structure. His two main "allegories" are given in the first two cantos: the descent into Hades and the metamorphosis. His equivalent of the signs of the Zodiac is the recurrent archetypal figures and situations (e.g., the good ruler, whether he is Sigismundo or Kung). Then there is the third stratum: nonrecurrent events of Pound's own day, where nearly anything may enter the poem.

But in spite of these "openings," *The Cantos* are a closed structure based on analogy—not that analogy in itself is any more closed a relation than contiguity. Edmond Jabès's *Livre des Questions,* for instance, uses metaphor in a way that undermines its unifying function. But in *The Cantos* the pattern of analogy in the constant metamorphoses implies an original oneness. They describe a kind of emanation myth where the original *One* (which, as far as we can pin a label on it, seems to be Light, Pound's value-word) is subjected to Time. That is to say, it is reenacted in history, in a series of metamorphoses that become more and more diffuse until the only way to get back to the original unity is through death, the descent into Hades. Time is the villain of the piece. Time has to be redeemed, that is, abolished.[12] Thus the basic gesture of *The Cantos* is a pulling in toward a center, toward a oneness, a timeless condition of light, against the grain of the outward flow of history; whereas *The Maximus Poems* moves with history, expands, pushes outward into the manifold. The place that metamorphosis holds in *The Cantos* is held in *The Maximus Poems* by topography (of Gloucester), which in itself is a pattern of adjoining places and of expansion.

Olson's attitude to history is the opposite of Pound's. He fully accepts the flux, the process, and does not hanker for a mythical past. Even in his most Poundian moments, when he inveighs against "pejorocracy," this is a condition that is there from the beginning, as the important fight for the fishing stage shows, or this explicit passage:

> the newness
> the first men knew was almost
> from the start dirtied
> by second comers.
> —(*Maximus* 135)

Or when Maximus says: "I who hark back to an older polis" (20), he adds immediately: "I'd not urge anyone back. Back is no value as better. . . . Back is only for those who don't move" (22).

Olson's attitude to history is much the same as his attitude to space. From the first, from *Call Me Ishmael,* he thinks of space as large, as the possibility of movement: "I take SPACE to be the central fact to

man born in America, from Folsom cave to now. I spell it large be-
cause it comes large here. Large and without mercy" (15). This idea
of large spaces invites two reactions. You can dig in "like a tent stake
to survive"; and in "The Gate and the Center" Olson has some good
things to say for this reaction. But Olson's own is the alternative, to
push (Olson's favorite word) outward and onward. The "Figure of
Outward" is not a casual motto. The theme of the open is ever present
in *The Maximus Poems:*

> the opening out
> of my countree
> —(*Maximus* 47)

> It is undone business
> I speak of this morning,
> with the sea
> stretching out
> from my feet
> (53)

It occurs most frequently at the end of a poem. Thus the theme of
the open contradicts the closure of the poem and takes on a vector
function toward the next section. It makes us aware that the poem as
a whole is continuing to open out.

This same sense of an open-ended process dominates Olson's sense
of history. History is not diluting. On the contrary, it is energy, proc-
ess, life: "Frequently I employ the expression history promiscuously
with life. That's my point. A function is how a thing acts. There is a
natural proper or characteristic action of anything. That is its func-
tion. As of a human life I say it is its history. It is the how," Olson says
in *The Special View of History*.[13] Or again: "Only thus, by the way, can
one say mortal—not as a 'lifetime,' not as flesh going toward death
and resurrection, but as *history:* that you live. An active. The dynamic
is, not the energy exploded, wasted, used, whatever is done with it.
But that it is there, to be used" (*Special View* 17). Where Pound turned
to the past, Olson looks to the future, to the energy still available:
"the Primordial—the absolute—is prospective . . . events are absolute
only because they have a future, not from any past" (16).

Even when Olson uses a pattern of recurrence, as, for instance, all the navigators in "On First Looking out through Juan de la Cosa's Eyes," we do not see an archetype worn down by history.[14] It would almost be easier to accuse Olson of singing progress: Behaim's globe, which begins the poem, ignored the Western Hemisphere, and Saint Brendan's mythical island could hardly make up for that. Then we hear of cod fishers likely to have reached Newfoundland, but only Columbus's cartographer had both halves of the map:

> But before La Cosa, nobody
> could have
> a mappemunde
> —(*Maximus* 77)

However, the poem does not chart progress. The effect is, rather, one of wave after wave of energy pushing outward, of ever-renewed efforts to cross seas and make maps, from Odysseus and the historical Greek navigator Pytheas to Corte Real, Bertomez, Cabot, Verrazano, and Columbus.

The figure that sums up this push outward, this energy, is the Diorite Stone, which, in "The Song of Ullikummi," keeps growing and growing until finally the gods themselves have to do battle against it. Maximus identifies with this stone ("I stand on Main Street like the Diorite Stone"),[15] and Olson calls it "the vertical, the growth principle of the Earth."[16] This vertical is not toward transcendence. The nature of stone, its solidity and weight, keeps it safely on the earth; but it expands and pushes outward as irresistibly as Maximus's body pushes out of his clothes:

> Holes
> in my shoes, that's all right, my fly
> gaping, me out
> at the elbows
> —(*Maximus* 14)

If we now look back to the "Projective Verse" essay, we understand better the importance of what Olson calls "the process of the thing," of writing, that "ONE PERCEPTION MUST IMMEDIATELY AND DIRECTLY LEAD TO A FURTHER PERCEPTION." It is the principle of the Diorite Stone, of growth outward. Not growing inward, deeper, by finding more to say about the same thing, metaphors for it, symbols, analogies, but instead turning to the adjoining thing, contiguity, further perceptions. Again, if we now look at the statement that "FORM IS NEVER MORE THAN AN EXTENSION OF CONTENT," we realize that it does not simply mean that form is determined by content (the credo of organic form), but that it *literally extends* the content, makes it grow, projects it outward into neighboring areas. I have no evidence that Robert Creeley, who formulated the statement, meant it this way, but Olson certainly does, for he goes on to say that although content gives the first impulse, this extension will change the content. Content is not a factor of the open; it is form that makes a text grow:

> From the moment the projective purpose of the act of verse is recognized, the content does—it will—change. If the beginning and the end is breath, voice in its largest sense, then the material of verse shifts. It has to. It starts with the composer. The dimension of his line itself changes, not to speak of the change in his conceiving. (*HU* 59)

It is high time to look at *The Maximus Poems* to see if their structure bears out Olson's theoretical preference of contiguity over similarity. I have already mentioned the central place of the topography of Gloucester. A central place, by the way, does not contradict the "Figure of Outward": you push outward from a center. Expansion is not the same as dispersion. Gloucester is present from the first page, not just metaphorically, as "the nest," but with a concrete place, its flakeracks. It is present in its vegetation, the tansies (and if you object that this flower grows elsewhere, Olson focuses on a particular field), in Olson's own house, its streets, through which we follow the light from a certain corner with a big elm toward the post office and Main Street. And so on until, toward the end of the first volume of *Maximus Poems*, the lines on the page twice break into actual mappings. In the letters in which the city of Gloucester is not present with streets and buildings it is present through its ships. The map is not only a pattern of pure contiguity, it is open on all sides—in the case of Gloucester, toward both land and sea.

The topography is only one layer, though, the horizontal one. At every point of the map there live people and there are traces of history:

> And I know who lived where I lived
> before the small-pox took them all away
> and the Pilgrims
> had such an easy time of it
> to land
> —(*Maximus* 49)

The site of the first house in Gloucester, Roger Conant's, leads to the story of Endecott's moving to Salem, which in turn leads to other stories involving Endecott. For the place and the history both have innumerable tendrils that interconnect. And to allow the fullest branching out, to allow the maximum number of tendrils that will lead to other places, events, and people, Olson constantly breaks out of the lyrical mode into narrative, both in verse and prose, narrative that admits more circumstances and details, so many more possible connections to other events.

Therefore, when the names of people recur, they do not usually stand for the same thing, in relation to the same values. Moulton, for instance, first appears in the context of seeing ("polis is eyes"), appears as the experienced fisher who knows his trade, knows "how to swim," knows not to try to pick out a fish in the sun blaze as greenhorn Maximus does, hurting his eyes (*Maximus* 26). Later this experienced fisherman comes back in a story of greed that also makes him ruin his boat. There are exceptions, of course. Ferrini keeps cropping up, always as a negative figure, an example of a man going wrong.

But the most important example of how Olson uses a story in *The Maximus Poems* is the story of the fight about the fishing stage, the founding of Gloucester. It is announced, in Letter 11, through a place, a rock that bears the plaque:

> "In the Early History of,
> A Notable Exemplification of
> Arbitration"
> —(*Maximus* 48)

The only other thing we learn right here is that the "Short Chimney," Miles Standish, would have died right there if Conant had not ordered Captain Hewes to lower his guns. This brief, rather enigmatic reference is completely intertwined with personal matters, young Maximus/ Olson climbing the rock ("the rock I know by my belly and torn nails"), his father lying in the cemetery in which Standish would have been the first to lie. Curiously, the father's grave there is as conditional as that of Standish:

> Mister Standish
> wld have been the first to lie in the cemetery where
> > my father does,
> > at least where I say he does,
> > where I wanted him to,
> > > —(*Maximus* 48)

We have already heard about Conant in connection with his house (in the previous letter). Letter 15 will tell us how Miles Standish is chosen as navigator over John Smith, which leads to a poem written by Smith, which leads to the mention of other poets.

The next time the fight is mentioned (Letter 23) we get the background of the quarrel in the form of a catalog: date, name of ship (conjecture), tonnage, master (conjecture), "left 14 men Cape Ann," names of the two bosses to oversee fishing and planting, respectively, and another list of what "planting" meant. Next we find the reason for the quarrel: Plymouth men had been there before and had set up a fishing stage, which they considered their property. The rest of the letter does not connect this event with others but discusses its significance. This is, of course, a matter of analogy. We have the fishermen who settle, that is, who stake their lives on a particular environment, versus the fishermen who come for a season, exploit the resources of the place, and go away again—a kind of exploitative attitude that leads straight to its more recent analogues: "nascent capitalism . . . sliding statism, ownership getting in to, the community as, Chamber of Commerce, or theocracy; or City Manager" (*Maximus* 101). And then there is a further analogy in the field of Olson's own craft: myth, poetry, *muthos*, which even among the Greeks was accused of being false, not factual, is here ranked with our fourteen fishermen as well as with Herodotus's principle of history: looking oneself for the evidence. By contrast, Olson puts down logos, which supposedly deals with facts, as being like the absentee owner, abstract, remote from reality.

From now on, all the letters until Letter 30 talk about the fight. But if we think that we are ready for the story of the fight since we know the background, the stakes, and the significance, we are wrong. Letter 24 goes into the life of those fourteen men during that first winter, but especially embeds the picture in the contemporary Gloucester:

> around what campfires
> these fourteen Englishmen
> managed
>
> where I as young man berthed
> a skiff and . . .
> —(*Maximus* 103)

Or this other passage: "Stage Head where now lovers / have a park," which branches out into a little anecdote about a certain Pat Foley, who was spied on while making love, and only within a parenthesis leads back to the fourteen men:

> when Pat sat spooning (where leisure
> occupies shore
>
> where fishing worke
> was first set up, and fourteen men . . .
> (102)

"Within" a parenthesis is not altogether accurate because, as so often, Olson does not close it. Just as he prefers parataxis to more hierarchical complex sentences, he uses open parentheses not to indicate lesser importance but simply as a branching off.

This same poem ("a Plantation a beginning") also continues the economic comment, but this time not with analogies to later conditions but with the facts that had direct bearing on the activity of those men, were contiguous with it: "the fishing, Gloucester / was good." But the cost of the ship and of having the men ashore was such that even so "It cost / $30,000 / to get / Gloucester / started" (*Maximus*

105). Again, a sidelight on John Smith, who this time sets up other fishing stages along the coast.

"Maximus, to Gloucester" (Letter 25) also weaves connections with the present. It introduces the historian Babson and his account of the settling with lists of names and England's hopes for money, but it also accompanies this backward look with a forward movement: the historian's widow, her progeny, her Gloucester property. And her houses recall Conant's house as well as the house of one of Olson's aunts.

Only after following John Smith and John White for a space, only after more details of the later money-grabbing attitudes and exploitation of the Indians at Stage Head ("So Sassafras"), only in Letter 27— "History is the Memory of Time"—do we finally get a full account of the fight, to be followed in the next two poems by more lists, a chronological chart, and a list of supplies for the fourteen men during the Stage Head winter.

So Olson tells a story not just in a gradual way, but also always allowing some detail to connect with other events before he goes on. When we finally get the actual story, it is already embedded in a web of references and circumstances that are not simply the background for a main event. Olson shifts his focus enough over all the areas that it would be very difficult to establish a clear hierarchy of background and foreground, except by cutting out a segment. (Let me recall his similarly antihierarchical syntax: sparing use of subordinate clauses, open parentheses that indicate a branching off rather than subordination.) Some of the interweaving is done by similarity, as the analogy between later economic attitudes and those in the fight, but most of the connections are to events, places, and persons contiguous in time or space. On the level of particulars, there are the frequent lists of items adjoining in some context, not to mention the sentences that trail off because some word has started a new train of thought, the open parentheses.

All of these instances of contiguity certainly carry out the principle of one perception immediately leading to another. There is in this kind of pattern a curious combination of stress on the immediate particular with a potential infinite, a total openness, that indicates a shift in the sense of form. To quote Duncan again: "I began to be aware of the possibility that the locus of form might be in the immediate minim of the work, and that one might concentrate upon the sound and meaning present where one was, and derive melody and story from impulse not from plan."[17] Olson's passages about form and knowing all go in this direction: "knowing as a halibut knows its grounds" (*Maximus* 19), out of immediate experience.

> and form only comes
> into existence when
> the thing is born
> (3)

Birth, *the* event with an outward impulse, is the locus of a form that is by definition *open*. Yet the impulse outward is not toward scattering but toward a larger and larger, an infinite coherence, as is also Stein's continuous present or Hodeir's perpetual melody. To let Olson sum it up (*Maximus* 68):

> He sd, "You go all around the subject." And I sd, "I didn't know it was a subject." He sd, "You twist" and I sd, "I do."

Obviously, it is the "going around" which is the "subject"—not one thing in the center, but the whole network.

Within this web of constant new openings, of taking up a thread here, letting another hang loose there, the single poems actually have rather strong closure, usually an A-B-A form, where the end comes back to the beginning thematically or even verbally. For instance, "I, Maximus of Gloucester, to You" begins its section 1 with:

> the thing you're after
> may lie around the bend
> of the nest

and ends:

> than that which is,
> call it a nest, around the head of, call it
> the next second
> than that which you
> can do!
> (1–4)

Letter 6 begins with "polis is / eyes" and ends with "eyes in all heads, / to be looked out of" (26–29). But Olson also uses this same device to link one poem to the next. The first poem begins (minus the adverbial phrase):

> I, Maximus
> a metal hot from boiling water, tell you
> what is a lance, who obeys the figures of
> the present dance
>   (1)

The second poem picks this up with:

> . . . tell you? ha! who
> can tell another how
> to manage the swimming?
>   (5; Olson's ellipsis)

Again, the second poem ends with the statue of Our Lady of Good Voyage, which is almost immediately taken up in Letter 3:

> so that my Portuguese leave,
> leave the Lady they gave us
>   (9)

In other words, the same kind of movement may lead us in a circle back to where we started and give us a sense of an ending and yet branch out from any point of the circle into another, which is again to say that the movement of *The Maximus Poems* is the knotting of a net.

But let me have a more detailed look at "Tyrian Business" (*Maximus* 35–40), which seems to contradict much of what I have claimed. It is more lyrical and more metaphorical than most of the poems. And its structure is based on similarity, namely, of kinds of movement. The poem has two parts, both of which start out with "proper" movement (the way man and woman should move, the contraction of the heart) and proceed to negative movement (regression, greedy grasping). The stages in between are, in part I, a more mental, metaphorical movement ("how to dance / sitting down") and the slide toward passivity (the woman craving to be dragged rather than moving herself, to be raped rather than to make love), which leads to regression into artificial, metaphorical wombs, diapers, drugs, the chaos-serpent Tiamat. Part II goes from the movement of the heart through that of air, sex, plants, a bird, to the movement of floating bodies. The latter is part of the story of the greed of Moulton, who tried to have his ship push a load of floating timber, which chewed up the blades of the ship's screw.

There are, however, a number of details that do not fit this structure, do not seem necessary. For instance, a passage like:

As a man is a necklace
strung of his own teeth (the caries
of 'em
   —(*Maximus* 37)

This does not fit until we realize that there is a second principle of organization, this time by contiguity, namely, the parts of the body. It begins with waist and breasts:

The waist of a lion,
for a man to move properly

And for a woman,
who should move lazily,
the weight of breasts
   (35)

We might include the buttocks suggested in the "sitting down" of section 2. Then there is the scalp of the woman who wants to be dragged over the ground, with a veiled reference to the sexual organs:

     And because nobody has dragged her,
she has everybody do it. She does it. She wants clean sheets,
each night
       (35)

Now negative views ("the body a shell, the mind also / an apparatus") and the metaphorical womb:

> There are so many, children
> who want to go back, who want to lie down
> in Tiamat. They sing:
> euphoria

> (35)

The voice is mentioned again. Then part II begins with the heart and the genitals. The latter are not mentioned explicitly. But the only sense I can make of the following passage is a rather limited inventory of sexual positions (even though my first association for "M" and "G" is Maximus and Gloucester rather than Man and Girl):

> (When M is above G, all's
> well. When below, there's
> upset. When M and G are coincident,
> it is not very interesting)

> (36)

The nose comes in through the nose-twist plant. The story of the bird, the toc, gives us tail, eye, and face. I have already quoted the passage about teeth. Then we are back to genitals. They are again referred to indirectly, via Samson's riddle about bees nesting in the gut of a lion (which animal is associated with man in the beginning of the poem):

> (the honey in the lion, the honey
> in woman

> (38)

However, the story of Moulton's greed is strictly without such references. Of course there are, by implication, arms and legs of the men working on the boat, but actually the only mention of such work is the phrase "we gaffed a half a dozen," which is completely submerged in the narrative and does not carry the weight the other references to the body do even when indirect. This breakdown of the pattern is significant. The similarity-pattern of kinds of movement had put greed in parallel with regression, but the absence of the human body in this narrative shows greed as a much worse kind of regression, because it is less natural than craving for the womb. We realize all the movement in this story is mechanical (water-wood-metal in interaction) or the abstract reaching out of greed.

However, both patterns—the sequence of parts of the body and the kinds of movement—fuse to answer the question that the poem poses and discusses mostly in the somewhat more abstract coda of each of the two parts. When the question is posed explicitly:

"felicity
resulting from life of activity in accordance with"
Which is the question: in accordance with what?
(38)

it is not answered explicitly, except that it is followed by Moulton's story, certainly a negative example. But the poem as a whole answers it: in accordance with the body, in accordance with the environment.

Nobody, not even Olson, can write entirely without analogies and metaphors. But he can and does put the accent on relation by contiguity, which allows him to combine the most insistent concern with particular experience, as Creeley notes, and an infinite context. For as the ability to experience is potentially unending, as there are always further perceptions, *The Maximus Poems* point toward a total inclusiveness that we have found perhaps in some novels and epics but rarely in a sequence of poems.

One last contrast should be mentioned. When contemporary French writers—Maurice Blanchot, Edmond Jabès, even theoreticians like Julia Kristeva—speak of the open, it is in terms of *rupture,* a burst, a gap, a fault, a breaking open. This is very different from Olson's outward growth. We can see two different conceptions of reality behind this: the French seem to regard reality as unsafe, as likely to break apart at any point. Olson, on the other hand, seems to trust in a reality whose truth consists exactly in its contiguous nature, a world that is coherent with itself in that it totally interconnects. Hence his confident judgments that some views are "truer," more in accordance with nature, than others. We can also see the difference as a function of geography: the limited, hemmed-in space of Europe, which can open only by eruption, versus the free expansion possible in the vast space of America. No doubt Olson would agree with this environmental interpretation. He is serious when he says in *Maximus IV, V, VI:*

I am one
with my skin
    . . .
geography
which leans in
on me

Mirrors and Paradoxes

This essay came out of translating Edmond Jabès's work and out of my fascination with circularity and interdependence. The "chicken-or-egg" pattern ("genetic paradox") that looms large in this essay is only one instance. Others are the interdependence, in literature, of form and content and of sound and sense—or, in the "hermeneutic circle," that of detail and whole. More fundamental yet: the interdependence of *langue* and *parole*. A speech act is not a simple individual application of an existing system. Conversely, sense and syntax cannot be defined independently of the speech acts that they presuppose.

Paradoxes "go round and round forever and never come to any conclusion," said Galileo.[1] Small wonder that they are not usually valued very highly in our culture, which prizes clarity, precision, common sense, facts, or even "objective certainty." Equivocal and dialectic, the paradox has been relegated to metaphysics and mysticism. Mystics of all ages have indeed welcomed the paradox as an epistemological tool in exploring a truth that is by definition beyond the limits of the human mind, beyond our craving for certainty and simple answers. But the equivocal nature of the paradox, its "double vision," also makes it a prime instance of "negative capability" that challenges our closed systems. Therefore paradox becomes "epidemic" in times of multiple and conflicting values like the Renaissance, as Rosalie Colie has pointed out, and, I would like to add, like our own century.[2]

One "epidemic" trend in twentieth-century literature has been the work that turns in on itself: poems about the composition of poems; novels, like André Gide's *Faux-Monnayeurs*, about a man who writes a novel about a man who writes a novel; plays like Luigi Pirandello's *Six Characters in Search of an Author*.

Such self-reference is inherently paradoxical. Even when a living person makes a statement about him- or herself, it is always ambiguous. Yet in life we usually have a context for the statement. We know additional facts. We have ways of checking the statement against outside information, against the point of view of others for whom the speaker is only an object, not subject and object at the same time. Within the frame of a literary work there is no such possibility. There is no "outside," no way of checking. We know we cannot trust what the subject says about itself. (I say "itself" because it is the novel or play rather than the author.) But our attempts to see "through" the statement to its object send us back to the subject's statement. It is all we have to go on. The subject that takes itself for its own object blurs the subject-object relation or, in our case, the relation of language and metalanguage.

It is not only that the authors are playing "the godgame, and just as the old dead God was supposed to have created man in his image, it follows that the fictive worlds of Modernist culture reflect the inner nature of their creators. The distinction between the maker and the made, subject and object, becomes blurred," as Maurice Beebe puts it.[3] The distinction becomes blurred in a particularly tantalizing manner: self-reference makes the reader refer back and forth between subject and object, between thing (person, word) and reflected thing (reflected person, "word") in an unresolvable oscillation.

I want to stress this point, this unresolvable ambiguity, because the phenomenon of the book dealing with its own process is often considered a closing in, a complete circularity. John Barth speaks of it as the "literature of exhaustion." But it is, on the contrary, an instance of *open form*. The circle cannot close. It is all the more certainly open, as the book's self-reference is more necessarily paradoxical than a person's: by the time the book reaches the reader, the process it shows as unfolding has come to an end. Clearly, this is a precarious genre. It shares the risk that the paradox takes "simply by its own existence."[4] For there is no such thing as a slightly flawed paradox. It either succeeds in juggling its two terms or, with the slightest imperfection, collapses and eliminates itself. Likewise, the books written about their own process of writing have to be breathtaking tours de force or they will be utterly trivial.

I would like to discuss an example of such a tour de force, the work of Edmond Jabès. The seven volumes of *Le Livre des Questions* are all books about the process of writing a book.[5] Paradox marks nearly all levels of the work from the literal paradoxes (which are abundant) via the paradoxical use of commentary and metaphor up to the macro-structure of self-reference. I hope to show that *Le Livre des Questions* takes this structure to a point where what seems to be play becomes the most radical quest of self-knowledge and what seems to be circular opens into an infinite spiral.

Jabès does not simply play the godgame and reflect on the world he creates. Neither does he play out the negative complement of the godgame: if I can create this world that seems so real, then I may in turn just be a fiction, a creation of another imagination. This doubt about the reality of the creator (which we find in Jorge Luis Borges's "Circular Ruins" and Samuel Beckett's trilogy *Molloy, Malone Dies,* and *The Unnamable*) posits another creator outside the work or, rather, an infinite series of such creators. This linear chain of "a is invented by b, b by c, c by d, etc." also implies a curiously quantitative and hier-archical notion of reality, since in every case the creator would seem to be "more real" than the created. "Reality," "God," the "original" creator is pushed off into an infinite distance but is nevertheless pos-tulated and connected with the work we are reading by this chain of successively less powerful creators.

Jabès also has doubts about the reality of the author. However, he does not relate it to a reality (or other fiction) outside the system of his work but to the reality of the words within it. Throughout *The Book of Questions* it is ambiguous whether the writer uses words or whether it is, rather, the words that use the writer as an instrument to come into being. The writer lures them onto the page, but they come fol-lowing their own law, fighting their own battles, making love and leav-ing again. Once the elements have been brought together, the writer is eliminated: "I am absent because I am the teller. Only the tale is real" (*LdQ* 60, *BQI* 58).

I shall come back to the question of reality. But even the view of the writer as a catalyst rather than as a demiurge seems enough to upset some minds. It seems a threat to our wishful image of rational man in control of his world. Giancarlo Carabelli, for instance, has accused Jabès of escaping from his place in history into mysticism.[6] There is no doubt that Jabès's attitude toward words, as so much else in his work, is indeed rooted in mysticism, in the Kabbalah to be precise. The Kabbalah gives a central place to language and the book. Every configuration of letters is an aspect of God's creative power. Everything is contained in the four letters of the name of God. Hence using any word means actually *reading* the language of God.

But Jabès is no mystic. He is not even a religious writer in the narrow sense. His "God" is a metaphor (for death, for the void, for all that transcends man and challenges his existence) rather than a living being or force. Besides, God does not exist.

It is uncomfortable to find that we are sorcerer's apprentices who cannot control the sign systems we invented. Language is not necessarily a tool we can "use" for our own purposes. More than that: words are not even altogether in the service of their meanings (which are supposed to be prior to the sign). For what is the "own law" of words in these books but the law of their "body" of sound and letters? And which writer has not experienced how a rhyme, a rhythm, an assonance may "take over" and make us say something other than what we first intended? Let us not forget that alongside the concept of the writer as maker, the *poeta faber,* we have long known the passive artist who is "ravished" by the muse.

But I have overstressed passivity. The relation of writer and word is more involved:

> I settle down in my work, but the work is unaware of it. The more I care about what I write, the more I cut myself off from the sources of my writing. The more sincere I want to be, the faster I must let the words take over: I cannot refuse to let them exist without me.
>
> And yet I am at the origin of their existence. I am, therefore, the man who conceived the verbal being which will have a fate of its own on which, in turn, my fate as a writer depends. (*LdY* 60, *BQI* 224)

Even without taking into account the further complications (the reader will enter into the relation; the author becomes the book: " 'I' is the book" [*Y* 19, *BQII* 12]), this is a paradoxical state. The writer, whose reality is doubtful, is at the origin of the existence of the words. Yet the words exist without him and are real. Moreover, the writer depends on them for his existence as a writer.

This is not exactly the logical self-contradiction of the famous Cretan who says that all Cretans are liars. It is rather a kind of "genetic paradox" where the contradiction is in time. But it is as equivocal as the truth or falsehood of the Cretan, because the two contradictory dependencies, the two contradictory temporal sequences, cannot be resolved. They are so balanced that one relation never outweighs the other, that we cannot take one without reference to the other. The relations are as if infinitely mirrored in each other as is the case with the logical paradox.

Mirrors are the obvious image for self-reflection. It is no surprise that Jabès's work is full of them. In *Le Livre de Yukel*, for instance, we hear the story of "Le miroir et le mouchoir" (*LdY* 37–39, *BQII* 203–05), the story of Mardohai Simhon, who claims that the scarf he wears around his neck is a mirror. At his death the scarf is found to cover a huge scar. There is a wound at the origin of self-reflection, of self-consciousness: the wound of existence, of individuation, of "otherness," the wound of the Jew. But reflection not only grows out of the wound, it can also wound in turn. It pretends to confirm us, to let us see ourselves as others would. But in doing so it turns us into a multipliable object and confronts us with an image that looks back at us, questioning our identity and reality: "The scarf reflects a face, and you think it is of flesh. . . . But my true face, brothers, where did I lose it?"

A discussion by a group of rabbis follows the anecdote. It goes through a dizzying number of interpretations of this appearance-reality problem. Let me just isolate two examples. In one interpretation the soul is the mirror in which we and our bodies are reflected. "But the body is the place of the soul, just as the mountain is the bed of the brook [*source*]." Another genetic paradox, parallel to that of writer and words: the body is the condition for the existence of the soul and at the same time is merely a reflection in it, a mirror image. As Jabès always plays on multiple meanings of words, we cannot go wrong in taking both meanings of *source:* body and soul are not only compared to mountain and brook, but also the body becomes the bed of the source, the origin, that is, the origin of the origin. Our paradox is spelled out clearly.

More important yet is Reb Alphandery's comment: "A double

mirror . . . separates us from the Lord so that God sees Himself when trying to see us, and we, when trying to see Him, see only our own face." The meaning of the double mirror is clear. Having created man in His image, God sees Himself when he tries to see us. We, in turn, cannot help seeing our own face when we try to see God, because we have made God in our image. Given the atheistic stance of the book, we find again our same paradoxical pattern: we create God in our image while considering ourselves created by God in His image. But whereas God sees Himself, we see only our face. Unambiguous self-knowledge is only possible for a God. Note also that this double mirror completely separates the two planes. If we cannot see God, God cannot see us either, only Himself. We are confronted by two self-contained sets of reflection that, by their very nature, activate our desire to transcend them. So that God together with His mirror image (man) is a reflection of man aspiring to the condition of godhead, in other words, self-knowledge.

This is the quest of *The Book of Questions:* man's quest to know himself, the book's quest to know its process. Of course, there is not going to be any answer. While questions seem by definition transitive, seem to progress, to lead somewhere, here they lead only to more questions: "The Jew answers every question with another question." When a despairing disciple asks, "So why should we even begin?" the rabbi turns the joke back on him: "You see, at the end of an argument, there is always a decisive question unsettled" (*LdQ* 125–26, *BQI* 116). The questions in these books do not engender the answers they intend and pretend to engender. They only perpetuate their own form. The questions, too, face mirrors, are mirrors, even though the question as such is not a paradoxical form. There are no answers. We begin to see the rather disturbing implication that there is no creation either, only reflection; that there are no beings, only images.

Man's mirror and instrument of self-knowledge is, above all, language. Therefore we must turn to *Yaël,* the book that openly allegorizes the relation of man and woman as the relation of writer and the word. Throughout the book, Yaël—the woman and the word—has the function of a mirror.

This becomes clear in the writer-narrator's relation to the "other." He is jealous of the "other." The "other" stands for other men as well as for other writers who would also have a relation to the word. But he is more than that. In a scene where the narrator and Yaël make love, the narrator and the "other" are identified in the woman's mind. At least, this is what the narrator thinks:

> Was it me or *the other* embracing her? *The other,* no doubt, whom Yaël always spoke to, always looked at with so much kindness that it hurt me deeply. However, that morning or that night, I do not remember which, something strange happened which I cannot get out of my mind. I was no longer the same. I was no longer myself. I was *the other* or, rather, I finally took his place and was so excited, so grateful to the auspicious hour and the whole world that I lost control and pressed Yaël to myself so long that she collapsed without a sign of life. (*Y* 94, *BQII* 68–69)

We pass rapidly from the identification of the two men (which the writer at first attributes to the woman's imagination) to a different plane where the writer recognizes the word as a mirror that doubles him into "moi" and the sufficiently different "other" that he becomes in his writing: "First, my relations with *the other*. It began with Yaël suddenly turning her eyes from their object to take in a world where I was not" (*Y* 124, *BQII* 89).

There is an exaltation of insight as well as the pleasure of taking the place of the other in the love scene above. For although "between me and me, Yaël cannot choose" (*Y* 137, *BQII* 98), she prefers the other. The word prefers its creation:

> You are hostile towards me as you are towards all that you have not created.
>
> You only accept what comes from yourself. You only take what your own hands offer.
>
> You love *the other,* not for himself, but against me. (*Y* 136, *BQII* 97)

Thus the jealousy of the "other" turns out to be the writer's resentment of the fact that he cannot impose himself totally on the word, that the word transforms him while he tries to express *himself*. Expressing oneself becomes as impossible as knowing oneself. The blurring of the creator and the created (both are "I") is only the first step.

The curious part is that the "other I" is created by the mirror of the word. The author (at least part of him) is created by the word. And yet, he says, *I* am at the origin of *its* existence.

In the exaltation of insight into his double self, the writer imagines he has killed Yaël. A fusion of the two selves would indeed eliminate the word, our mental mirror. (In the chapter "The Three-paneled Mirror," the fusion of life and death destroys the mirror.) But there cannot possibly be such a fusion: we would cease to be human with the loss of our double, of our self-consciousness.

Two pages later the narrator would strangle Yaël. Not just because she cannot be true (the word implies the possibility of ambiguity and lies), not just because he rages against the "other" as a false self, not even because his fusion with the "other" makes the mirror super-fluous, but because the torment of the doubling is unbearable:

> I was no longer *the other*. He stood behind me. I realized that the immense distance Yaël had tried to put between us canceled the apparent distance between *the other* and me, so that I was the nightmare she fought by clutching her lover across my hands which did not let go of her neck. (*Y* 96, *BQII* 70)

The fusion was illusory. But what is more interesting is the comment on the respective distances between the protagonists. Only with the mirror at a distance, in an unreflected state, could the distance be-tween the two selves be abolished, could man be at one with himself. But once you have looked into the mirror this is impossible. So man's task becomes "to be oneself in the other" (*Y* 146, *BQII* 105), in the reflection that the word creates of him in the book. And perhaps he succeeds all too well in this ambiguous task. Perhaps the writer is al-together transformed into his book, dies into the other.

> [Y]ou said to me: "Is this you?" Entering into your game I re-plied: "No." Then you threw yourself screaming into the arms of *the other*: "He's changing. He's forced to change too. It's not him. It's you." (*Y* 127, *BQII* 91)

The other will die with the author and the word in the book, which is the only place where the word can die: "You will die in the book where I am dying with *the other*, after God" (*Y* 152, *BQII* 109). God, being a reflection of man, dies first as the light goes down on the mirror. But this death in the book is a death awaiting resurrection by a reader whose eye will create a new virtual space in which the game of reflection can continue with the reader taking part. For he will look for himself while acting as a mirror for the author's mirror image in the book.

There is also a literal mirror in the book, a mirror with three panels. Yaël is about to give birth. "In the first mirror she smiles," thinking about her child. The doubling of the mirror is set in parallel to the doubling of procreation. The second mirror is split by Yaël's scream (or an object she hurls to attract attention) at the moment of parturition. The child is stillborn. Hence, "in the third mirror, the void engulfs the room." This sequence is commented thus:

> In the first mirror, O woman, the lie relished its spite.
> In the second mirror, O woman, the lie blew up.
> In the third mirror, O woman, truth questions itself.
> —(*Y* 67, *BQII* 49)

It is the truth of death and the void that questions itself in the mirror faced with the panel in which the lie of life is smiling. It is the treachery of mirrors to contain both the earthly paradise (*Y* 31, *BQII* 21) and death. But their fusion in the birth of death, in the birth of the stillborn child, shatters the mirror.

It shatters the mirror because the game of reflection depends on alternation, on "the alternating of All and Nothing which appearance tries to mask" (*Y* 58, *BQII* 41). It cannot be resolved without going straight to the void. Appearance, the game of reflections, alternating between all and nothing is, of course, lies: "the lie of images. Mirror of a mirror, the universe lives by reflections" (*Y* 58, *BQII* 41). Jabès's mirrors say: all mirrors are lying. Jabès's words say: all words are lying. But this lie or, rather, this oscillation between lie and truth that these paradoxes create, is the condition of life, of existence:

> Beings and things exist only in the mirrors which copy them. We are countless crystal facets where the world is reflected and drives us back to our own reflections, so that we can know ourselves only through the universe and what little it retains of us. (*Y* 161, *BQII* 114–15)

This new double mirror where the world is reflected in us and we in the world also recalls the end of *Return to the Book:* "Man does not exist. God does not exist. The world alone exists through God and man in the open book" (*R* 100, *BQI* 402). The world exists, but only in the book, only through us and the mirrors we have created with their endless back and forth, perhaps only through the terror we feel at midpoint between the reflections and that is perhaps the locus of creation.

But the "real" world? If it exists, it is undecipherable and therefore totally inaccessible to us. All we know how to do is decipher, read signs: "Our lot is to interpret an undecipherable world" (*Y* 116, *BQII* 84). Thus Jacques Derrida is wrong after all when he finds at the end of his important essay "Edmond Jabès et la question du livre" that under all the questions of *Le Livre des Questions,* there is one non-question: "the unshaken certainty that being is a Grammar; and the world through and through a cryptogram to constitute or reconstitute by poetic inscription or deciphering; that the book is the origin [*originaire*]; that everything is *in the book* before being *in the world*."[7] This sounds convincing. But at least in *Yaël* the book does not give birth to the world. The child whom the writer and the word would have is stillborn. Jabès does indeed posit the *illisibilité radicale* of which Derrida speaks. However, it was very likely Derrida's observation (which was first published in 1964 when only the first *Livre des Questions* had appeared) that sharpened Jabès's eye to the implications of his work. For while the mirror structures of question and commentary as well as their ground of silence are present from the beginning, the explicit statements I quoted come after Derrida's essay. It shows how enclosed we are in the mirrors of our sign systems that both Derrida and Jabès can posit this radical illegibility only in semiotic terms, though of course negated: un-readable, un-decipherable. It is because Jabès's thinking is bold enough to come to this absolute borderline where our signs are impotent, where we can at best *point* or *scream,* that his writing naturally turns "back on itself." There is no way forward after this point. And it is on turning back to examine its own process that the thought and the writing of *The Book of Questions* conclude that "being is a Grammar" insofar as it is accessible to us at all. It is in the light of man defined as a sign-making animal that we must look at the way Jabès uses commentary and metaphor.

Commentary is the main procedure of *The Book of Questions,* commentary on a story that is not told except through the commentary. Even in his two latest volumes, *Aely* and *El, ou le dernier livre*, which do not have the pretext of a story, the structure is still commentary—this time on words, on the stories of the earlier volumes, on the earlier volumes themselves. But the commentary structure is most obvious in the three volumes of *The Book of Questions* proper, where he overtly uses the Talmudic tradition and has a host of imaginary rabbis doing the commenting. The rabbis have names but are not individualized. There are dozens and dozens of them. Most of them do not speak more than once, although a few of them are allowed to dispute for several pages. But even the latter do not become characters; they remain voices. It becomes clear that the important thing is not the particular comment rabbi X might make but the fact of commentary as such.

Commentary by its very nature draws attention to the process of signifying. Reduced to a formula it could be written "A means B." Add to this that the basic technique within the commentary is metaphor, which doubles the signifying function: we have a signifier, which stands for a signified, which in turn stands for another signified. A is B is (talked about in terms of) C.

Moreover, metaphors are used in such profusion that their original function of linking two terms is eroded. It is true that there are key metaphors and recurring clusters.[8] But on the level of texture, Jabès rarely develops one metaphor fully or even stays within one semantic field. The images change rapidly from one area to another. Consider, for instance, this passage:

> Childhood is a piece of ground bathed in water, with little paper boats floating on it. Sometimes, the boats turn into scorpions. Then life dies, poisoned, from one moment to the next.
>
> The poison is in each corolla, as the earth is in the sun. At night, the earth is left to itself, but, happily, people are asleep. In their sleep, they are invulnerable.
>
> The poison is the dream. (*LdQ* 54, *BQI* 53)

The first paragraph sets up childhood as a scene of life, fertility ("ground bathed in water"), and, of course, play. The toys, the little paper boats, can turn into scorpions, can poison as well as amuse. In the second paragraph the poison is no longer in the scorpions but in flowers. No difficulty yet. We see the parallel: beautiful, loved things contain the possibility of hurt.

However, the poison in the flower is likened to the earth in the sun. Suddenly poison and earth are set in parallel, whereas the beginning gave us a piece of earth as metaphor for childhood, as what is threatened and killed by poison rather than being poison. The relation of poison and earth in the two paragraphs is diametrically opposed. Not only do the images range from toy to animal to plant to geology, but their logical relation changes as well. The metaphors cannot be organized into a system where their elements would always correspond to the same concepts. They are not stable. At first glance we might consider this a confused, inept use of metaphors. But Jabès is so consistent that we cannot help recognizing an intention: he uses metaphors in a way that subverts their function. We might say he uses them paradoxically.

This is not to say that the passage does not make sense. There is a certain consistency of thought that becomes clear with "the poison is the dream." The poison is the element of libido, of anarchic and potentially destructive freedom present in play, in nature, and can at least be imagined on the cosmic level. But this coherence is created by strangely sliding images and relationships.

Even when the relation of terms does not change, when the linking function of the metaphor is not blatantly subverted, the images change with breathtaking rapidity. In the space of one page we find a conversation compared first to a glass of wine, a drink at the sources of the soul, then to a boat in the raging sea, then to a horse, a tree, a bee (these last three are connected by the image of the circle: the horse in a circus, the rings of the tree, the bee living around its honey-probe), and finally to an apple (*LdQ* 117, *BQI* 109).

Again, this might at first seem simply a naïve pleasure in analogy, an excessive piling up of images and comparisons. (I should perhaps mention that I use "metaphor" in Jakobson's wider sense of all relations that are based on similarity, whether comparison, simile, image, or metaphor proper.) But the richness undermines itself. If there are always more images, then no one image means anything. We are left with the *gesture of analogy* rather than one specific similarity, just as we found the *gesture of commentary* rather than one specific statement.

There is a parallel to this in mystical symbolism. Gershom Scholem points out that for the Kabbalist, everything is endlessly correlated with everything else, everything mirrors everything else, with the result that symbols signify nothing in themselves "but make something transparent which is beyond all expression."[9]

What Jabès makes transparent is not the numinous—in spite of the frequency of the word "God." It is the structure of language, of signification (which is obviously not beyond expression, although it is usually outside our consciousness). He makes us aware of the imaginary line between signifier and signified by constantly crossing it, by constantly saying "A means B," "A is like B." "A stands for B." True, these relations are not exactly identical, but they are similar. The gesture of analogy and the gesture of commentary could be subsumed under the gesture of signification. But if we are made aware of the structure of signs and signification, we are made aware of something ambiguous.

The ambiguity deepens when we consider that the formula of commentary I gave ("A means B") needs to be qualified. For while it is adequate on the level of microstructure, where the rabbis often comment on a given text, anecdote, and so forth, on the level of macrostructure the "story" is not given. Therefore B is a commentary on an A that does not exist prior to the commentary, which comes into being only through the commentary. This means that the commentary has to create its own pre-text for being. We have encountered this relation before. It is again the "genetic paradox" of the relation of writer and word, man and God, body and soul.

So the *Book of Questions* shows us on all its levels, explicitly and implicitly, thematically and by its method, that man, faced with an undecipherable world, creates his own world of signs, which is legible and inhabitable but has no bridge to "the real world," or "being." It is a set of mirrors where the signs perpetuate themselves. There are no referents. There are only endless questions, endless commentaries. The text is missing.

It is this knowledge that our words are our world that makes Jabès listen so intently to his words, makes him try so passionately to discover "their own law." One could nearly say of *El, or the Last Book* that its whole text is an attempt to comment and explain the "natural" affinity of certain words. *L'arbre est dans le marbre* ("The tree is in the marble, he said. The fruits of eternity are seasonal" [*El* 79, *BQII* 407]). In French the similarity of sound is immediately perceived. It may take a moment longer, but not much more, for the eye to take in how literally the word *arbre* is contained in the word *marbre*, or how to unscramble *Privé d'R, la mort meurt d'asphyxie dans le mot* ("Deprived of the air of its *r, la mort,* death, dies asphyxiated in the word, *le mot*" [*El* 39, *BQII* 371]). But the excitement comes when the association of signifiers also works on the semantic level, though we know we would not have associated the concepts without the physical similarity of the words. Reversing thus the assumed priority of sense over sound, Jabès gives us a last paradox, the paradox of the linguistic sign. He shows us the indissoluble unity of signifier and signified while demonstrating that the two are not one. The word is indeed our true mirror: it shares our own dual nature. And even though it is denied a referent, even though it may all be stabs in the void, there is real blood. "A saber stroke in the void, this is the image of my life and writing I would like to leave behind, he said. And if drops of my blood have more than once soiled the ground, you must understand that each of them is an unknown book" (*El* 122, *BQII* 442).

Palmer's *First Figure*

Michael Palmer's *First Figure* is his fifth volume of poetry, not counting chapbooks. One of our finest poets at the height of his power, he brings together and unifies tendencies that have divided poets into opposing factions. The epigraph from Paul Celan, "Niemandes Stimme, wieder," announces the book's theme even by the fact that it is left in German—"nobody's voice, again"—in a language the reader may not understand. We are entering a meditation on language that will not stay within the range of comfort: "Once I could not tell of it / and now I cannot speak at all."

The poems seduce us immediately by their fluidity, their serene, dreamlike tone. Palmer's early volumes streamed with images, seamless in spite of their disparity—their music bringing to mind the Surrealists' descent into our inner space. But I don't think Palmer ever had André Breton's trust that the unconscious might heal the dichotomies of our waking lives. On the contrary, he has focused more and more precisely on the wounds inflicted by consciousness, on the way an act of attention alters the object, on the fault within our perception, our language, our mind. So images have partly given way to abstraction, statement, and meditation, and to an analysis of the way imagination works in language. In the poems we seem to move, still with the ease of a dream, among parts of an argument as large as the mind itself.

In the first line of the book we encounter the man who "painted the mountain over and over again," the master of the fragmenting, constructing stroke, the stroke that constructs through taking apart, through questioning—Cézanne rather than Breton. Palmer's method from the beginning has been collage and construction. Even his first book, *Blake's Newton,* acknowledged "drawing or distorting phrases" from the philosopher Willard Van Orman Quine and others. Yet he does not manipulate language to show off his erudition and wit, though he has plenty of both ("You mean that's your idea of desire, with all those commas?"). He is too aware of how language shapes our consciousness to think of using it as a mere tool.

At times the interaction of the personal and impersonal in the act of writing becomes frightening: "You may use the paper with my name on it / to say whatever you want." It is frightening because it is the poet's ultimate glory to become absorbed into the language ("an ant is an ideal reader"). It means becoming "nobody's voice, again"—with all the paradox of identity and nonidentity implied in that phrase. Again and again, like lighted-up scrims, the words become transparent. Cézanne fades back into Plato's cave.

But of course neither the questions nor the impossibility of answers is as important as how this acute intelligence focuses on working all the way down into the region where the light gives out, and the poet has to accept the gifts of the subconscious:

I failed to draw a map and you followed it perfectly
because the word for "cannot" inscribes itself here
to define an atmosphere of absolute trust
which both fastens and unfastens us.

First Figure and Palmer's previous volume *Notes for Echo Lake* are his best books to date. Let me end with a whole stanza:

There are shadow figures of a new world
but I have no question to ask you. The watery gates
have already told everything
needing to be known
and the sentence is there
free at last to occur
in some other direction.[1]

Chinese Windmills Turn Horizontally

> Everything is the same except composition and as the composition is different and always going to be different everything is not the same.
>
> —Gertrude Stein, "Composition as Explanation"

It is not just because Lyn Hejinian is an outspoken admirer and follower of Stein that I put this quotation at the beginning. Aside from the foregrounding of language implied in its name, L=A=N=G=U=A=G=E poetics is a radical focusing of a much larger development: the shift away from the emphasis on analogy and metaphor toward emphasis on combination, a shift that began with Stein and has been worked at in a variety of ways by a variety of poets since. (Olson and "projective verse" are crucial here, Creeley's exploration of sequence in *Pieces,* Louis Zukofsky's grammatical rhymes, the spatial syntax of the "Concrete" poets, the tonal shifts of the "New York School," etc.)

In discussing her own work or Stein's, Hejinian definitely emphasizes combination, the relation *between* things, with particular stress on openness, on "rejection of closure." She talks literally about "words and ideas continuing beyond the work." Following William James, she connects this with the inclusiveness, the "porosity," of the mind, and with consciousness as a verbal plane with a vast "range of activity on its surface." Hence, language becomes "one of the principal forms our curiosity takes," also an exterior, a *site,* a landscape with "innumerable non-isolating focal points" so that "the vanishing point might be on every word."[1]

So when she proposes the paragraph in *My Life* as a unit representing "a single moment of time," she does not mean a literal time unit and what might have happened in it, but, again following William James:

a single moment in the mind, its contents all the thoughts, thought particles, impressions, impulses—all the diverse, particular, and contradictory elements that are included in an active and emotional mind at any given instant. ("RC")

There is no chronological or thematic organization. Each of these moments of the mind contains all of the author's thirty-seven years (just as each of the thirty-seven paragraphs contains its thirty-seven sentences), including present perceptions, reflections, and so forth.[2]

The quantitative organization is not perceptible in reading except as roughly even paragraph length. What is perceptible is a musical structure established by recurring phrases. A recurring phrase or sentence is a very strong rhythmic marker because of its size, more so when it is typographically singled out, and yet more when the phrase is memorable. Who can forget "As for we who love to be astonished"?

However, Hejinian does not just use the rhythmic, unifying effect of repetition here. She has the phrase appear each time in a changed context. As she says, she *recontextualizes* the phrase, giving it a new emphasis, and thereby

disrupts the initial apparent meaning scheme. The initial reading is adjusted; meaning is set in motion, emended and extended, and the rewriting that repetition becomes postpones completion of the thought indefinitely. ("RC")

Stein held that "there is no repetition," because the context is always made different by the mere fact of a phrase recurring. Hejinian changes her contexts beyond that. It is worthwhile looking at a few instances of this *recontextualization*. The first key phrase is "A pause, a rose, something on paper." It clearly describes a privileged moment, set off from the daily routine ("a pause"), involving something beautiful ("a rose") and "something on paper" (writing? reading? drawing?). The first time it appears it is mostly a feeling, a color, but likened to an important moment for the family, the father's return from the war:

A moment yellow, just as four years later, when my father returned home from the war, the moment of greeting him, as he stood at the bottom of the stairs, younger, thinner than when he had left, was purple—though moments are no longer so colored. (5)

Next, it is associated with music and, in contrast to the intense family scene, with solitude:

> You could tell that it was improvisational because at that point they closed their eyes. A pause, a rose, something on paper. Solitude was the essential companion. (15)

The following two instances are variations on the context of beauty and solitude. The narrator becomes more aware of her individuality, hence feels isolated, with the desire to communicate, but also realizes the privilege of solitude, of privacy.

> There is so little public beauty. I found myself dependent on a pause, a rose, something on paper. It is a way of saying, I want you, too, to have this experience, so that we are more alike, so that we are closer, bound together, sharing a point of view—so that we are "coming from the same place." (21)

> I have been spoiled with privacy, permitted the luxury of solitude. A pause, a rose, something on paper. I didn't want a party for my tenth birthday, I wanted my mother, who was there, of course, at the party, but from whom I was separated by my friends and because she was busy with the cake and the balloons. She kept a diary, but she never read it. (29)

The social frame widens along with the intellectual one:

> The ideal was of American property and she had received it from a farmer. It includes buying thrillers and gunmen's coats. A pause, a rose, something on paper. It was about this time that my father provided me with every right phrase about the beauty and wonder of books. (34)

Again, the context gets larger: the perception of natural phenomena takes on an analytical bent; foreign travel introduces a sense of history, tradition, of different ways of thinking:

> But because we have only seven days, the light seems to be orderly, even predictable. A pause, a rose, something on paper im-

plicit in the fragmentary text. The Mayan calendar has more days. (39)

L. S. Vygotsky has a useful distinction between sense and meaning:[3]

> The sense of a word . . . is the sum of all the psychological events aroused in our consciousness by the word. It is a dynamic, fluid, complex whole, which has several zones of unequal stability. Meaning is only one of the zones of sense, the most stable and precise zone. A word acquires its sense from the context; in different contexts, it changes its sense. Meaning remains stable throughout the changes of sense.

The meaning of Hejinian's phrase (privileged moment associated with beauty and writing) remains the same. But even just these few examples show how its sense changes in the course of the book. The privileged moment very much embodies the narrator's sense of selfhood, which began as a vague feeling, a "color" connected with her family. It changes as she becomes more conscious of her individuality and moves, both physically and mentally, from the enclosure of the family into wider spheres and into identifying herself through art.

It is this, and only this, that makes for a feeling of development, of time passing in this work that otherwise seems completely synchronic. It is remarkable, nearly paradoxical, that Hejinian is able to suggest change and growth through repetition, which we tend to associate rather with sameness and stasis. The method puts in a nutshell the tension between the synchronic presentation and the essentially diachronic pattern of (auto)biography that lies behind it. It also very beautifully embodies the nature of the subject of biography: the person is always both the same and changing with time and circumstance.

The method embodies even more strongly the tension between a pull toward closure (she wants "each sentence to be as nearly a complete poem as possible" ["RC"]) and a pull toward openness.

Hejinian's 1984 book, *The Guard,* makes this tension its theme.[4] More precisely, recurring phrases and contrasts very gradually map a field of opposing concepts that do not quite line up, so that the precise boundary of the opposition keeps shifting: captive vs. roving mind; concentration vs. interruption; order vs. disorder-generosity-confusion; inward vs. outward; concealing vs. revealing. Across this field, the poem roves and leaps, blurring the dualisms; on it, driven by a force that knows no boundaries, "Tossed off, serene, Chinese / windmills turn horizontally." The themes emerge gradually; the discontinuity strikes us first. Each of the first three lines seems to have a different frame of reference:

> Can one take captives by writing—
> "Humans repeat themselves."
> The full moon falls on the first.

The gaps between the lines are not, as in Pound, an abbreviated "this is like" that brings the two adjoining units closer together. Instead they show a mind taking leaps into multiplying contexts, in a *projective* rush to set many different fields in relation against the equally strong need to narrow down, to select, as she says in "The Person":

> Here I translate my thought
> into jump-language, to double fate
> But fate imposes its very interesting exercise: select[5]

Stephen Ratcliffe's "Two Hejinian Talks" are a model of careful reading that gives play to the multiple associations allowed for by such shifting frames of reference.[6] We don't usually read this way, but his analysis accounts for the sense of richness we have in reading Hejinian, even if we do not follow all the suggestions.

But because the discontinuity is obvious and foregrounded by the poet, I get interested in what nevertheless makes for continuity across the shifts and gaps, what keeps the work from disintegrating into "sentence-rubble" (Hejinian's phrase). In general, the more semantic similarity is played down, the more important similarity of sound, of grammar or any other formal pattern becomes. (And this kind of formal similarity is never included in even the most virulent attacks against analogy.)

It is true that with line 4 ("whatever interrupts"), which is so clearly in opposition to line 1 ("Can one take captives by writing—"), we get a first glimpse of a thematic field. But it is not foregrounded sufficiently to establish immediate continuity. Sound play, which seemed the most important "bridge" in *Writing Is an Aid to Memory*, is certainly present in *The Guard* ("The full moon falls," "of people . . . of pupils," "windows closed on wind in rows," "I'd seen the sea / . . . / The seance, or chance"). But syntactic patterns attract our attention right at the beginning (and of course Hejinian has alerted us to her reliance on "grammatical congruence").

If for a moment we consider sentence structure only (and take the dash as equivalent to the period), we find that sentences [1], [3], [5] are parallel: two-part structures whose first half varies, while the second half is always a prepositional phrase:

> [1] Can one take captives by writing—
> [3] The full moon falls on the first.
> [5] Weather and air / drawn to us.

Between them, sentences [2] and [4] consist of three words each, both are quotations with, in addition, some sound repetition in the verbs: "repeats" and "interrupts."

> [2] "Humans repeat themselves."
> [4] I / "whatever interrupts."

If I thought I had found *the* pattern, I was quickly disappointed: sentence [6] repeats the adjective-noun subject of "The full moon" with "The open mouths," but then sets up a quite different pairing. This in turn gets both repeated and modified. What Hejinian seems to work with is *partial* congruence, as we already saw in sentences [1], [3], [5]. We might add that the quotation marks introduce a discrepancy into the parallel of [2] and [4]. As "I" stands outside the quotation, sentence [4] breaks into two parts.

It is such *partial* overlap we find again and again, as in the theater game where each person must repeat one element of the partner's gesture but continue it differently.

Of course, there are additional complications. So far I have completely ignored that the text is in verse. The lines, which at first coincide with the sentence units, begin to go against them with line three:

> Can one take captives by writing—
> "Humans repeat themselves."
> The full moon falls on the first. I

"whatever interrupts." Weather and air
drawn to us. The open mouths of people
are yellow & red—of pupils.

The lines are not quantitative units but seem determined by rhythmic and semantic considerations. The latter are wittily at work in placing a break *before* the words "whatever interrupts." Like the quotation marks, the line break separates the "I" from that phrase and stresses its ambiguity. (Is the "I" part of the interruption? Does the "I" welcome or hate whatever interrupts?) The line unit also introduces an overtone-like secondary reading of "whatever interrupts weather and air" that would reinforce concentration, the mind taken captive by reading.

Again and again, the line units move against the sentence units. This is, of course, an old device to get a fluid rhythm, but the fact that the lines disturb and shift the parallelism of the sentences here reinforces and complicates the pattern of difference-within-sameness.

But they don't invent / they trace. You match your chair.
Such hopes are set, aroused / against interruption.

In each of these groupings, three phrases are separated by punctuation and line break. The beginning two are both rhythmically and syntactically parallel, whereas the third element deviates. But line break and punctuation mark appear in reverse order. This not only breaks up the parallel, but the line break in each case reinforces the opposition that is there on the semantic level.

As we read on, as phrases recur, the thematic fields gain strength. But as lines move against the sentences, the image clusters often move against and across the thematic oppositions. "The open mouths of people / are yellow & red" at first seems on the side of the roving mind, of curiosity and openness to whatever interrupts. It might even be brought about by the idea of weather and air drawn to us, into our open mouths. But the open mouths are visually related to caves, which "cooperate / with factories," and via the cave to:

The concave sentence—
one shaped like a dish

> —with a dip in the middle—
> to read it was like gliding in

This is clearly one of those sentences that *can* take captives. Moreover, the open mouths (which "are yellow & red") have already through their color been connected with factories ("It takes hollow red & yellow factories"), so that the mouths are clearly producing, speaking mouths. At the end of the poem we get:

> "I am a construction worker, I work at home"
> with stiff serenity . . . this
> is the difference between language and "paradise"

In any case, the image has crossed the lines of opposites. It cannot be pinned down for one side or the other and, in fact, helps blur the lines, redefine the territory. Again, the progression is by partial overlap, partial repetition. The color tie ("red & yellow") between the open mouth and the factory occurs in a different place from their being linked through the reference to "cave."

This partial overlap on all levels is an unobtrusive pattern, but it is enough of one to establish a sense of form. It is also a smaller-scale and *formal* variant of the *semantic* difference-within-sameness that we encountered in the recurrent phrases of *My Life*. As I said, it embodies the double pull toward closure and openness. Rather than always folding back toward a center, it makes the text breathe forward and backward at the same time. It establishes a continuity, but it is a sliding one with ever-shifting terms. Unless I'm simply tilting against Chinese windmills, it is Hejinian's most characteristic procedure. I close with a stanza plus one line from *The Guard:*

> Yesterday the sun went West and sucked
> the sea from books. My witness
> is an exoskeleton. Altruism suggestively fits.
> It's true, I like to go to the hardware store
> and browse on detail. So sociable the influence
> of Vuillard, so undying in disorder is order.

Shall We Escape Analogy

When I was beginning to translate *The Book of Resemblances,* I was asked for an essay on Jabès for a French issue of *Studies in 20th Century Literature.* I believed that writing an essay on Jabès at this point would interfere with the translation. Instead, I proposed an essay on Royet-Journoud and Albiach. It was printed in *Studies in 20th Century Literature* 13, No. 1 (winter 1989).

———————————

I want to talk about the refusal of metaphor that Claude Royet-Journoud and Anne-Marie Albiach dramatize in their work (the latter most explicitly in "Enigma," the first part of her book *État* [State]). It is a stance they share with a number of French (as well as American) poets, but as editors of the magazine *Siècle à mains* and, in Royet-Journoud's case, of the radio program "Poésie ininterrompue," they in fact did much to focus the concerns of their generation.[1]

I find this attitude of particular interest because, for the long stretch from Romanticism through Modernism, poetry has been more or less identified with metaphor, with relation by analogy. In linguistic terms, this has been an emphasis on the vertical axis of the speech act: the axis of selection, of reference to the code with its vertical substitution-sets of elements linked by similarity, rather than on the horizontal axis of combination, context, contiguity, syntax, and metonymy. By contrast, it is the latter that this generation of poets tend to foreground and, by implication, a view of the poem as constructing a world through its process, rather than expressing or representing an experience or world existing prior to its formulation.[2]

Opening books by Royet-Journoud or Albiach, we are immediately struck by the amount of white space on the page. "So much white! so much white!" wailed a reviewer of *Le renversement*.[3] It seems indeed a far cry from Breton's psychic automatism, which, in its desire to catch the functioning and speed of the mind, tended toward overflow. Here the stress is, rather, on what disrupts the flow, on the silence against which the words have to define themselves. Both Albiach and Royet-Journoud give white space, silence, a constituting function. "For thought to become act," says Royet-Journoud, "there must first be a pause."[4]

However, in spite of this statement, the strong presence of white space does not reflect an initial inhibition in the writing process of these two poets. It does not indicate a kind of mental stammering, not a fight against an overwhelming silence from which you painfully wrest one word or phrase at a time, not a pausing *before* words come about. Rather, both poets begin by writing "massive prose," a "negative dungheap" (*fumier négatif* [*O* 60]), by filling pages and pages of notebooks completely, from top to bottom. If it is not exactly automatic writing, it is at least a copious flow of words, which, as with the Surrealists, is an attempt to "put your head down on paper" (*O* 61). Royet-Journoud speaks of it as the condition for entering into the right mental space for writing, as a possibility of seeing. Then, there is the second stage: taking the axe to it, erasing, paring it down to the core that will become the poem. Thus we might say that the writing process of these two poets, besides producing a text, also *enacts* their attitude toward the Surrealists, that it becomes a theater where the historical reaction of one generation of poets to another is replayed. This may in part account for the violence with which Royet-Journoud talks about the process as "butchering" (*H*), though the frequent image of slaughtering and slaughtered animals in the poems goes deeper and has to do with his uneasy sense of the body, which is present only as an agent of language and writing (hand, wrist, thumb in a book) or as the object of cruelty and mutilation.[5]

The violence of the "cleaning" is consciously directed against all that is traditionally associated with "poetry," "literature," "beautiful language" ("that would be blue / the literary color / whereas we hold wake over a new form of obscurity" [*R* 67]). Royet-Journoud speaks of systematically cutting out metaphor, assonance, alliteration "as much as possible" in order to get down to a flat, literal language (*M*), to "the mystery of literalness" (*H*). So it is doubly programmatic when he writes a text with the title "Le renversement des images." He celebrates both the overthrow of images and the literal optical fact of the reversed image on the retina.

What we get instead of the expected poetic devices is a very careful architecture or orchestration of the page. The spatial relation of words and phrases takes on the greatest importance. Both poets have referred to writing as theater and to the page as a stage on which the word-actors execute carefully choreographed movements. "An ellipsis is the disappearance of a character," says Albiach in an interview with Joseph Simas.[6]

With Royet-Journoud, the positioning of lines goes a long way toward statement. Let us look at pages 16–17 of *The Notion of Obstacle:*

	premier passage.	|	
le dehors,		|	ce qui n'aura jamais lieu
	la pensée traversait le	|	
	rôles	|	

	first crossing.	|	
the outside,		|	which will never take place
	thought went through	|	
	the roles	|	

On the left page the position, as much as the vocabulary, pairs "first crossing" and "thought went through the roles" against "the outside." The right page lines up "which will never take place" with "the outside." When a magazine, in printing Keith Waldrop's translation, lined the pages up by the top of the text—that is, put the line "which will never take place" opposite "first crossing"—the author was most upset. It became clear that he saw the two facing pages as one unit and saw "which will never take place" in a strong relation to "the outside" rather than to "first crossing" or even to any line immediately preceding it on its page. Indeed, Royet-Journoud's world is inside language, where passage and movement of thought are events that definitely take place, whereas the outside can be questioned and denied. More important, the spatial arrangement is used to establish relations between terms and to replace, as much as possible, relation by metaphor or other forms of analogy.

In general, the pared-down, naked lines gain strength from being set in tension with the large white spaces, which remain a field of energy through the reduction, still holding the charge of what had been there. In Albiach's case this is true even in a spatial sense, as she likes to let phrases keep the original position on the page that they occupied in the first draft. With both poets, those devices that remain, and especially the repetitions, take on enormous weight. For instance, again in *The Notion of Obstacle,* we read on two facing pages (50–51):

	| le mur
	| lettre inachevée
	|
lettre	| dans la bouche
	|
	| de pleine terre
dans la bouche |	
	|
de pleine terre |	
	wall
	| unfinished letter
	|
letter	| in the mouth
	|
	| of full earth
in the mouth |	
	|
of full earth |	

The repeated "letter/in the mouth/of full earth" becomes insistent and gives to the semantic complex of "obstacle" (wall, incompletion, full earth) a haunting death association, even though the grammar tries to elude the expected *bouche pleine de terre* (mouth full of earth). It also gives the letter a solidity (both as wall and as being of the full earth) that is strange only if we do not accept language as Royet-Journoud's primary reality.

Among the unwanted poetic devices, metaphor bears the brunt of the attack. Its problematic is Royet-Journoud's main theme. He takes in its widest sense the old problem of the human being as sign-making animal who is conscious of the gap between thing and representation (a split that metaphor raises to the second power), between event and language ("immediate description was impossible" [R 15]), and yet (or therefore) is nostalgic for an undivided, unreflected, immediate and "real" life, *unio mystica* or paradise lost.

"I would love to be here," writes Royet-Journoud in his first book, *The Reversal* (42)—here, in the *cercle nombreux,* the crowded circle of beasts and beings, in the midst of "life." Instead, the speaker finds himself always among images, masks, roles, simulacra, make-believe, rehearsals, and representations. The very air is theatrical ("a theatricality of air / in the outfield of repetition" [N 22]). "Shall we escape analogy" he asks at the center of his first book. Without a question mark. We would like to. We may try. But the answer is clearly: no. The mirror is not a stage. It is a prison. The sentence: life. His screams get frantic in their attempt to grasp it in spite of everything, all of it, right now, here, as it happens, in the instant before it dies: *Prenez-le vivant* ("take it [him] alive" [R 71]).

Should this not be possible when the tongue seems to reconcile the two worlds, when it belongs to the sign as well as to the body, is both inside and outside us, personal, organic, yet also a system shared by the whole culture? The poem "Entrait" shows us the tongue as our "tie-beam," both concrete and abstract. It comes with the ground, a given of geography. It is a muscle and as such under the rule of sleep (*M* 87). It is the opening onto where the task can perhaps be accomplished, the gap abolished, where language is perhaps immediate and of the body. *Il respire au dos du sens* (*N* 87). An ambiguous phrase: he breathes on the back of sense, riding it as you would an animal? Or he breathes in back, behind the back, of sense, of interpretation, that is, on the other side of the mirror? In either case: here he *breathes*. But the tongue becomes a wall in the mouth. The sign wins out over the body: "dead tongue / around the mouth" (*N* 84). And the body is its own obstacle as is language. Royet-Journoud pares away at it, makes it sparse and austere. Yet he knows the obstacle is all there is, just as we can approach the infinite only through fragments, through the objects that, as his most recent title holds along with Ludwig Wittgenstein, "contain the infinite."

"Cold" is perhaps the most frequent word in these poems, used both literally and metaphorically: "the cold as story" (*O* 45). The word cannot hold on to life. Warmth itself appears as a fiction ("His childhood is a fiction of warmth" [*O* 55]). The best the poet can hope for is that his work will "look alive" (*N* 63). Emmanuel Hocquard has argued that this phrase, *Cela fait vivant*, could, besides the more obvious "This appears to be alive," be shorthand for *Cela* [*ayant été*] *fait* [*de mon*] *vivant* ("having been made in my lifetime"), thus bearing both on the process of writing, the thing done in my lifetime (out of my lifeblood, Albiach would say) and on the product that resembles something alive. But in either case, the life (whether the subject's, the author's, or that of the represented object) is absent, and resemblance is all we are left with.[7]

This ties in curiously with Royet-Journoud's preoccupation with the emptiness of the center: in the book it is the gutter between the left and right page, which is of course blank. He connects this explicitly with the fact that the pronoun "I" does not occur at all in *The Notion of Obstacle* and very rarely in his other books. And it is in the center of his first book that he placed the sequence called "Middle of Scatter" (*Milieu de dispersion*) with its manifesto question: "shall we escape analogy." In the following two numbered sections, he opposes a discomfort with resemblance and with the "lie" that is literature—"resemblances cramped him / he talked about this impossibility of lying" (*R* 49)—to his parameters of life: movement, place, looking, and, on the next page, the need to grasp. But the movement, the passage, is toward absence: "He watches himself pass" (pass by, pass away). And here, in the movement toward death, we have "perhaps / the opposite of fable." Again, I am taking my cue for relating these two couplets from their alignment on facing pages:

> il s'absente | peut-être
> Il se regarde passer | l'envers de la fable
>   —(*R* 54–55)

It is easy to agree with Hocquard not only on the strong, even violent, sense of dispossession in Royet-Journoud's work, but also on the "Schopenhauer intuition of the identity of the living and dead, an inaptitude of the living to be lived (thought) outside death."[8]

However, what Royet-Journoud articulates in his poems is less an identification of the two states than a constant passage between them. In talking about paring his initial prose down to verse (*M*), he used the image of a restorer of paintings who finds in a crack, in an accidental feature of the painting, the traces of an earlier painting underneath. So he begins to scratch at the paint, to provoke further accidents in order to reveal, to make legible the hidden painting. But whereas the restorer must choose between the first (accidental surface) and the second (virtual) painting, the poet is interested in the process, the passage from the accidentally given to the virtual image. This analogy for his working process holds also for the passage from life to death, from the accident of being to representation, from words to what the tension between them sets in motion. "You write to give movement" (*M*), he says quoting Saint Augustine to the effect that there is no location, only comings and goings. (He might also have quoted Whitehead that there are no facts, only events and occurrences.) Now words are "boats" par excellence, ferrying us back and forth between inside and outside, "between sleep and fable" (*O* 44, 52), between birth and death. And this traffic, which includes "the traffic / of objects of memory" (*O* 40) as well as light passing from one "middle" to another (*O* 78) might just possibly create (or regain) "a place that is neither inside nor outside," but made of passage, and which he calls "pre-birth" (*pré-naissance, H*). Hence also the will to incompletion that makes him end his last book with the line: "he sets about undoing the whole" (*O* 93).

Albiach is also concerned with the interrelation of body, language, and silence. But while only the obstacle seems sure with Royet-Journoud, with Albiach the body is certainty and matrix. It would not "like to be here," it is. We become aware of her words as of a pulsing of energy, vibrant, and vibrantly female. There are mysterious female presences, "elles," all through *Etat*, unidentified, but as powerful as witches.[9] All energy in *Etat* is sexual, if not as overtly as in her first chapbook, *Flammigère*, which opens with *la taille du sexe*, "the size of the penis" (at least I assume it is the penis, size not being much of a factor in the female organ). Still, there are many phrases like "can't // without sensuality" (*E* 73).

"I live the text as a body [*je vis le texte comme un corps*]," the author says in an interview (*AP*): literally, as the physical aspect of breath, of Voice (giving body to the "obsessional memory music, the permanent secret opera"), and of syntax, which, she often stresses, has a physical contiguousness; but also as a body, which inscribes its rich "enigma / the imponderables of desire" (*E* 13), its "inexhaustible novel" of drive and impulse (*E* 29), "the pedigree of / thirst" (*E* 104). Here, words are not just written, they are "engendered" (*E* 99) by coupling words, and song becomes blaze, or "incantescence" (*MV* 23).

> The discourse only seems abstract, in reality it wants to be concrete, with givens, for example like that of *the fall of a body* . . . it is above all *a poetry of desire*. . . . and not even afraid of a certain lyricism or the baroque (*AP* 14).

The rapid shift from desire to literary categories, which I find rather funny, is characteristic of Albiach's statements. There will be more examples of how totally her world is a world of texts. (In fact, does not her "concrete given," the fall of a body, quote Valéry?)

The energy wants to spread, expand, couple, and engender, but is not allowed to, is dammed up. The obstacle? On the thematic level, it is causality, rationality, "logical aridity" (*E* 115), thinking in terms of geometry, which is strongly present throughout the poem in the vocabulary of angles, measurement, and numbers as well as in the logical articulations, the frequent repetition of "because" and "if." These aspects of the mind, which "have only market value" (*E* 101), act as censors on mystery and the unconscious, silencing its joys and desires:

nos censures
pour la nudité blanche de la lettre

Cette maturation
et pleinement cadence
un trait d'union

"abaisser la paume sur la luxure des dalles"
—(*E* 31)

our censure
for the white nakedness of the letter

This maturation
            and fully cadence
a hyphen

"to lower the palm onto the lust of flagstones"

(This is the whole page; the three groups of lines are more spread out vertically.) The "censure" in the first line is for the "white nakedness of the letter"—again, a strong suggestion of the letter as a female body. However, the next lines celebrate this body, "this maturation / and fully cadence / a hyphen," giving us the three terms of organism, song, and grammar. There is an added advantage in French that the word for hyphen is literally "line of union," a line that unites and connects. Then, in the final line, "to lower the palm onto the lust of flagstones," the white body stretched out on the ground becomes a "line of union" indeed, desire overflowing the boundaries of the inanimate, and moving certainly into the baroque.

Here, in the horizontal, "the mysteries might speak" (*E* 32). But the calculating spirit can even harden the body by perverting its gestures through "knowledge of poses" (*E* 29), which is the ultimate perversion. Mystery "has no place in this parallel," but will denounce it and the "military mode of its evolution" (*E* 38).

But on the level of writing, the obstacle that dams up the energy only to increase its force is the white space and the constant interruption of discourse, as, for instance, when the skewed grammar keeps us from reading lines as continuous. We have already encountered "this maturation / and fully cadence," where the adverb instead of the expected adjective alerts us to a caesura, to erased words in between. Another example would be the beginning of the "Manifesto" (*E* 37):

la violence	violence
dessinent le drame	are sketched the drama
l'esthétique prend	the aesthetic hardens
et puissance de gestes	and strength of gesture

Here it is the third-person plural of the verb (*dessinent*, literally they sketch, design, outline, etc.) that keeps us from a simple, continuous reading. Violence and something else outline drama. It is also ambiguous whether *prend* is used intransitively—the aesthetic sets, takes, hardens—or whether there is another ellipsis: aesthetics takes what? shape? bribes? In either case, though, we have a caesura.

But more important yet is the white space. A strong impression of an earlier, fuller text persists in the pages of *État*, of a more coherent argument that spreads to cover the whole page. But most of it has been eaten into by silence, erased, with only part of a sentence left here and there, broken off more abruptly than in Royet-Journoud's work, the cut edges rough, giving off sparks like live wires. Sometimes only a solitary quotation mark or comma has survived without surrounding words:

> It is through the effect of the *white space* that I try to destroy the *given syntax*. To this end I seem to interrupt the discourse, leaving sentences unfinished, *in suspense*. The *white space* intervenes and takes on the form of the unsaid words . . . it projects its own discourse on the page. . . . which is an alternate to and yet inherent in the discourse of the text. (*AP* 15)

Thus Albiach can speak of "syntactical white space" or the "syntactical support" given by the white space. It is not merely negative, it also functions as a counterpoint. Hence her refusal to see her work as fragmentary. She speaks instead of "parallel discourses," of the play of alternation, of "questions and answers that make it all into theater" (*AP* 17).

What gives the white space its final importance as *matière constitutionnelle*, as constituting matter—which it is for Albiach as much as for Jabès or Royet-Journoud—is that it is directly based on rhythm, hence on breath, on the body: "I calculate the white space according to the strength of the text, but also according to that of the breath I have in my body to pronounce this or that word" (*AP* 14).

The cut, the caesura, imposes a vertical dimension in tension against the natural horizontal tendency of the line—and of the stretched-out body in its heaviness. It also cuts off the expected predications, specifics, explicitness, and opens onto speculations about the parallel strands of nonarticulation, of counter-voice, of silent words that could complement the given text, a vertical set of options similar at least in their relation to the given text.

This effect is paradoxical in Albiach's work because the linguistic aspect of the vertical, the substitution-sets above every word (with their relation by similarity, which is the basis of metaphor), is problematic. Ironically, and quite possibly tongue-in-cheek, she also gives us her attack on analogy in terms of an analogy, an image, that of a falling body:

> État is the book of a *FALL,* of the loss of verticality. The body on the ground is the prey of grammatical elements or of the "fire," for example, sustained by adverbs and conjunctions. (*AP* 16)

The rapid transition from body to grammar may surprise, but if the text is a body for Albiach, this is a total and reversible identification. The body is text. She is as much caught within the system of language as Royet-Journoud. Even when speaking of a possible political dimension, in the context of the exploitation of the body, she says:

> The body is for me a term of writing, tied to images, to discourse, to syntax. It is not a matter of a body as an entity (or monad), but of a body with its grammatical attributes. (*AP* 16)

Thus the fall in question is clearly the fall from metaphor into the horizontality of contiguity, where grammatical elements, connectives like conjunctions and adverbs, are dominant and sustain the "fire" of the writing process, the desire of words for one another.

The religious overtones of a fall from grace are no doubt intended, as is, perhaps, even a pang of regret at the loss of the beauty of images, of what traditionally has been considered poetry. When the "fall" is first mentioned in the poem, it is a *chute en arête,* which punningly evokes a fall backward, a *chute en arrière,* but has the meaning as well of a most uncomfortable "fall onto a ridge," which I read to represent the austerity of Albiach's enterprise. That the fall is indeed from metaphor is made explicit in the "Manifesto:"

obtuses dans le sang obtuse	in blood
que l'on dit métaphore	said to be spilled
répandue	metaphor

une déliberation	a deliberation
de normes	of norms
de formes	of forms
l'énigme	the enigma
ansi surcroît mon regard	thus overgrows my view
	—(*E* 37–38)

Metaphor's blood having been spilled, the vertical having been lost, we find the body stretched out on the ground as we already encountered it earlier. The horizontal is qualified as an earlier state, an "antecedent." So the fall, in a reversal of the religious precedent, is a return. (Remember the *chute en arrière* buried under the text.) Horizontal, the mystery of desire joins the mystery of early childhood, but also that of death ("this absence"). Mystery overgrows my eyes, the sense of sight, which can operate at the greatest distance and is therefore most "abstract," most associated with rationality. Here, in the horizontal, the enigmas could still speak—if it weren't for "confusion and this absence:"

Antécédent:	Antecedent:
l'horizontal	the horizontal
dans l'énoncé	in the speech
à l'horizontal	horizontally
les énigmes s'énonceraient	enigmas would speak
n'était-ce la confusion	were there not confusion
et cette absence	and this absence
	—(*E* 32)

Also, the body falls not only onto the earth, but also *with* the earth, and this trajectory is credited with the possibility of cutting through the subject-object division:

trajectoire de l'objet	trajectory of the object
où la trajectoire	where the trajectory
retrouverait le sujet	would rejoin the subject
	—(*E* 35)

This trajectory is "matter of a different kind" (*E* 36), because, I speculate, it is the motion of bodies in harmony, horizontal, thus avoiding the hierarchical split of subject and object. Later, the same elements appear in a variant configuration; "the inescapable / destruction / of metaphors" is set in relation first to the important arrival (written in capital letters) of one of the mysterious "she's" (*DE SA VENUE*) and then to simplicity, "extension without relation / by comparisons / for which we have no criterion" (*E* 57).[11] Of course, we might argue that the relation by contiguity is no more "simple" than that by similarity, but in Albiach's text the horizontal extension stays closer to matter, to the body, whereas metaphor has notoriously been our main tool for speculations about the metaphysical for which we have no criterion, and which takes us out of our depth. (We should remember the "as above so below" argument, God writing the "Book of Nature," what Olson called the upward "suck of symbol.") The true mysteries, for her as for Royet-Journoud, are the mysteries of the literal: "anything evident is mystery for her [or for him]," *toutes les évidences lui sont mystère* [*E* 14]).

Metaphor is destroyed "for benefit of other / modes / graphisms" (*E* 57–58). An example of what these might be appears on page 53, where a "PORTRAIT" is announced and followed by "only an imprint remains." While we may be reminded of the imprint of the Buddha's foot, it is more important that once the body has fallen out of the verticality of metaphor, the portrait, which is a likeness by definition, is replaced by the imprint, whose relation to the body is by contiguity: the contact of body and ground and, not likely by accident, the contact of the body of letters with the paper, the imprint that results in the book we are reading. (*État* is indeed printed by letterpress.)[12]

With the fall from metaphor, the play of associations in the virtual (metaphysical) dimension is curtailed—at least theoretically. With both Royet-Journoud and Albiach, the articulating of relationships by spatial arrangement goes some distance toward nonmetaphorical writing, but Albiach's constant caesuras, as we saw earlier, keep reasserting the vertical while seeming to deny it and open the door to speculations about the virtual, nonarticulated parts of the discourse. I suspect that she is perfectly aware of this, that she is playful (as in her attack on analogy in terms of an analogy). She, too, knows that we cannot escape analogy; that every linguistic act involves *both* selection from the code, the vertical substitution-sets, *and* combination in the horizontal dimension of contiguity; that all we can do is put our *emphasis* more on one axis than on the other. But I also find that in reading *État* I do not usually stop to speculate on what the missing words might be, but rather just take in the fact of the interruption, of the silence. I stay with what is physically present: the parallel strands of articulation and nonarticulation, of voice and nonvoice, of event and silence, the play of alternation that, as the author says, makes it all into theater (*AP* 17).

One last note on this "theater" of writing: Jabès has written much about the author being rejected by his work—and his work is one of those Albiach says she writes "in the reverberations of" (*AP* 19). In *État*, this rejection takes a complex form. The author is "devoured" by the writing, by "the cruel game between language and body, writing and desire. . . . A force comes into being which I desire and which gives birth to a body of a different kind" (*AP* 16). This other body is what plays out the theater on the page, whereas the author becomes a mere spectator, opposite the action (*opposition: je* is the title of a section). Nowhere in *État* can we find a direct first-person statement like the "I scream" (*Je crie*) in *Flammigère* (11). The "I" is present but problematical. It often appears in quotation marks: " 'I' persist with the fire" (*E* 83).

We have already encountered "fire" as the writing process sustained by elements of grammar, by connectives and conjunctions. The writer persists in playing with fire, for in writing "the body risks its own existence" (*AP* 16), is devoured by, but also persists *with* the fire, is sustained by the very process that devours her. The drama of writing is a ritual. Albiach mentions an image of Kafka's that has stayed with her: a wrist circled by a gold ring "at the same time scar and ornament: as for the elaboration of sacrificial writing . . . as if the writer were to be sacrificed to the body of the text" (*AP* 16). It is the wrist, whose movement is the crucial physical basis of writing, that is dressed up for sacrifice. And with the living author sacrificed to the other body, to the text, we have come full circle: only the sign system exists; the body is textual. But we have added a religious dimension, even without the help of metaphor and symbol. Language, in atheistic times, is one of the forms of transcendence we have left.

Sebald's *Vertigo*

W. G. Sebald's *Vertigo* is unlike any other book I have read. The four parts do not fit our genre expectations. They are not quite stories, not quite essays, but Sebald's own mixture of personal narrative, investigation report, quotation (both textual and pictorial), and meditation.

The theme is the vertigo we feel in moments when reality shows itself to be unstable or uncanny. It is traced through instances when "fact" clashes with memory or perception, with the complex layering of knowledge and expectation that enters into it. This nonmatch is further complicated when we try to transform experience into writing, as all three "characters" (Stendhal, Kafka, and the first-person narrator) do. The insight into our inability to hold on to "reality" pervades the characters and the book with a tone of melancholy.

Pictures are used throughout, in a strikingly original way. The pictures are not illustrations but reference points placed at precise points of the text. They seem to constitute a reality check, as they seem a more objective record, closer to documentation, to the pole of "fact," than writing can be. But of course this is deceptive. The pictures, especially as they largely represent photographs or paintings, open onto the same *mise-en-abîme* of mediation and perception as the writing. In the end, they actually exacerbate the vertigo we feel as we move in the web of text and image. I like especially the way the first piece, "Beyle or the Strange Fact of Love," makes the pictures part of the sentences, most strikingly on page 15, where a picture of Stendhal's eyes is used *instead* of the word "eyes."

Each of the four stories narrates a journey. The first, "Beyle or the Strange Fact of Love," is about Stendhal, then still the seventeen-year-old lieutenant Henri Beyle in Napoleon's army. We follow him across the Alps, into some adventures with women, and into the battle of Marengo—experiences he will later mine for *The Charterhouse of Parma* and *On Love*. The writing of those books enters only marginally into the story. But we are with Stendhal when he revisits the battlefield later in his life and is shocked and made dizzy by the unreliability of his memory—an experience that becomes the real germ of his later writing.

The second story, "All'estero," is a first-person narrative of two trips to (Vienna and) Italy, which the narrator undertakes partly to alleviate his depression and partly to do research on a little-known episode in Kafka's life, his journey to the Italian spa known as Riva. During the first trip, the narrator is obsessed with Casanova's imprisonment in Venice and gets into a quasi-paranoid state of mind where small perceptions take on ominous meanings till he sees himself as the likely next victim of a terrorist group, the "*Organizzazione Ludwig*," and takes flight. The second trip becomes a brighter revision of the experience, where the terrors are cleared up and real problems (like the loss of a passport) are easily resolved.

The third story, "Dr. K.'s Journey to the Baths of Riva," is the result of the narrator's research in the preceding story. A lovely vignette of Kafka in the routine and society of the spa, battling with his terror of love (his relation to a fellow patient, to Felice, his memory of following a "repulsive" man through the streets of Prague). At the end, the story compounds the layers of fictionality by taking us into a scene from Kafka's story "The Hunter Gracchus."

Finally, in the fourth story, "Il ritorno in patria," we follow the narrator to his native village in the German Alps and through his efforts to recapture the past. The story is a moving blend of childhood memories, German village life, and the melancholy realization that we cannot recover the intense meaning that things had in our childhood.

Vertigo is a wonderful, fascinating book—an adventure of the mind. It should definitely be translated and made available to American readers.

Guest's *Rocks on a Platter* and *Miniatures*

Barbara Guest is one of our most important poets. She is usually considered part of the New York School. Among the poets of that school, she is closest to John Ashbery, whose tolerance of diffusion she shares. But she has developed a style completely her own, combining a kind of Mallarméan tracing of philosophical tenuousness with a formal sense much like an abstract painter's.

Rocks on a Platter is an electrifying fusion of poem and poetics. It is as remote from the direct self-referentiality of much recent poetry as it is from the statements worked into, say, Wallace Stevens's "Notes toward a Supreme Fiction."

Instead, Guest creates an airy, hovering, mind's-eye perspective that allows her to alight rapidly and effortlessly in any area of life and art, the concrete and the abstract, the raw and the cooked, fusing them into astonishing and delightful combinations ("pollen indoctrinated," "the moss of subjectivity") and, even more importantly, showing their essential unity. As one of her epigraphs says, "to live is to defend a form." Guest gives us a shimmering, if brittle, sense of life, where mind and body are equally vibrant and equally tenuous.

She does this with an amazingly light, playful touch. Consider the opening: "Ideas. As they find themselves. In trees?" Or: "the pear-shaped manuscript is endangered."

It is actually difficult to quote examples, because the airy spacing is essential to the poems' limpid tonality as well as to the sense of the tenuous, the perishable, the mortal. For Guest's "frail sentence" is "moved by / the seismic sway of existence." The vibrancy implies an ever-present threat.

This book shows the mature Guest in full power. It is another step away from her early emphasis on the visual, toward more literary/ philosophical explorations. In short, I think this is an extremely important book of poetry. By all means publish.

Almost all of what I wrote about *Rocks on a Platter* applies to *Miniatures* as well. Here, there is less explicit stress on poetics, but the concern with form and with art is just as strong—it is an essential ingredient of Guest's work.

Again there is the delightful light touch, the sheer fun as she evokes "spirits" from anywhere in our culture. The historical charge she works into her poems does not weigh them down as "cultural baggage," but creates a sparkling community across centuries.

> ("Petticoat:"
> She ran down the middle of the road throwing her hands up
> to Heaven.
> Longinus, Leviticus, mathematical wonder.
> . . .
> The Morse Code arrived in petticoat blue, the steam engine.)

Again there is the fusion of the concrete and abstract capacities of language that make all of her later work so vital, so remarkable—and so important a model for many younger poets.

I love the structural crescendo from "Miniatures" via (tongue-in-cheek) "Pathos" to the single longer poem "Blurred Edge," which engages with a full range of life, from anguish to form, from objects to the intangible, from mood to geometry, from drama to sand! It is a crescendo that does not culminate in a big orchestral bang, but in Guest's typically subtler pointing toward the indeterminate, toward an "unworded distance at edge."

With *Miniatures*, Guest continues to mine the rich vein of *Rocks on a Platter*. This book refines, pushes even further toward the tenuous and toward open form, but always, amazingly, with perfect balance and within a humorous human perspective. It seems the perfect sequel.

From White Page to Natural Gaits

Notes on Some Recent French Poetry

Toward the end of 1997, *American Poet* asked me to present a mini-anthology of current French poetry for their spring issue. The following is the introduction to my selection of texts by Anne-Marie Albiach, Pierre Alferi, Dominique Fourcade, Emmanuel Hocquard, Anne Portugal, and Jacques Roubaud.

———————

The 1997 poetry *event* in France was Claude Royet-Journoud's *Les natures indivisibles,* the long-awaited final volume of his tetralogy (which for more than ten years had been a tetralogy in three volumes!)

Royet-Journoud had, with Anne-Marie Albiach, focused his generation's reaction against image and metaphor in their magazine *Siècle à mains,* but especially with his manifesto "shall we escape analogy"—without question mark—placed at the center of his first book, *Le renversement.* I had for a long time considered this (along with the stress on discontinuity, on white space) a reaction against Surrealism, just as I took the current American equivalent as a reaction against Pound and Imagism. But I have come to suspect that the experience of war—World War II and the Algerian war—is a more crucial factor, even if during the former the writers were either small children or not born yet.

The sequence "Erreur de localisation des événements dans le temps," in Royet-Journoud's new book, confirms my suspicion. The events behind the poem were these: In October 1961, during the Algerian war, Algerians in Paris defied the curfew in a large demonstration that included women and children. The C.R.S. (Compagnie Républicaine de Sécurité) mowed down some three hundred of them and tossed the bodies in the Seine. The event was censored out of existence. In the same week of October 1961, demonstrating Frenchmen were chased into a Métro tunnel that was closed at the other end. In the press of bodies, five people suffocated. This caused a great scandal, which was much written about.

When people are asked about the scandal of 1961, they invariably mention the second incident. This replacement of one memory by another, less atrocious one is referred to by the title, "Error of Localization of Events in Time." The poem "of course," says Royet-Journoud, in no way talks about this. So the poem, too, replaces words about the event by other, less atrocious ones. And, refusing representation, it allows no recourse. Though after our conversation some lines became heavier for me:

he is dead in the sentence
cold reaches its target

she speaks blackwards
no image will remain
a blind ball strikes the walls noiselessly
grass is uncertain like the color and
the stifling of numbers
         —(trans. Keith Waldrop)

Royet-Journoud's texts are always "survivors." He (as does Albiach) always begins by writing "massive prose," a "negative dung heap" filling pages and pages of notebooks. If this is not exactly Breton's psychic automatism, it is at least a copious flow of words that, as with the Surrealists, is an attempt to "put your head down on paper." Royet-Journoud speaks of it as the condition for entering into the right mental space for writing, as a possibility of seeing. Then there is a second stage: taking the axe to it, erasing, "cleansing," paring it all down to the core that will become the poem.

Now in his maturity, he has compacted his texts in an almost Beckettian manner. The sparse constellations on the page explode with contained power.

"This way of proceeding by subtraction, so amazing." Is this a comment on Royet-Journoud? No. This is Dominique Fourcade on Degas's monotypes. But yes, it also applies to Royet-Journoud and most of all to Fourcade's own poetry, especially when he sets this process of condensing in tension with the other crucial feature of the monotype: that you not only "subtract" ink, but you also paint directly in the ink, without preliminary sketches and with great speed—before the ink dries.

Degas as Fourcade's alter ego can be seen all through the new book, *Le sujet monotype*, which is itself an embodiment of this tension. It is not so much that there is prose and verse but that both have this urgency, this sense of being pared back and at the same time shooting out as if from a gun (invoked already in his *Rose-déclic*). His lines shoot straight to the edge of the page and off, to the edge of the French language. And beyond: into a space between English and French in the next book, *IL*, where the "s" of "snow" becomes part of the French word: *le s dans neige*. And back to conversations with Degas. All on a ground of uncertainty whether writing exists, is possible. And even when it happens, it is precarious: *le site du poème s'évanouit à peine le poème écrit*, "the poem no sooner written than the site of the poem vanishes."

Dominique Fourcade received the Grand Prix National de Poésie this past year.

The word as body. Pitted against silence, the threat of death, the "Violence of the White Page."

What makes the white space important for this group/generation is not only that it reacts against Breton's psychic automatism, which, in its desire to catch the functioning and speed of the mind, tended toward overflow. Nor is it only a literary matter that these poets hark back to Mallarmé. It is after World War II that the whiteness begins to dominate and that Mallarmé's sense of crisis (of verse, of language) seems a premonition of the total crisis of society in our century.

And most of all, the negative space, silence, is a constituting matter of the poem in that it is based on rhythm, on breath, on the body.

"I live the text as a body," says Albiach. She lives it literally, in the physical context of breath, of voice, of syntax as a physical next-to-each-other of words broken off by silence. But the body is also the site of the "inexhaustible novel" of drive and impulse (Albiach, *E* 29). Not just Fourcade, but many other practitioners of the white page have also turned—have been driven?—to prose.

Jean Daive began his many-volume "novel," *La Condition d'infini,* in 1995. In 1997 he published volume 5, *Sous la coupole,* which is really a book-length prose poem, an extraordinary lyrical, incantatory evocation of Paul Celan. There is a curious exchange where Celan admires André Du Bouchet for knowing the *Littré* (the French equivalent of the *Oxford English Dictionary*) by heart. Daive, irritated, replies, "that's not what matters," and Celan says: "But it *is* what matters." Daive then comments: "It is what matters because a person who lives and entertains all the tensions of a floating language has an almost biological need to turn to a person who can lock the word into its most radical definitions." One recurrent image will stay with me: Celan out shopping, carrying a net bag with a single lightbulb in it.

Emmanuel Hocquard has long led a campaign against the "false seriousness" of French literature—recently, by writing mock detective texts and using a private eye, Moebius, as persona. And he has turned his immense inventiveness to collaboration and mixed media: *Le voyage a Reykjavik* chronicles an imaginary voyage to Iceland that really chronicles the methods of the painter (Alexandre Delay) and the poet with a combination of video stills, photographs, and text.

Hocquard's earlier books had an archeological feel, as if excavating shards of a civilization that we could still lament as a disappeared whole. Now the private eye searches for clues in the visual world of the present. It proves as fragmentary as the past and even more resistant to interpretation. The detective is called Moebius for a good reason: the photographs, seemingly documenting a hard reality, quickly become ambiguous, show the same absence of any shared system of reference.

Jacques Roubaud, the master Oulipist, spent most of November 1997 in the United States. He gave readings and lectures and participated in a collective translation project organized by Benjamin Hollander at the Djerassi Foundation, where he vainly tried to engage the cows in conversation and had to conclude they did not understand his accent. He also took pleasure in confounding us translators with puns (like *nuage: nu âge*) and the awkwardness of "duration" versus *durée*.

While Roubaud continues to write poems with mathematical patterns, he has also produced a veritable explosion of prose. Aside from smaller books, he has two extended fiction projects. He is halfway through the cycle of six comic novels around the figure of "la belle Hortense." The other, an autobiographical series that began with *Le grand incendie de Londres* in 1989, seems like a compendium of all modernist and postmodernist techniques: multibranching, incisions, parentheses, footnotes, convolutions, cross-reference, multiple-choice, narrative, essay, you name it. The year 1997 brought the third volume, *Mathématiques,* which to my great relief contained no hard-core mathematics. The scope of these books is amazing. They range from personal history to Fermat's theorem, via a disquisition on croissants and a theory of prose in terms of making jam!

The Oulipian procedural tradition is thriving among the younger women, notably Michelle Grangaud and Michèle Métail. Grangaud writes anagrams or, more recently, *Poèmes Fondus,* where she "melts" down into haiku the sonnets of Joachim Du Bellay, José Maria Hérédia, Charles Baudelaire, Gérard de Nerval, and Stéphane Mallarmé. A curious, shadowy presence of the older poets comes through in the vocabulary, as Mallarmé's in:

> Ce sens bu dans un
> bloc de mots en vols du noir
> nu avec sa voix.
> (100)

Unlike in "S+7" texts, the effect is not parodistic. It rather seems to take up residence in the gap between East and West and the gap between centuries—or, rather, the resonance between them. Who would have thought a Du Bellay sonnet had this in it:

> Le droit n'est pas droit.
> Propos encore propos,
> le la n'est pas la.
> (45)

Pierre Alferi's *Allures naturelles* seems a programmatic title for the younger generation of poets. There is a new primacy of rhythm, flow, "natural" movement, replacing the stress on discontinuity, fragmentation. Alferi combines an analytic/scientific tone with a movement that seems driven yet impeded, seems to oscillate in a field of conflicting forces, contrapuntal harmonics, and jazz dissipation. While he is perfectly capable of compacting seven-liners of seven syllables each into the strongly allusive bouillon cubes of *Kub Or,* his new volume, *Sentimentale journée,* is back to "natural" movement, this time on the model of conversation. It is not a Jabès dialogue lost between the silences of pre- and post-dialogue. Rather, it is a collection of quasi-improvisatory riffs that stop short of communication or "sense," but chart nuance, difference, overtone of the said and unsaid.

Olivier Cadiot's work has a rare combination of carnival and catastrophe, of verve, humor, innovation and provocation. His game is always grammatical, but the arrow hits and a real corpse decomposes. I am happy that he has been translated by Charles Bernstein, whose playfulness is Cadiot's match [*Red, Green & Black* (Potes & Poets)]. Watch out for *Future, ancien, fugitif,* forthcoming from Roof Books. [*Future, Former, Fugitive* came out in 2003.] It is a book that, among other things, "contains a complete list of what to do in case of exile, a memento on table manners, a method of dialogue in one voice.

Norma Cole is in the process of translating Anne Portugal's *Le plus simple appareil.* (I wonder, is she going to call it *The Full Monty?* or *With Nothing On Nor On Her Mind?* or *In the Altogether?*). [The book was published as *Nude* in 2001.] It is a playful, lively, free-style, geometric ("let us now try to limit Susanna to a rectangle") and inventive poem on a pretext of Susanna and the Elders. Portugal is delightfully anti-literary, ironic, and down-to-earth. "In poetry, one must break the notions of the sacred," she says. "For me, poetry . . . is first and foremost physical."

For the very young (along with some poets well known in France), look at the current issue (no. 16) of the Canadian magazine *Raddle Moon.* It is a special issue devoted to "22 New (to North America) French Writers." The translations are all by poets.

All during the summer of 1997, postcards for the sixtieth birthday of Anne-Marie Albiach circulated in the United States and were signed by a large number of American poets. The initiative came from Kevin Killian, who as far as I know is not a personal friend of Albiach's. The birthday itself was celebrated by a public reading in San Francisco. The "love affair" between French and American poetry is clearly continuing. Here is another, more directly literary example: when Emmanuel Hocquard translated the sequence called "Baudelaire Series" from Michael Palmer's book *Sun,* he had the feeling of "writing a book I was not writing" and "continued" his translation by writing a book of poems of his own, *Théorie des Tables,* which is "imprinted" by Palmer—and which Palmer then, fittingly, translated into English in his turn [*Theory of Tables* (O.blek Editions)].

Scalapino's *New Time*

Leslie Scalapino is one of our most radical innovators in poetry. *New Time* is amazing writing, difficult but rewarding.

As in all of Scalapino's books, there is a strong sense of "the social," especially in its urban form: "the outside is one's awareness." But where earlier books, like *The Front Matter, Dead Souls* had an extremely strong presence of urban chaos with its constant jump-cut sensory overload, here "the social" has become more abstract. We do get an occasional glimpse of people:

> people sprawled leaning on wall (of subway underground in passing it)—they can't rest // can in subway underground, but not at all, they aren't resting.

But we don't get characters so much as activities, states of mind, and feeling ("there's no entity but there's action"): working small jobs, fatigue, not having time to oneself, fighting, traveling, all building up to a sense of isolation and alienation. This is played against violent dream images like the airplane on fire and against the utopian "new time," in which action would be transparent for consciousness and the boundaries of inner and outer abolished ("there is no inner").

Formally, *New Time* works above all with constant qualification and modification of statements and phrases. While this procedure has its roots in Gertrude Stein, and while both poets use it to trace the process of thinking, Scalapino pushes more relentlessly at the boundaries of the sentence. Also, her structure owes less to Cubism than to Serial music. Her repetitions do not pull inward, toward a center, but move centrifugally through shifting contexts.

Reading this book, I feel I am taken on a journey over unstable ground, syntax and grammar shifting subtly under my feet, the movement outward, into regions yet unmapped, but that we've always known —in the way of a truth so deep down we can't normally get at it.

There is no other poet like Scalapino. Even if one associates her with the L=A=N=G=U=A=G=E school, one will find similar theoretical positions, but no poetry that is anything like Scalapino's.

Zukofsky's *Le Style Apollinaire*

Louis Zukofsky is one of the few really important poets of our century. Anything he has written should be published.

I am not up on Apollinaire criticism but would think that this work from the early 1930s has considerable interest for the field. There are many insights into Apollinaire's style, the fascination with speed and technology he shares with his contemporaries, his quasi-anthropological stance ("the poet studied his race as tho it were 'primitive' " [121]), and many interesting points of comparison, ranging from Rimbaldian rhyme schemes, Alfred Jarry, and Villon to Dante and Longinus.

The main importance, though, is for American poetry: the book shows a stage in the formation of Zukofsky's aesthetic. It seems to me a work where the author analyzes a kindred spirit in order to clarify his own thinking. Many of his statements about Apollinaire go beyond the ostensible subject, toward developing a contemporary aesthetic. Issues of composition are central. Also the lens, the most crucial image for Objectivist poetics, appears already here.

An example: Zukofsky sees the main difference between Apollinaire's and Jarry's writing in "Apollinaire's artistic instinct for the natural simultaneity (rather than the unity) of intelligence" (21). This curious concept of "simultaneity of intelligence" feeds into the "manifold aesthetic" in chapter 3 ("& Cie"), which is the "meatiest" as far as Zukofsky's own writing is concerned. Here, he uses Dante's polarization of composition into action and passion from *De Vulgari Eloquentia* (91) to develop a modern aesthetic of the inclusive and manifold, in which the distinction between poetry and prose is dialectically sublated into "writing" and discussed in terms of a different polarization: construction and utterance/sounding (94). The latter is of particular interest because the *sounding* of a text is something rarely even thought of outside poetry but is here applied to prose in a very interesting way.

What is most remarkable is the form of the work. It consists almost entirely of quotations. A conventional critical book would take the reader by the hand and lead him or her along the thread of its argument. It would provide lengthy transitions between quotations. It would explain why the texts are quoted. Zukofsky's comments tend to be elliptical; for example, "Of one whose work was often filtered with the light of mediaeval intelligence, it might be said for the convenience of insight that the destiny of his writing was not unlike the destiny of love as Cavalcanti defined it" is followed by the poem in question (43). Often he simply says: "*Collate:*" and then juxtaposes two or more texts. In other words, he invites the reader to enter the reading process in an active manner and leaves it to the reader to figure out the relations and rationales of quotations and juxtapositions.

This is in exact parallel to Zukofsky's own poetic procedure: he cuts out all unessential steps to arrive at an extremely condensed text. It is also a tendency he shares with Apollinaire, whose "dialectical sensibility . . . telescoped into a choice of words without the accretion of rendered corpulence" (107) he clearly appreciates. We are used to this procedure in poetry. In a critical book, it is a radical divergence from the accepted, conventional style.

In short, this is an unusual, idiosyncratic book of great interest. I definitely recommend publication.

II

TRANSLATION

The space between two languages is a space like no other.
—Anne Carson

Writing anything at all is a work of translation exactly comparable to that of transmuting a text from one language into another.
—Paul Valéry

The Joy of the Demiurge

When Goethe has Faust sit down to translate Saint John's gospel, Faust is restless and discontented. Concentrating on how to render *logos* clears up some of his own attitudes and problems. In fact, his solutions anticipate the course of his life and the play. "Translation is evidently something of importance, not only to the reader but also the translator himself," Leonard Forster throws out.[1]

I have often asked myself why I go on translating instead of concentrating exclusively on writing my own poetry. The woes of the translator are all too well known: little thanks, poor pay, and plenty of abuse. To this traditional triad we may add that American publishers at present seem even less eager for translations than for original poetry—if this is possible. I am not speaking of commissioned translations, of course, but of the situation where a translator chooses to translate a work of literature.

Occasionally, translating has helped me when my own work was stalled, much as it helped Faust. But this alone would hardly have sustained me through the volumes of Edmond Jabès's *Livre des Questions*. Is my choice to continue translation a matter of wanting to assume the noble role of the mediator? Maybe. But if I cared most about the readers, I would serve them better by teaching them the language. Is it a matter of personal circumstances? As an immigrant to the United States, I came to a point where I could not go on writing poems in German while "living" in English. Translating (from English to German, at that time) was the natural substitute. What finally made me bold enough to try writing in English is difficult to trace (except for some foolhardy encouragement), but writing in my adopted language came before translating into it, so that even my particular state as a person between languages cannot altogether account for my persistence in this seemingly unrewarding, nearly impossible activity.

The reason must lie deeper, must lie in my relation to the original work. Renato Poggioli holds that "like the original poet, the translator is a Narcissus who in this case chooses to contemplate his own likeness not in the spring of nature but in the pool of art."[2] This simile amuses me because it makes me, who claims to be both poet and translator, a veritable nymphomaniac of narcissism contemplating my own likeness in anything at all! But Poggioli is right. Only, he does not go far enough in his indictment. As I read the original work, I admire it. I am overwhelmed. I would like to have written it. Clearly, I am envious—envious enough to make it mine at all cost, at the cost of destroying it. Worse, I take pleasure in destroying the work exactly because it means making it mine. And I assuage what guilt I might feel by promising that I will make reparation, that I will labor to restore the destroyed beauty in my language—also, of course, by the knowledge that I do not actually touch the original within its own language.

The destruction is serious. Translating is not pouring wine from one bottle into another. Substance and form cannot be separated easily. (I hope we do not have to go again over the false dichotomy of *les belles infidèles,* which assumes that one could be "faithful" to a poem by rendering ugly or dull what it "says.") Translating is more like wrenching a soul from its body and luring it into a different one. It means killing. "We grow old through the word. We die of translation," says Jabès in *Retour au Livre.*[3] His words are not an author's facetious despair at bad translation, but part of a more serious meditation on time and the word, on the book of flesh. Death, it is true, is more certain than resurrection or transmigration. There is no body ready to receive the bleeding soul. I have to make it, and with less freedom than in the case of the most formal poem on a given subject. I have to shape it with regard to this soul created by somebody else, by a different, though not alien, aesthetic personality.

Let me stay with the analogy to metempsychosis for a moment. It does not hold very far. In translation, the progress of the "soul" is not toward greater perfection. Alas, the new body will never fit altogether. Nor is the goal Nirvana, although Walter Benjamin, arch-Hegelian in spite of himself, envisages the afterlife of the original work as a *progress* through translation into "a higher and purer linguistic air, as it were,"[4] a step further toward "pure language" stripped of all the characteristics of particular languages. This concept of a "pure language," of a central relationship between languages through "what they want to express," is indeed confirmed by the fact that translation is possible at all. However, the progress of the work through translation is not toward this abstraction, but, on the contrary, toward another embodiment in a concrete, particular language. Or we might say that the work moves *through* "pure language" understood as translatability into another concrete embodiment. Here "pure language" would function as a kind of black box like Eugene A. Nida's "transfer mechanism," which I will talk about later.

However, "soul" is an uncomfortable word, both too vague and too laden with religious associations. Perhaps we can turn the idea of the afterlife of a work of literature toward biology and consider translation as the offspring of the original, less handsome than the parent, but true kin. (This analogy, which also does not bear to be pressed very hard, has curious implications for the time gap that often exists between the original publication and the translation and that compounds the cultural differences.) The first task of the translator would be to find the "genetic code" of the work, to get from the surface to the seed, which, in our terms, would mean getting close to the nucleus of creative energy that is at the beginning of a poem.

Concretely, this means that translating is more than a triple matching of words, grammatical structures, and cultural contexts, which in itself would already be a formidably complex process. Nida speculates that it is likely that "the message of language A is decoded into a concept, and that this concept then provides the basis for the generation of an utterance in language B."[5] If we widen "concept" into "conception," this statement is, I think, accurate for literary translation and applies both to detail and, most importantly, to the structure of the work as a whole. In other words, the *unit* of translation is the whole work rather than the single sentence or line—let alone the single word, as Benjamin suggests.

This last idea is so absurd that we need to consider its background. Benjamin makes a stand against translations that try to sound as if they were works written in the host language, in which the transfer is unnoticeable. He invokes Goethe as an ally and Friedrich Hölderlin as a counterexample. Instead, Benjamin wants the translator to "expand and deepen his language by means of the foreign language."[6] I share this desire. I, too, like "some strangeness in the proportion," a trace of the foreign in the translation. But if it gets *too* strange, it will not affect its medium but will simply be rejected as quirky. This was the case for Hölderlin's translations from the Greek, which are Benjamin's model along with interlinear Bible translations. I hardly need to remind anybody that no interlinear version ever became a translation event as the King James version did, which indeed expanded the scope of English prose. Following the foreign syntax word for word seems to me to show rather dubious respect for the original.

In our own days, Celia and Louis Zukofsky's *Catullus* provides an example of this attempt,[7] compounded by the desire to keep also the sound structure, nearly phoneme by phoneme. Their translation, says the preface, "follows the sound, rhythm, and syntax of his Latin—tries, as is said, to breathe the 'literal' meaning with him." This most ambitious and impossible undertaking to transfer *everything intact* has brilliant successes like "Miss her, Catullus" for the famous "Miser Catulle." Here, both the single sound and the whole poem enter into the translation, because "missing her" is indeed at the root of Catullus's misery. But when the line goes on with "don't be so inept to rail" for *desinas ineptire,* I am much less convinced. Even just the preponderance of Latinate words in their translation makes for a heaviness that to my ear is much worse than giving up the sound structure (whose effect in English is at any rate very different from what it is in Latin). But if it is a failure, it is a grandiose one and immensely fascinating. When I find, for instance:

minister wet to lee, pour the Falernian

for:

minister vetuli puer Falerni
(27)

I am immediately tempted to try this kind of surface transformation as a method to mine foreign texts for strange combinations of words. But I do not think English usage will be much affected, nor will translation practice—although Anne-Marie Albiach has used the method to translate Zukofsky's "A 9" into French (in *Siècle à main* 12, 1970).

Faust's effort to translate the first line of Saint John goes through four versions. "In the beginning was the *word*" and "in the beginning there was *sense*" [*Sinn*] are both speedily rejected in favor of "in the beginning there was *strength*" [*Kraft*], which is finally narrowed to "*act*" [*Tat*]. If I may for a moment forget the function this sequence has in the play and pretend that it refers to translation, I find here a perfect support for my view. Neither the single word nor the sense, the meaning, can be the center of translation. Neither element can be at the beginning of a text. It must be the *Kraft*, the energy or, more specifically, the *creative act* that brought the particular words and meanings together and that will have to be duplicated by the translator.

This also means that beyond a few rules of thumb there is as little prescription for translation as for original writing. Nida sets up a neat diagram of how a message in language A is *de*coded by the receptor and *re-en*coded into a message in language B. But in the center of the diagram is the process he labels "transfer mechanism." Regarding this process, he has to admit that "if we understood more precisely what happens in this transfer mechanism we should be better able to pin-point."[8] It is the crux of the problem that we do not understand the central process of translating any better than we understand the creative process in general.

The parallels between the two processes of writing and translating are often overlooked, because on the surface they seem to work in opposite directions. Translation starts out from a given articulated structure and works down to what I have called the genetic code of the work or its creative core; whereas original writing would seem to begin with a vague energy and work wholly toward the articulation of surface and structure. To state it this way, however, disregards the destructive aspect of all creation. There are always structures that are undone in the process of writing. It is perhaps most obvious on the level of detail, when time-hallowed combinations of words are broken apart to form "fresh" ones or when the traditional combination of elements in a genre is disarranged. On the most general level, the structure of experience is transformed. Jabès has the narrator of *The Book of Questions* ask his protagonist: "Have I betrayed you, Yukel?" The answer has to be: "I have certainly betrayed you," for writing cannot but betray experience:

It is I who force you to walk. I sow your steps.
And I think, I speak for you. I choose and cadence.

For I am writing
and you are the wound.
Have I betrayed you, Yukel?
I have certainly betrayed you.[9]

I could marshal nearly all the symbolists here, who were very explicit about the destruction inherent in creation, from William Blake's "printing in the infernal method, by corrosives . . . melting apparent surfaces away, and displaying the infinite which was hid," in *The Marriage of Heaven and Hell,* to Mallarmé's letters to Lefébure, which proclaim that "destruction was my Beatrice." Translation makes the destructive aspect more obvious, because the structure of the original work is perceptible; whereas, for instance, the experience or experiences transformed into a poem cannot be traced by any means. This might make us hope that analysis of translation would provide significant insight into the creative process in general because some of the elements are more measurable. But I fear that the difference in the process of choice (which is so limited in translation and so infinite in the case of original work) takes this hope away—not to mention the creative core of both processes, whose resistance to analysis throws us back to images and analogies.

The fact that the original work is evident in a way that experience underlying a poem is not gives translation a sense of reference. This brings me back to Benjamin. Translation at its best, says Benjamin, "does not cover the original, does not block its light, but allows the pure language, as though reinforced by its own medium, to shine upon the original all the more fully."[10] I agree with this except for the part played by "pure language." The work, rather than moving toward this abstraction, "pure language," seems to me to undergo something more like erosion. It is weathered by the passage into another language as a statue might be by the passage of time. The extremities— puns and other wordplay, very specific cultural connotations—are particularly vulnerable, but everything is worn down to some extent. Yet there are compensations. Have we not all admired some of those worn faces where the original traits were only a suggestion, but as such, in their indistinctness, infinitely fascinating? Thus—and here I agree with Benjamin—a translation that can suggest the lost beauty of the original is preferable to a smooth replica that pretends to be the original itself. This means, however, that while this kind of translation does not block the light of the original, it is not completely transparent either. The ravages of time and translation will be visible. Even the most faithful of translations will bear the mark of the translator, of her time, of her cultural background. "One cannot translate in a vacuum," says Richmond Lattimore.[11]

Michel Leiris tells the story of a young dervish who stands out by his piety and mystical gift.[12] The old monk who is his spiritual director tells him: "you are very advanced in the mystical life, but not yet at the last stage. There is another border. You are ready for it: if you want you can see the face of God." The young monk is violently disturbed and for a long time refuses the suggestions of the old monk. He is not worthy, he says; the idea of finding himself face to face with God fills him with horror. Eventually, though, he complies and sets out for the old ruined mosque. When he is not back the next day, the old monk goes to look for him and finally finds him looking ravaged, terribly upset. Did he go to the mosque and through the prescribed prayers and rituals? He did. Did he see the face of God? He did. What did the face of God look like? At this question the young dervish remains silent and starts to tremble. Pressed, he finally answers, shaking with terror: it was his own face.

This sacrilegious joy of substituting one's own face for God's—without for all that making it any less God's—is the real reward of the translator, though he or she, too, may (innocently or hypocritically) seem to be frightened by it.

Silence, the Devil, and Jabès

"There is no muse of translation," declared Walter Benjamin.[1] The Brazilian poet Haroldo de Campos (who otherwise follows Benjamin) counters with a fanfare: "If translation has no muse, one could however say that it has an angel."[2] The angel, we learn, is Lucifer, and a good translation should by rights be called a "transluciferation." I think Benjamin would have approved of the angel of light in this function, since his highest claim for translation was that it allows the light of "pure language, as though reinforced by its own medium, to shine upon the original all the more fully." Although I have difficulties with the construct of "pure" language, I am happy to claim Lucifer for translation as bearer of light, as the father of lies, and as the one who says "no," who will not serve.

De Campos's *non serviam* is particularly directed against the "seemingly natural relationship postulated as dichotomy between form and content" in which the content is considered dominant in the way of an "inner presence" or spirit. Benjamin had already scoffed at this emphasis on translation as "inaccurate transmission of an inessential content," for "what does a literary work 'say'? . . . Its essential quality is not statement or the imparting of information." I would add also the opposite danger, a mechanical understanding of form. We have all read translations of poems that boast of keeping rhyme and meter but that also make it difficult to believe that the poem was worth any attention to start with. Neither de Campos nor Benjamin considers this, and when they speak of translation as a "reproduction of form," their understanding of form is the intentionality of the work (Benjamin's *Art des Meinens*) rather than any rhyme scheme. De Campos translates Benjamin's word for reproduction, *Wiedergabe*, literally, a "re-giving" of form, and thus stresses in good Luciferian spirit that the original form must first be destroyed in order to be reshaped. He describes this process as a dionysiac orgy of signification that "dissolves the Apollonian crystallization of the original text back into a state of molten lava."

I wholeheartedly accept this, along with the more commonly remembered aspects of the devil image, because I have long held that translating involves envy, usurpation, and pleasure in destruction—vices and crimes, "negative," "satanic." I have often quoted this analogy:

> A psychoanalyst—dead now many years—showed to certain of his friends and patients photographs of ancient statues in perspectives that stressed the action of time: missing limbs, worn surfaces, features eaten by long erosion. His subjects—so he reports—were invariably uneasy, both attracted and repelled at the sight of these beautiful and ruined objects. Clearly, they felt themselves guilty, having in their hearts willed always death and torture and a slow grinding away of the human form.
>
> Now hard stone offered them mutilations in a dream of unchanging timeless flesh. Here an arm with perfect biceps, broken above the elbow. There a face, ideal, erased as if by sand. Nose, ear, nipple are particularly vulnerable, but chins, cheeks, everything goes, crumbled little by little or suddenly cracked. They stir in the unconscious, these damages—so the good doctor was convinced—not only guilt, the guilt of connivance, but also a longing for reparation, the restoration of destroyed beauty.

The passage is from a literary work, Keith Waldrop's *Quest for Mount Misery*,[3] but the reference is factual. The experiment took place.

Both phases of the viewers' feelings are found in the translation process. Only, my guilt is not just of connivance: I myself take over the action of time, grind away the form of the original work. Worse, I take pleasure in destroying it, because it means making it mine and perhaps simply because there is pleasure in destruction.[4] Yet I not only long for but also promise to make reparation, to restore the destroyed beauty in my language.

The destruction is serious. Sound, sense, form, and reference will never again stand in the same relation to one another. You have to break apart this seemingly natural fusion of elements, this seemingly natural presence. You have to break it apart no matter what your theory is. And unlike in writing, you must have a theory, because you constantly have to make decisions as to which elements of the original you will privilege. Even if the translator should not feel Luciferian, even if she wants to serve, she can only, in each instance, serve one element at the expense of another.[5] We must wrench apart. We must kill.

However, before I get too dramatic about the devilish side of translation, let us remember that a crucial "no" to what already exists is inherent in the urge to make, that destruction is part of the process of creation. There is always a whole range of structures that are undone. Artistic conventions, customary ways of perception, and, most basically, the structure of experience are transformed. The narrator in *The Book of Questions* asks his protagonist:[6] "Have I betrayed you, Yukel?" and has to answer: "I have certainly betrayed you." Writing cannot help betraying experience. I would therefore move to declare Lucifer the angel of all human creativity, not just of translation.

I would like to give two examples of "nose, ear, nipple" in Jabès's work, of the parts particularly vulnerable to the action of translation: wordplay, passages that develop from givens of the particular language, and so forth:

> *Quelle différence y a-t-il entre l'amour et la mort? Une voyelle enlevée au premier vocable, une consonne ajoutée au second.*
>
> *J'ai perdu à jamais ma plus belle voyelle.*
> *J'ai reçu en échange la cruelle consonne.*
>   (*Le Livre des Questions,* 155)

> What difference is there between love and loss? A fricative taken away, two sibilants added.
>
> I've lost it forever, my lovely *v*
> I got in exchange the cruelest sound.
>   (*Book of Questions: Vol. I,* 141)

In this passage as elsewhere, Jabès posits language (more precisely, the French language) as the basis of our thinking. Why does there seem to be a close relation between love and death? Not because of our evolutionary connection with the amoeba, which literally dies into its offspring, as Georges Bataille holds (though he may well be right), but because the two words (in French!) have a surprising number of letters in common. It was essential to find words in English that overlap at least somewhat in their letters rather than keeping "love" and "death," which only share one "e," making it impossible to establish their connection on the basis of a linguistic closeness. I was fortunate to have "loss" available, which shares at least half its letters with "love" and is close enough to the semantic field of "death." True, the description of the difference in English lacks the simplicity of the change from vowel to consonant that it has in the French. Operating with "fricative" and "sibilant" is both more technical and less precise. I shift to the level of pronunciation by ignoring the mute *e* in "love" (considering it would complicate my description to the point of being cumbersome), but at the same time I pay no attention to the fact that the *pronunciation* of the *o* is not the same in "love" and "loss." However, what makes up for this is that the text, within two pages, goes on to a passage about the Nazi SS, indeed the cruelest letters, the cruelest sound in the context of a work that on one level is about the holocaust. It is a spectacular piece of translator's luck.

Less importantly, I also could not parallel the internal rhyme (*belle, voyelle, cruelle*) with which Jabès laments the loss of his vowel in the following couplet. I substituted a different kind of sound repetition (the assonance and consonance in "lost, forever, lovely, v"). I was pleased that I was able to make the repeated sounds the "l, o, v" of "love," and thus keep present through sound what is declared lost, as Jabès does.

The second example is one of failure. Here I had no luck at all, I could not even find an approximation and finally decided to leave the wordplay in French.

"Sais-tu, dit-il, que le point final du livre est un oeil et qu'il est sans paupières?"

Dieu, il écrivait *D'yeux.* "D pour désir, ajoutait-il. Désir de voir. Désir d'être vu."

Trait pour trait, Dieu ressemble à son Nom et son Nom est la Loi. (*Aely,* 7)

"Do you know that the final period of the book is an eye," he said, "and without lid?"

Dieu, "God," he spelled *D'yeux,* "of eyes." "The 'D' stands for desire," he added. "Desire to see. Desire to be seen."

God resembles His Name to the letter, and His Name is the Law. (*Book of Questions: Vol. II,* 203)

Much discussion of translation focuses on this kind of salient problem. However, I think that their solution (which requires a combination of luck and ingenuity) is no measure of the quality of a translation. It is possible to have brilliant equivalents for puns and still produce a translation that misses the tone or rhythm of the work.

This brings me to my main point: what is the *unit* of translation? In contrast to Benjamin, I am convinced that it is not the word, not even the line or sentence. I used to think it was the whole work, which is also what de Campos has in mind when he wants the original in a state of molten lava. The fluidity of this image comes close to the essential working of the process, although on the conscious level there are thousands of small decisions. Still, thinking in terms of the whole work, if you cannot do what the original does where it does it, you can at least do similar things in other places. You can rotate which aspect you privilege in each micro-decision and thus approximate the original at least as a whole.

I still hold with this. But I have recently come to think that the unit is even larger, that it includes what Hans-Georg Gadamer calls the "third dimension" of a work of literature:[7]

Nothing that is said has its truth simply in itself, but refers instead backward and forward to what is unsaid. Every assertion is motivated, that is, one can sensibly ask of everything that is said, "Why do you say that?" And only when what is not said is understood along with what is said is an assertion understandable.

This resonates strongly with the work of Jabès, who has always stressed the importance of silence, philosophically as well as literally, in the white spaces in his text, the margins that let the words breathe. I was especially reminded of *The Book of Dialogue:*

There is *pre-dialogue,* our slow or feverish preparation for dialogue. Without any idea of how it will proceed, which form it will take, without being able to explain it, we are convinced in advance that the dialogue has already begun: a silent dialogue with an absent partner.

Then afterwards, there is *post-dialogue* or after-silence. For what we managed to say to the other in our exchange of words— says virtually nothing but this silence, silence on which we are thrown back by any unfathomable, self-centered word whose depth we vainly try to sound.

Then finally there is what could have been the actual dialogue, vital, irreplaceable, but which, alas, does not take place: it begins the very moment we take leave of one another and return to our solitudes. (7)

Both Jabès and Gadamer take dialogue as *the* manifestation of language, not just the literal exchange between two persons. Gadamer accepts Plato's definition of thought as "the inner dialogue of the soul with itself." Writing and translating as dialogue are familiar metaphors, though I shall want to modify the assumptions about the partner: in writing, it is not so much the future reader as language itself, or, we could say, the potential work that in this process gradually assumes shape. In translating, it is more than just the original.

But there is a crucial difference between Jabès's "silence" and Gadamer's "unsaid." Jabès takes the silence that "we write on,"[8] with which we are lastly in dialogue, in an existential way. It is everything that is "other," nonhuman, everything that challenges us who are defined by language, by the word. But it also challenges us to assert ourselves in our definition. It is our ultimate motivation to use words. So when Jabès's *Livre du Partage* defines writing as a translation from silence ("the silence which has formed the word") into more silence ("the silence of the book: a page being read"), we know he is also talking about our lives. But it takes words to make the silence visible: "Writing is an act of silence, allowing itself to be read in its entirety" (45–46; *Book of Shares,* 31).

Here the translator is either struck by despair (how can we possibly translate silence?) or realizes that the problem is so large that it is not one of translation. Because, on this level, the crucial act is to engage, through the nearly infinite space of language, in a dialogue with its final limits, which are also ours: silence, death, the void, or, if you like, God. It is not very important whether we do this in the space of our own language or at one remove, in the very curious space between two languages.

In contrast, I take Gadamer's "unsaid" not as this ultimate silence, but as what is potentially sayable within a language but not articulated in a given utterance. It is a *space* for the utterance rather than an ultimate limit, a threat of non-space. This becomes clear in Gadamer's main example, a question we cannot answer unless we understand why it is asked, what is intended by it:

> A question that we do not understand as motivated can also find no answer. For the motivational background of a question first opens up the realm out of which an answer can be brought and given. Hence there is in fact an infinite dialogue in questioning as well as answering, in whose space word and answer stand. Everything that is said stands in such space.

Curiously, Gadamer's example for the person who does not fully understand this silent, motivational background is the translator. So that in translations this space, this third dimension, becomes felt through its absence:

> Everybody knows how the translation makes what is said in the foreign language sound flat. It is reflected on one level, so that the word sense and sentence form of the translation follow the original, but the translation, as it were, has no space. It lacks that third dimension from which the original is built up in its range of meaning. This is an unavoidable obstruction of all translation.

Well, not everybody knows this. On the contrary, "the" translation exists even less than "the" poem or "the" story. Some translations make what is said sound flat and some do not. But there remains the interesting notion of the motivational background of the literary work.

I like Gadamer's use of "space" here, partly because it has always been my sense of language. Especially, changing my language from German to English made me very aware of moving in a different space or, rather, in and between two spaces. (I even wrote a poem about being an amphibian.)[9] I have also had the sense that in translating I was letting another person's space invade me or that I in turn was pushing into the author's space, trying to reach something like its center, the point of conception of the work, though I had not considered how much this involves another space beyond the work.

But a space can be explored, even this space of the unsaid. If we can translate Gadamer's statement into terms of practice, he seems to be pleading that the translator have read as much as possible *around* the work in order to get a feeling for the language as well as for the literary and cultural context of the original and, most importantly, for the relation in which the work stands to its linguistic and cultural context. This is hardly a revolutionary demand, but it is one that Jabès might call a pre-dialogue with the work.[10]

Nobody will be surprised that I found it helpful to read in the *Mishnah* when I began translating Jabès's *Book of Questions* with its texture of rabbinical commentary. I knew Jabès's earlier poems. They are in the wake of Surrealism, of which I had read much and of whose relation to language I had a pretty good sense. But the *Book of Questions* fuses this with an altogether different tradition. I felt I needed to become at least somewhat familiar with the form in which orthodox rabbinical commentary had been received into English. Herbert Danby's translation did not give me the language I was looking for (I found its diction several notches too elevated), but it gave me a sense of the rhythm of question and answer and further question and commentary and commentary on the commentary, which lies behind the *Book of Questions*.[11]

But I would expand the requirement. I would not limit my reading to works explicitly or implicitly part of the tradition of the original. The whole *musée imaginaire* of literature may be involved in the "pre-dialogue" with the work. For instance, when I read Georges Limbour's *Les Vanilliers*, I was strongly reminded of the tone of early John Hawkes novels. So, although there is no direct connection between the two writers, if I were to translate Limbour I would steep myself in Hawkes, because there seems to be a similar relation to language. They seem to stand in a similar "motivational space." I would say the translator should be as well read as possible in *both* languages, should be conscious of the cultural "air" breathed by herself and by the original author, their differences and affinities. For I think that far from not having a space, translation stands in a very complex space, which includes the "unsaid" potential of *both* languages and their relation (cf. Benjamin's "central kinship of languages" that makes translation possible at all) as well as what *was* said in the original work and has been rendered unsaid by the translation. For if there is anything certain, it is that the original is part of the "motivational space" of its translation.

This would mean that the destructive phase of translating does not just break apart elements and melt them down to a state of lava still contained in a kettle, but that it pushes the work out of the boundaries of the said, down into the tectonic stresses and heat of the volcano, if I want to follow out de Campos's metaphor, into the nucleus of creative energy where the work was conceived, where the author's dialogue with the infinite space of (a different) language took place. Only there can it take place again, as a more complex dialogue with the original and its space as well as with the space of the translator's language. Only there can the translator become "the one saying it again."

In order to achieve this, to come near recovering this "realm out of which an answer" or a translation "can be brought," the translator, says Gadamer, "must never copy what is said, but place himself in the direction of what is said (i.e., in its meaning) in order to carry over what is to be said into the direction of his own saying."

With the stress on "the *direction* of what is said," Gadamer rejoins Benjamin, whose definition of form is "mode of intention" and who sees the task of the translator as "finding that intended effect upon the language into which he is translating which produces in it the echo of the original" (76).

The sense of transitiveness, of direction and intention, while not exactly a recipe, is a helpful *orientation* for the translator. It is a plea for a complex understanding of form as the *relation* in which the original stands to its language and traditions, its motivational space, as well as for finding a way of re-creating, or at least echoing, this *relation* in the translator's language and tradition.

Jerome Rothenberg once argued in conversation that Japanese haiku should be translated in the idiom of Wordsworth because they occupy parallel cultural positions. This intriguing idea at first sight seems to go in the direction of what I have been saying. But it does not. First of all, the translator would be working with *three* motivational spaces, two of which he does not naturally inhabit. But even without the problem of archaism, this argument privileges the relation to the historical cultural space over that to the language. This attitude makes for *too* smooth a transfer into the conventions of the target language and does away with the transitivity built into translation, the echo of another language. I agree with Benjamin that it is preferable to let the other language stretch and expand the possibilities of English (as the juxtapositions and extreme condensation of haiku have done through the mediation of Arthur Waley and Pound).

I would like to end with an example of such a too-smooth transfer, but one that confounds my theoretical convictions. It will be a reminder that translation is a creative act, that in spite of the need for theory, its territory cannot be charted beyond a few rules of thumb, any more than that of other kinds of creation.

Here is the first stanza of poem 394 by Osip Mandelstam in a literal version by Clarence Brown:[12]

Limping automatically [or involuntarily] on the empty earth
with her irregular, sweet gait,
she walks, slightly preceding
[her] quick girlfriend and the youth one year older [or
younger] than she.
The straitened freedom of [her] animating affliction
draws her on.
And it seems that a lucid surmise
wants to linger in her gait—
[the surmise] that this spring weather
is for us the first mother [i.e., Eve] of the grave's vault
and [that] this will be forever going on.

And here is W. S. Merwin's version:

Limping like a clock on her left leg,
at the beloved gait, over the empty earth,
she keeps a little ahead of the quick girl,
her friend, and the young man almost her age.
What's holding her back
drives her on.
What she must know is coming
drags at her foot. She must know

that under the air, this spring,
our mother earth is ready for us
and that it will go on like this forever.

The word-by-word rendering of Clarence Brown shows us that Man-
delstam's stanza works exclusively with statement, with abstraction.
Merwin changes the poem significantly by adding the image of the
clock. Theoretically I disapprove. Adding to someone else's writing is
a bad idea to start with. Worse, adding an image to a stanza that avoids
images and works with statement falsifies the original's relation to its
language. The change assimilates Mandelstam into Merwin's own id-
iom and "cultural air," into a poetry dominated by images, which is
still widely considered "mainstream" American poetry. On the other
hand, when I read the stanza I am enchanted. The image is so apt,
fitting both the limp and the sense of approaching death. The rhythm
is so alive, the caesura of the line breaks between the forward and
backward movement ("What's holding her back / drives her on" and
"what . . . is coming / drags at her foot") so marvelous that I cannot
help but surrender all theoretical opposition and enjoy the poem.

Still, I prefer a translation in the image of the mutilated statue. If
a translation cannot avoid ravages ("chin, cheeks, everything goes"),
it can through these ravages point beyond itself and suggest the lost
beauty of the original. Thus it can approach Benjamin's ideal trans-
lation, a true "transluciferation," which "does not cover the original,
does not block its light." And to come back to Gadamer, if translation
can reach such transitiveness, if it can point beyond the limits of what
it says and, at its best, even beyond the limits of its language and tra-
ditions, it not only has a space to resonate in, but it also enriches this
space, this third dimension, for all the literature in the target lan-
guage. This may well be what Keith Waldrop's prose poem about the
psychoanalyst calls the "beauty in the ruin as ruin."

Irreducible Strangeness

In August 2001 a Danish-American Poetry Conference, "In the Making," was held in Copenhagen. The following talk was presented in a panel on translation.

Either the translator leaves the author in peace, as much as possible, and moves the reader towards him; or he leaves the reader in peace, as much as possible, and moves the author towards him.[1]

These words are from Friedrich Schleiermacher, the German Romantic theologian and philosopher, on the various methods of translation. He is in favor of leaving the author in peace rather than adapting the foreign work to what the reader is used to. This debate is lively right now in the United States. Lawrence Venuti has written three books in defense of "foreignizing," as he calls it.

But the debate has been going on for a long time. Goethe saw these two possibilities as part of a historical process. Actually he posited three stages of translation following one another:[2] The first is simple and prosaic (*schlicht-prosaisch*) and wants to know what a work "says." This kind of translation has been reigning through the seventeenth century. The second stage, which he calls "parodistic," adapts the foreign work's spirit to our own culture. This stage Goethe assigns to the early eighteenth century and especially to the French—with a definite dig at their arrogance of wanting to make everything according to

French taste. It is still the dominant mode in English-speaking countries, as Lawrence Venuti has shown. Translation of this kind is praised as "transparent" or "seamless." It reflects the values of our science-dominated culture, Venuti says, by "valorizing a purely instrumental use of language and . . . immediate intelligibility."[3] Looked at from a political angle, this appears less harmless than "parodistic" would indicate: at the very least it domesticates, at worst it is imperialist and colonizing.

In Goethe's third and highest stage, finally, the translator tries to make his work identical with the original. These versions at first encounter resistance among readers, because a translator who "attaches himself so closely to his original more or less abandons the originality of his own nation. The result is a third [term] toward which the taste of the public must first be educated."[4] This he sees going on in Germany in his time, with the nationalistic aim of making the German language suppler by listening to foreign cadences.

This "third" is of the greatest interest. It is important that in contrast to the domesticating, colonizing model, this kind of translation follows the foreign work so closely that it almost abandons its own language and culture. It is, in Schleiermacher's phrase, "towards a foreign likeness bent."

Its locus is definitely new ground somewhere between the two languages, stretching the border of the target language beyond where it was before. Emmanuel Hocquard calls the new ground a "blank spot" on the map of one's language: "a particular language within French, which resembles French without being altogether French." So that translation actually means "gaining ground," gaining new territory between languages.[5]

(I part company with Goethe when he goes on to say that the last, the translation that tries to identify with the original, in the end, tends to approach the interlinear and thus close the circle. This owes more to Goethe's love of circular patterns than to an understanding of translation. But it is no doubt one source of the value Benjamin places—at least in theory—on literal word-by-word rendering of syntax.)

Both "domesticating" and "foreignizing" translations aim to enrich the target language and culture, though the latter has a more respectful attitude to the foreign culture. To continue the colonial metaphor: one method imports raw material to manufacture something good and English out of it, the other tries to import the foreign artifact and points at the foreign culture as something interesting.

Of course there are many ways to be "foreignizing." Which particular features of the foreign language a translator tries to keep depends on the nature of the particular foreign text. The most radical example I know is Celia and Louis Zukofsky's monumental *Catullus*, which tries to keep the sound of the words, almost phoneme by phoneme, while also conveying the meaning. The grandeur of this impossible ambition to transfer *everything intact* is overwhelming. So is the Zukofskys' sheer persistence: they do not just tackle one poem or two in this manner, but *all* of Catullus.

I am fascinated by this focus on sound (which is also a bit quixotic because we don't even know very well what Latin sounded like) and by this project of "breathing the 'literal' meaning." There are brilliant successes. For instance, the famous opening, *Miser Catulle* (something like "poor old Catullus"), becomes "Miss her, Catullus?" Here, both the single sound and the whole poem enter into the translation because "missing her" is indeed the root of Catullus's misery.

When I look at Catullus 85:

> *Odi et amo, quare id faciam, fortasse, requiris.*
>   *nescio, sed fieri sentio et excrucior.*

(literally:

> I hate and love, why I do so you may well ask.
>   I don't know, but I feel it happen and suffer.)

and find:

> O th'hate I move love. Quarry it fact I am, for that's so re
>   queries.
>   Nescience, say th'fiery scent I owe whets crookeder.

I am amazed that the English does indeed sound like the Latin, amazed by the sheer strangeness of diction that nevertheless manages to suggest some of the Latin's meaning. I am intrigued by the particular English words Zukofsky *heard* in the Latin, by the meanings and associations the unexpected ones set in motion: "quarry," "fiery," "owe," "crookeder." I am in awe of this work, delighted that it exists. But I am also glad it is not the only Catullus in English.

In fact, I tend to think of it as Zukofsky rather than as Catullus. I do not think of the method ("his monstrous method," says Guy Davenport) as a window onto a foreign text, whereas it definitely is a way of extending the possibilities of poetic speech in English and especially of drawing attention to the materiality, to the physical nature of words. In other words, when a "foreignizing" translation gets this extreme, it flips over into an emphasis on the target language, in terms of a subversive poetics. However, it is through the presentation *as* translation that the point is made. In short, I think of Zukofsky's *Catullus* as an extreme possibility, as a monument rather than a model.

In my own translation process I very much go through all three stages that Goethe saw as a historical sequence:

A preliminary stage of intense reading together with my first round of writing (which is interlinear, almost word for word) attempts to understand the work—though not just "what it says." The understanding I am after is also different from a critic's analysis. It aims more at retracing the author's steps, his creative process. As Valéry puts it:

> Translating . . . makes us try to step into the vestiges of the author's footprints; not to fashion one text out of another, but to go back from this one to the virtual epoch of its formation, to the phase where the state of mind is that of an orchestra whose instruments awaken, call out to one another, try to be in tune before the concert.[6]

Haroldo de Campos speaks of "dissolving the Apollonian crystallization of the original text back into a state of molten lava."[7] Curiously, philosopher and critic Wilhelm Dilthey saw the hermeneutic process exactly in these terms, as

> uncovering the meaning of a text by re-creating the whole process of the genesis of that text. The conceptual premise behind it is Aristotle's distinction between *ergon* and *energeia:* Interpretation of a work, as Dilthey understands it, consists in "translat-

ing the *ergon*—the completed object—back into the *energeia* that brought it forth."[8]

In the second round, I do not look at the original. I must separate myself from its authority. I treat the mess of the first draft (which is not quite English, often makes no sense at all) as if it were a draft of my own, though with a sense of the text's intentionality in mind. I try to re-produce, re-create it in English, make a poem of it. The importance of this stage of separation cannot be exaggerated, and I am still grateful that I was very early pointed in this direction by Justin O'Brien.[9]

In the third round, I go back to dialogue with the French and try to wrestle the English as close to the original language as possible.

It is difficult to say if one stage is more important than another. Each only seems possible once I have gone through the preceding one. I can write an English text only once I have "understood" the French. I can get close to the French only once I have a text that can stand by itself as a text in English. In my Jabès translations, much of the work at the third stage has been on syntax, on letting the sentences approach again the length of the French ones, on trying to catch the rhythm of the paragraphs.

I would say it is a matter of finding, for each individual case, that fine line between being as foreign as possible and sounding as good as possible in English. It seems to me analogous to the problem of aesthetic distance: you want to be as cool, as far from sentimentality as possible—while still being able to engage the emotions. Another analogy would be open form, which wants to be as open as possible, but still have as much closure as necessary for it to be recognizable as form.

Translation's ultimate task may be to bear witness to the *essentially* irreducible strangeness and distance between languages—but its immediate task is exactly to explore this space.

III

POETICS

A made thing made of words
> —Robert Creeley

The thinking force gathers in a word like light clouds appearing in a serene sky.
> —Wilhelm von Humboldt

Alarms and Excursions

In fall 1988 Charles Bernstein curated a series of talks on "The Politics of Poetic Form: Poetry and Public Policy" at the New School for Social Research in New York, which was published in the book of the same title (New York: Roof Books, 1990).

I was grateful for the occasion to, if not sort out, at least *set* out my confused and contradictory thinking on the relation between creation and political/social thought and action. But it was only once I found a form that allowed unresolved contradiction, "a form to accomodate the mess," as Beckett says, that I was able even to begin writing.

"Alarums and excursions" is an Elizabethan stage term for off-stage noise and commotion that interrupts the main action. This phrase kept running though my head while I tried to think about our topic, because all that occurred were doubts, complications, and distractions. So I decided to circle around this mysterious interaction of private and public that is poetry with theses (things I believe or *would like* to believe), alarms (doubts), and excursions into quotes, examples, and so forth. I numbered the theses to give an illusion of progression that will only make their contradictions more obvious.

Let me start with some of the assumptions of this seminar.

THESIS 1

Shelley: Poets are the unacknowledged legislators of the world.
Oppen: Poets are the legislators of the unacknowledged world.

Excursion

This astonishing kind of importance is often ascribed to poets and writers (mostly by writers?). Sartre, for instance, held Flaubert responsible for the failure of the Commune of 1870, because he never wrote about it.

In the recent French discussion on whether Heidegger's Nazism invalidates his philosophical work, Jabès assigned a responsibility to writers that is commensurate with this kind of importance:

> I believe a writer is responsible even for what he does not write.
> To write means to answer to all the insistent voices of the past and to one's own: profound voice, intimate, calling to the future.
> What I believe, hear, feel is in my texts which say it, *without sometimes altogether saying it.*
> But what do we *not altogether say* in what we say? Is it what we try to keep silent, what we cannot or will not say or precisely what we do want to say and what all we say hides, saying it differently?
> For these un-said things we are gravely responsible.[1]

Alarm

But I am not only astonished, I am this uneasy with our two quotes, with the poet as legislator, no matter of which world. It sounds to me like a hangover from the times when the poet occupied a priestly position. But in our time, poetry has no such institutionalized function, and I must say I am not sorry. Or is it a male aspiration? I certainly have no desire to lay down the law. To my mind, writing has to do with uncovering possibilities rather than with codification. My key words would be "exploring" and "maintaining": exploring a forest, not for the timber that might be sold, but to understand it as a world and to keep this world alive.

Counter Alarm

My uneasiness means perhaps only that I prefer a different image while I grant poetry the same importance. After all, poets work on the language, and language thinks for us, or, as Valéry puts it more cautiously:

> I am almost inclined to believe that certain profound ideas have owed their origin to the presence or near-presence in a man's

mind of certain forms of language, of certain empty verbal figures whose particular tone called for a particular content.[2]

EXCURSION

When Confucius was asked what he would do first if he were ruler, he said that he would improve the use of language:

If the words are not right, what is said is not what is meant. If what is said is not meant, work cannot flourish. If work does not flourish, then customs and arts degenerate. If customs and arts degenerate, then justice is not just. If justice is not just, the people do not know what to do. Hence the importance that words be right.

Bertold Brecht also tells how Confucius practiced this by changing just a few words in an old patriotic history, so that "The ruler of Kun had the philosopher Wan killed because he said . . . " became "The ruler of Kun had the philosopher Wan murdered"; "the tyrant X was assassinated" became "the tyrant X was executed by assassination." This brought about a new view of history.[3]

ALARM

The two decades before Hitler came to power were a period of incredible literary flowering, upheaval, and exploration in Germany. All the Dadaists and Expressionists had been questioning, challenging, exploring, and changing the language, limbering up its joints. So the German language should have been in very good condition. Yet the Nazis had no trouble putting it to work for their purposes, perverting it to where what was said was light-years from what was meant. So, while language thinks for us, there is no guarantee that it will be in a direction we like.[4]

THESIS 2

The main thesis of this whole seminar is that (a) poetry has social relevance. It is not just an ornament or just private, an expression of personal emotions. (b) Its relation to society is not just reflective or mimetic, not just articulating what oft was thought but never so well expressed. It can make the culture aware of itself, unveil hidden structures. It questions, resists. Hence it can at least potentially anticipate structures that might lead to social change.

EXCURSION

It is difficult to be aware of our own social and historical position, let alone to know how far our works are expressing the explicit or implicit givens of our society and how far they make them conscious and possibly contribute to their changing. The borderline between private and public is elusive. On the one hand, there seems to be a fairly high *quantitative* threshold for something to have effect. On the other hand, I suspect that nearly everything we do has some social effect, simply because we are members of a society. (What could be more private than making love? But if the couple is heterosexual and not careful, their lovemaking may produce a citizen.)

So even if poetry were just expressing personal emotions, it would have a social function—namely, acknowledging the importance of the emotions even though (or because) they often hinder our smooth functioning within a social order.

In contrast, ornament or entertainment is a conservative function widely assigned to literature, which our initial thesis does not consider. I once got a rejection slip that said: "I do not find your poems comfortable." I was comforted by this statement. There are poems which are "comfortable," immediately recognizable as poems. And when they celebrate unquestionable values like love or nature, they make people feel good and give them the illusion of being in touch with something "higher," some transcendental poetic essence. It gives them what Roland Barthes calls "the good conscience of realized significance."[5]

I might want to argue that even these poems, for all their reinforcing of the status quo, still present a small challenge by stepping out of the frame of what is useful. But I am willing to bracket these poems and believe with our THESIS 2 that poetry's function is critical, questioning. Georges Bataille sees *transgression* as literature's essential quality. Jabès calls it subversive:

Subversion is the very movement of writing: that of death.[6]

ALARM

Jabès takes this subversion immediately to a level where it is seen as the very principle of change, hence of life, rather than directed against a particular social order:

Did I already know that opening and closing my eyes, lying down, moving, thinking, dreaming, talking, being silent, writing and reading are all gestures and manifestations of subversion?

Waking upsets the order of sleep, thinking hounds the void to get the better of it, speech in unfolding breaks the silence, and reading challenges every sentence written.[7]

There is much support for art's social function as a conscious-making counter-projection. For instance Theodor Adorno says:

Art does not recognize reality by reproducing it photographically, but by voicing that which is veiled by the empirical forms of reality.[8]

Writing becomes action through this unveiling.

ALARM

While part of me wants this social function, any such consideration is far from my mind when I am writing. George Bataille's notion of art as a glorious waste of excess energy seems to me much closer to what is going on.

THESIS 3

The function of poetry is to waste excess energy.

EXCURSION

Let me summarize briefly the main tenet of Bataille's "general economy," which should really be called "economy on the scale of the universe," as given in *The Accursed Share*.

He starts from the given of excess energy derived from the sun and sees the whole history of life on earth, and especially the appearance of humanity, as "the effect of a mad exuberance."

It is in the principle of life that the sum of energy produced is always greater than that needed for its production.

The living organism . . . receives in principle more energy than it needs to maintain its life: the excess energy (wealth) can be used for growth of a system (e.g., an organism). If the system can grow no more or if the excess cannot entirely be absorbed into the growth process then it has to be lost without profit, spent voluntarily or not, gloriously or else catastrophically.[9]

On the level of the individual human being, once the body is fully grown, we get the explosion of sexuality liberating enormous amounts of energy that are either wasted or used for procreation, extending the body's potential for growth.

The most general and thorough waste of energy is death. Therefore, on the level of societies, war is the obvious catastrophic spending. For Bataille, the two great wars of this century follow quite logically a relatively peaceful century devoted to industrial growth. Unemployment he calls passive spending or, rather, passive reduction of the excess. The glorious ways of wasting the excess are great feasts; conspicuous luxury; sacrifices; rituals like potlatch, in which wealth is literally destroyed; monuments like pyramids and cathedrals that are far in excess of their practical function as tombs or places of worship; and of course all forms of art.

THESIS 4

Bataille's general economy, his notion of waste and excess, explains the persistence of poets and poetry in the face of meager rewards. It makes more sense than putting the poem in a context of useful production, let alone supply and demand, even though it does enter the world of merchandise once it is published and distributed.

EXCURSION

Marx/Engels: "A writer is a productive worker not in as far as he produces ideas, but in as far as he enriches the bookseller who distributes the work."[10]

The Internal Revenue Service shares this view absolutely. When Burning Deck, the small press Keith Waldrop and I run, applied for nonprofit status, we were told: "If you sell books, you are a business. You may be a bad business, but you are a business." In any case it is obvious that the energy that goes into writing a poem is enormous and totally out of proportion to any gain it might bring, even if it should get published by a commercial press, even if we include nonmonetary gains like reputation, approbation of a group, and so forth.

ALARM

Poetry is an extreme case in that not even the most successful poet could live off of his or her book sales. So a poet knows from the beginning that he or she will have to make a living in some other way, whereas a successful novelist can hope to live by writing. However, the more "difficult" among successful contemporary novelists (John Hawkes, Robert Coover, John Barth, Walter Abish, Angela Carter) all seem to teach at least part-time.

As for a publisher or bookseller being enriched, this holds for some books, but I doubt that it ever holds for poetry, and obviously not for the small presses and their distributors, which have no hope of even breaking even and must rely on grants or patronage. I would like to see the bookseller who gets rich by stocking small press poetry. In other words, the whole small press world, rather than getting rich at the poets' expense, is like the poets engaged in wasting energy, time, money—wasting it beautifully.

Why do they do it?

THESIS 5

There are more crazy people around than you would think.

ALARM

Nobody can be crazy all the time and still be sane. The process of writing, let alone distribution, cannot be *pure* waste. There has to be a balance between the contradictory tendencies toward growth and toward spending.

EXCURSION

Let us for a moment imagine two writers embodying the extreme points of the two orientations. Bataille's distinction between warrior and military societies seems a good analogy ("La part maudite" 60). A warrior society (e.g., the Aztecs) engages in wars that do not necessarily enlarge its territory. Their wars are exercises in pure violence, conspicuous combat without calculation of profit. What matters is fighting and waste worthy of the gods. A military society, by contrast, is a business enterprise for which war means expansion of territory, power gain, empire building. The latter society will be gentler, more rational and civilized, in contrast to the intense ferocity of the Aztecs. It will also be more apt to survive

Likewise, for what we might call the reckless writer, the essential is the writing, the intensity of the process, of the present moment, the anxiety and glory of *making* something that did not exist before, creating a structure that holds together. The key word here is the *present,* being unconstrained by any considerations of the future in which the work might be read, appreciated, or sold. It is a moment of being most completely myself, whether we call it unalienated or mad. In contrast, if I am concerned with building a career, I write as an investment rather than spending (though I still spend more energy than justified by the material returns). My eye is on the market, maybe just on the approval of a group—in any case, it is on the future. I voluntarily submit to the order of reality, to the laws that ensure the maintenance of life or career, whereas the reckless writer would, in these terms, and at least at the moment of writing "rise indifferent to death."

ALARM

Nobody is pure. For all of our anarchic intensity, sooner or later we want our manuscripts published. We want to be both reckless *and* read. It is once again a case of Valéry's famous two dangers that threaten the world: order and disorder.

EXCURSION

Barthes's *Pleasure of the Text* applies this same distinction to reading. Reading as *jouissance,* an orgasmic pleasure, versus reading as an educational activity, an effort of understanding and interpretation. Again, only as an abstraction can we separate the pleasure in the effort of understanding from the purer orgasmic pleasure. But Barthes has given us an interesting word.

THESIS 6

The social function of poetry is pleasure.

Pound said: ecstasy, the kind of pleasure that is an enormous anarchic and subversive force, which is why societies and religions (including those of Capitalism, Marxism, and Freudianism) are suspicious of it and try so hard to regulate it.

ALARM

Subversion by pleasure does not at all fit our initial thesis of a more constructive critical role. But it might well fit with the notion that writing and the writer do not really have a place inside the social structure at all, but are outside it, opposite.

EXCURSION

Jabès writes throughout his work about the "non-place" of the book and the writer. This non-place (which perhaps rejoins Oppen's "unacknowledged world") is a more radical idea than the mere distance from the exercise of power that is thought to qualify intellectuals to speak on matters of politics. It goes further than marginality. It goes into otherness. Roland Barthes, while admitting that he occupies an official pigeonhole ("intellectual"), calls his inner sense of his position "a-topian," being outside even the notion of place. He explicitly contrasts it with u-topias, which traditionally are a direct reaction to an actual situation and propose an answer or counter-model. An a-topia is strictly negative.[11] Even Adorno joins in, seeing the task of art not in function, but in nonfunction.[12]

ALARM

Is this wishful thinking? Is it a desire to deny how deeply we are part of our society, how impossible it is to escape the place that birth, education, profession assign to us? Is it not trying to make a virtue out of personal alienation? Perhaps this is partly true. But it proceeds from the essence of literature, which is negative, not "real," a mere "as if," especially as it is no longer endowed with priestly function. But for this very reason its existence alone constitutes an alternative to what is and hence a criticism of it.

So we have circled around to

THESIS 7
which reaffirms THESIS 2:

By its very nature of being "other," literature *cannot help being critical,* cannot help being "an action against the inadequacy of human beings." This is Brecht's formulation. He draws the conclusion that "all great men were literary."[13]

It is high time we get to the question of how a poem could bring about this action.

THESIS 8

Not by direct communication with a reader. For one thing, it is impossible to know our readers (beyond maybe five friends). I am in a dialogue when I write a poem—not with a prospective reader, not even the "ideal reader," but with language itself. Of course I hope that eventually there will be readers who through my poem will in their turn enter into a particular dialogue with language and maybe see certain things as a consequence. We might approximate this as a diagram where the circle represents the language environment shared in varying degrees by author and reader.

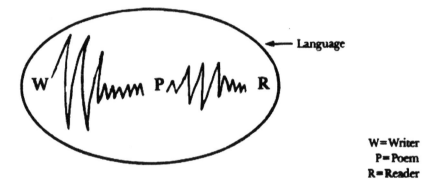

W = Writer
P = Poem
R = Reader

I mean the words "dialogue with language" quite literally. When I begin working, I have maybe a phrase, maybe a rhythm, an energy running to words. As soon as I start *listening* to the words, they reveal their own affinities that pull the poem into their own field of force, often in unforeseen directions, away from the semantic charge of the original impulse.

THESIS 9

A poem is primarily an exploration of language.

This view is shared by Jakobson and Valéry:

When the poets enter the forest of language it is with the express purpose of getting lost; far gone in bewilderment, they seek crossroads of meaning, unexpected echoes, strange encounters; they fear neither detours, surprises, nor darkness. But the huntsman who ventures into this forest in hot pursuit of the "truth," who sticks to a single continuous path, from which he cannot deviate for a moment on pain of losing the scent or imperiling the progress he has already made, runs the risk of capturing nothing but his shadow. Sometimes the shadow is enormous, but a shadow it remains.[14]

When I say poetry is an exploration of language, it is not a retreat from the social, because language is the structure that is shared by society and this otherness that is poetry. It also does not mean that there is no reference. It means only that reference is secondary, not foregrounded. The poem works by indirection, but the poet's obsessions and preoccupations will find their way into the text. Jabès again: "What I believe, hear, feel is in my texts which say it, *without sometimes altogether saying it.*"

EXCURSION

In the early stages of my writing, all the poems were about my mother and my relation to her. I decided I had to get out of such an obsession. This is when I started to make collages. I would take a novel, take one or two words from every page, and try to make a structure. When I looked at them later, the poems were still about my mother. This made me realize that you do not have to worry about content: your preoccupations will get into the poem no matter what you do. Tristan Tzara has a famous recipe for making a Dada poem by cutting words out of a newspaper and tossing them in a hat. He ends with: "The poem will resemble you."[15]

THESIS 10

The poem will not work through its content, not through a message, which in any case would speak only to the already converted, but through its form.

Excursion

Brecht:
The presentation has to be unusual to get the reader out of the shelter
of his habits, so that he pays attention and understands and, we hope,
will react less in accordance with norms.[16]

Adorno:
[Because] art is by definition an antithesis to what is . . . it is sepa-
rated from reality by the aesthetic difference. . . . It can only act on it
through its *immanente Stimmigkeit,* the intrinsic rightness of the rela-
tion of its elements [i.e., through its form]. Only as a totality, through
all its mediations, can the work become knowledge, not in its single
intuitions.[17]

Excursion

I would now like to give two examples of poems with explicit social
content. The first is from Charles Reznikoff's *Testimony:*

1

Forty feet above the ground on a telegraph pole,
the lineman
forced the spur he wore into the pole and,
throwing his other leg around it,
leaned over

to fasten a line with his nippers
to the end of a crossarm
by a wire around the glass cup on a pin.

The line, hauled tight
hundreds of feet ahead of him
by means of a reel,
broke,
and the crossarm
broke where it was fastened to the pole:
he fell headlong
to the stones below.

2

It was a drizzling night in March,
The street lamps flashed twice:
a break in the connection,
and all hands were looking for it.

When the policeman saw him first,
the colored man was carrying a short ladder
that the hands used
in climbing the electric-light poles.
The policeman next saw him hanging on a pole,
his overcoat flapping in the wind,
and called to him but got no answer.

They put the dead body on the counter of a shop nearby:
the skin was burnt on the inside of both his hands;
his right hand was burnt to the bone.
The insulation was off of part of the "shunt cord" he had car-
ried
and his skin was sticking to the naked wire.

3

There were three on the locomotive:
the flagman, the fireman, and the engineer.
About two hundred yards from the man—
stone-deaf—
the flagman commenced ringing the bell;

within about a hundred yards
the engineer commenced sounding his whistle:
thirty or forty short blows.

The man did not get off the track or look around.[18]

Reznikoff's poem seems to contradict what I said about indirection.
But by operating with distance, without any kind of commentary, ex-
planation, or even just fuller details, Reznikoff goes against our ex-

pectation of empathy. He lets the flat language of the news note stand
as is, but accumulates the instances into a testimony to a society that
not only causes such daily disasters in the name of industrial progress,
but also reports them in this manner.

The German poet Helmut Heissenbüttel often uses Gertrude Stein's
technique of avoiding nouns and replacing them by words with an
implicit reference to context, like pronouns, connectives, auxiliaries,
and dependent clauses. He often uses this refusal to name for social
and political comment. The unstated words assume the aura of the
taboo; the relative clauses, the "it"s and "that"s imply hedging. The
following is an excerpt from the poem "Final Solution":

> they just thought this up one day
> who just thought this up one day
> it just occurred to them one day
> whom did it just occur to one day
> someone of them it just occurred to someone of them
> someone of them just thought it up one day
> one day just someone of them just thought it up
> or perhaps a number of them thought it up together
> maybe it occurred to a number of them together
> and how did they do what had occurred to them
>
> if you want to do anything at all you've got to be for something
> and not just anything you just think up but something you can
> be for alright or at least something that many like to be for or
> at least something you think many like to be for
>
> and so they just thought it up one day
>
> they thought it up and they hit on it when they wanted to start
> something but what they hit on wasn't something you could be
> for but you could be against or better yet something you could
> get most people to be against because when you can get most
> people to be against something you don't have to be very spe-
> cific about what you are for and the fact that you don't have to
> be very specific about this has its advantages because as long
> as they can let off steam most people don't care what they
> are for

and so they hit on it when they'd started to just think up something like that

they hit on the idea that what you're against must be something you can see touch insult humiliate spit on lock up knock down exterminate because what you can't see touch insult humiliate spit on lock up knock down exterminate you can only say and what you can only say can change and you never really know which way it will turn no matter what you say against it.

and so they hit on this and did it

so they hit on this and did it and when they had done it they tried to get most people to go along and when they'd gotten most people to go along they hit on the idea that what you're against can still change as long as it's still around and that only what's gone can't change and so they forced those they'd gotten to go along to destroy what they'd been gotten to be against to regard it like Malaria mosquitoes or potato bugs which you've got to exterminate.[19]

It is true that we are given a reference in the title, but what the poem is "about," the reference it constructs, is not so much the "final solution" itself, but the postwar German feeling about it: the wish not to talk about it, the wish it would go away, and yet its inescapable presence in the mind, in the relentlessness of the poem. Its power lies exactly in the fact that the text does not state what it was "they" thought of, what it was they could get people to be against. Nothing but this circling around an unnamed middle could convey so much ambivalence.

THESIS 11

For a form to be unusual, it has to go against expectations by breaking some convention, some rule, some established tradition, some law, whether literary or more general.

EXCURSION

Bataille:
Men differ from animals by observing laws, but the laws are ambigu-

ous. Men observe them, but also need to violate them. The transgression of laws is not from ignorance: it takes resolute courage. The courage necessary for transgression is an accomplishment of man. This is in particular the accomplishment of literature whose privileged moment is challenge. Authentic literature is promethean.[20]

Or, as Tzara put it more succinctly: we must "destroy the pigeon holes in the brain and in social organization."[21]

The possibilities for breaking laws in writing are of course infinite. I would like to talk briefly of two very fundamental targets of attack—logic and meaning.

EXCURSION

I am certainly not the first person to say poetry is an alternate logic. It is not illogical, but it has a different, less linear logic that draws on the more untamed, unpredictable parts of our nature.

This is part of what I think my *Reproduction of Profiles* addresses. It works with a logical syntax, all of those "if-then" and "because," but constantly slides between frames of reference. It especially brings in the female body and sets into play the old gender archetypes of logic and mind being "male," whereas "female" designates the illogical: emotion, body, matter. I hope that the constant sliding challenges these categories.

What I worked on consciously, though, was the *closure* of the propositional sentence. This was a challenge to me because my previous poems had worked toward opening the boundaries of the sentence by either sliding sentences together or by using fragments. Here I accepted complete sentences (most of the time) and tried to open them up from the inside, subvert the correct grammar and logical form by semantic slidings. Needless to say, the opening of closed structures would also be a thought pattern that could be useful in a social context, but while we write, we are, as Cervantes says in *Don Quixote*, working on the back of a tapestry, working out patterns of colored threads without knowing what the picture on the front is going to look like.

EXCURSION

Steve McCaffery has applied Bataille's economics to an attack against the privileged position that meaning holds in literature.[22] He makes "meaning" the equivalent of wealth, the reward and "destination of the de-materialization of writing," which for him is what makes a text into merchandise. So his idea of a "general economy" of writing is the destruction of an absolute, fixed meaning. This can range from the "nomadic meaning" of metaphors and any other kind of multivalence to sound poems and texts that refuse meaning or at least delay it. As an example of the latter he quotes from Charles Bernstein's *Poetic Justice*, where we recognize the meaning of "inVazoOn uv spAz," but not without having been slowed down by the unusual spelling and capitalization.

This seems to me closer to Ezra Pound's economics than to Bataille's. McCaffery introduces an abstract-concrete dichotomy—abstract meaning versus the concrete sound and shape of the words—and then uses the analogy of money, wealth, which is abstract, symbolic energy, to discredit meaning. In Pound's work, anything concrete is good. Gold, the concrete metal, "gathers the light against it." But money and all banking operations are abstract and evil, whereas Bataille wants the waste of energy in all its forms, not just the symbolic ones like money, but human lives, work, anything.

However, I agree that one of the important tasks of poems is to short-circuit the transparency that words have for the signified and that is usually considered their advantage for practical uses. For the philosopher, "a symbol which interests us *also* as an object is distracting."[23] It distracts from the reference, from what is symbolized. But this is exactly what poems want: to attract attention to the word as an object, as a sensuous body, to keep it from being a mere counter of exchange. For Jakobson, it is the poetic function of language to make words "palpable,"[24] and Sartre's *What Is Literature?* accepts as the basic difference between prose and poetry that poetry treats words as things rather than signs, that it is more like painting or music than like prose.[25]

ALARM

I have not kept clear borders between genres in this essay. Many of the statements are not just about poetry but about literature in general or even all the arts. However, Sartre has put his finger on a crucial difference, and we need to rethink all of this in terms of poetry versus prose.

EXCURSION

Let me give you one more example from a book of mine, *The Road Is Everywhere or Stop This Body:*

Exaggeration of a curve
exchanges
time and again
beside you in the car
pieces the road together
with night moisture
the force of would-be sleep
beats through our bodies
denied their liquid depth
toward the always dangerous next
dawn bleeds its sequence
of ready signs[26]

Here the target is more strictly grammatical. The main device is that the object of one phrase turns into the subject of the next phrase without being repeated. I was trying to extend the boundaries of the sentence, to have a nearly unending flow playing against the short lines that determine the rhythm. And since the thematic field is cars and other circulation systems, I liked the immediate effect of speed.

In retrospect, however, I realized that this device comes out of my feminist preoccupation. The woman in our culture has been treated as the object par excellence—to be looked at rather than looking, to be loved and have things done to rather than being the one who does. Instead, I propose a pattern in which subject and object function are not fixed, but temporary, reversible roles, where there is no hierarchy of main and subordinate clauses, but a fluid and constant alternation.

ALARM

There remains the huge doubt, the nagging suspicion of a quantitative threshold. Maybe our poems offer a challenge to the ruling grammar, offer some patterns of thinking and perception that might not be bad possibilities to consider. But how many readers does a small press book reach? Even if all one thousand copies of a typical press run get sold, even if they all reach readers, how much effect is this book going to have on society? None, I am afraid. I suspect it takes similar patterns appearing in many disciplines at the same time, even though in this essay I have acted as if there existed nothing but society on the one hand and writing on the other. For instance, many of the characteristics of innovative art that bother people to this day (discontinuity, indeterminacy, acceptance of the inescapable human reference point) were anticipated in science by 1900. The fact that they are still an irritant in art would seem to show that it takes art to make people aware of the challenge to their thinking habits, or that the challenge has to come in many areas. It also gives us an inkling of how *slowly* mental habits change.

EXCURSION

One last word on the development of the small presses, which is a curious and more tangible example of interaction with society. In the early 1960s, when Keith Waldrop and I were graduate students wanting to start a magazine, the quotes from printers were completely unaffordable, but we found we could buy a small letterpress for one hundred dollars. We had stumbled into a moment of technological development when offset printing had become cheaper than letterpress, so print shops all over the country were dumping their machines. More and more small presses sprang up. Not all printed letterpress, but in the early days a good many did because this particular technology was accessible (as computer typesetting is now). I remember a bookseller in Ann Arbor, Michigan, whose eyes lit up when we told him we had purchased a press: "With a mimeo you can start a party, with a printing press a revolution." The small press phenomenon is perhaps not quite a revolution, but it very quickly became more than just a few kooks printing little books. Over the past thirty years small press publishing has snowballed into an alternative to commercial houses—to the point that it gives the latter a good conscience about taking even fewer financial risks! They now say: a small press can do this better than we could! But small press publishing has also had enough impact to make a conservative agency like the National Endowment for the Arts admit that our literature would be much poorer without it and to offer occasional grant help.

Whether all of this will produce a revolution in our thinking or amount only to a little putsch remains a question.

Split Infinite

At the end of 1992, *Denver Quarterly* asked its contributors: "What place, if any, do the old theological/religious issues, images, and implications have in contemporary poetry?" The request arrived when I had just finished a poem that evoked the religion of my childhood. The poem, "Split Infinites," became interwoven in the following brief text and provided the title, though reduced to the singular.

I had violently rejected Catholicism and then spent years translating Jabès's work, where the word "God" occurs constantly. True, it is an unbeliever's god, a metaphor for the void, but working with Jabès's sentences nevertheless led me not back to belief, but away from my allergy to religion and toward being able to think about metaphysical matters.

I had also come to realize that for me language had taken the place of God.

The essay appeared in *Denver Quarterly*'s spring 1993 issue titled "Facing (up to) God."

———————

I have been tempted to say with Freud: "I myself cannot discover any 'oceanic' feeling within me." Not. Or maybe no longer.

Attempts at recollection succeed soonest with corresponding loops. A small square with tramlines in several directions, bounded on one side by a church. Adding up dark cobblestones against more unguessable events.

I am spending a good part of my time translating Edmond Jabès. I am fascinated by the way he can use the word God, can engage the whole metaphysical complex. It is something I cannot do in my own writing. So that translating becomes a way of "writing" what I cannot write.

It works for me because Jabès's God is an unbeliever's God.

"The very condition of His freedom: *not to be*."[1]

Jabès's God. A metaphor. Shorthand for what we find as we try to know ourselves, as we test our limits and try to think the unthinkable, know the unknowable—"and screw the inscrutable," as one preacher had it.

"The ladder urges us beyond ourselves. Hence its importance. But in a void, where do we place it?"[2]

Lilies with heavy pollen powdering priestly fingers. Indiscriminate application of adjectives. The next day my throat was swollen. To the degree that sex is in the mind I threw snowballs.

The Faustian impulse. The urge to push at our boundaries. God, an invention larger than the inventor. "We are God's reflection," but on the other hand, "God is sculpted."[3] By whom do you suppose? So we *can* pull ourselves up by our own bootstraps?

"In creating, you create the origin that swallows you." "A double mirror separates us from the Lord so that God sees Himself when trying to see us, and we, when trying to see Him, see only our own face."[4]

God as void, infinite, nothingness, silence, death, desert. As ultimate otherness. God as metaphor. For all that calls us into question. Our primal opponent. The center we long for, which, we think, would give meaning to our lives. The center that all of Jabès's books circle and circle, but that remains unreachable. Of course. Because it is empty. There is nothing there.

The towers of the church rose into red shifts. The snowflakes drifted slowly in the opposite direction. God blesses those who are careful. Not to step too far into rejoicing.

But if there is no center, is there a periphery?

> " 'Can we be like Him, Who in His essence, is without likeness?' asked Reb Eliav.
> "He was told: 'Are we not the image of the void which has no image?' "[5]

We'd done it twice already. Mother moved slowly with a small hook. But the longing for the father is incontestable. You feel a splinter and you don't know where it came from.

No comfort. No gospel. No "good tale: more at spell." The double mirror, which is also the mirror of self-consciousness, is a wound. At best, a scar. The center is empty. It becomes tangible only in the negative, in the totalizing claims to define it, give it a content, which cannot but turn into tyranny and intolerance. In Jabès's books it becomes tangible in its grotesque historical parody, the concentration camp.

With what effort the vines grew erect on the slopes of the valley. To live with all five senses. Muffled by snow. Tense flesh of lilies thick to the touch.

Jabès's truth, that we are always face to face with the void, leads to vertigo. By the addition of a single letter: *verité: vertige.* A vertigo of metaphors, fragments, aphorisms, all contradictory, canceling each other out:

> "The word is a horse. Its gallop whirls up the dust on the road. It forces the passers-by to lower their eyes."
> "Your words have become our mounts, master," said Reb Lindel. "But we have not gone far. We went in circles, as in the circus. No doubt, we are wretched horsemen?"
> "The tree goes in rings to its full height, and the bee around its honey-probe. Did not Reb Azar write: 'The road of knowledge is rounder than an apple?' "[6]

The relations between the terms keep shifting. No one metaphor is central or even more important than another. In the end, we are left with gestures: the gesture of analogy rather than any particular analogy, the gesture of signification rather than any particular meaning, the gestures of endless commentary and interpretation. A wild whirl to cover the abyss. Vertigo. Our gestures, too, are empty. But they have a resonance that grows out of the consent to emptiness. As do instruments. As does language, depending on the blank space that is the matter between words, that allows them to be. As, I would add, does the womb, the "empty" organ that is the locus of birth: the *Lawn of Excluded Middle*.

Narrow rooms. When we say infinite we have no conception but our own inability. Therefore the name of God is used. The I has no sharp boundaries inward.

~

It is not true that I have no oceanic feeling. I have this kind of feeling about language. The ocean of language. Robert Duncan said that "Jabès lives in the French language as if it were the Sea."[7] Don't all poets? If we take "the French" out? "Thought-diver," says John Taggart.[8]

Sitting down to write. On the one hand, I feel I am coming to myself, out of the daily scatter of tasks, jobs, people. On the other hand, I am terrified. The page is the void. Nothing will ever break the clear white surface.

"To create is to make a pact with nothingness."
—Clark Coolidge[9]

Worse, the emptiness is not outside, but inside me. There is no self to come home to. Or a vertigo of selves, of makeshift constructions, canceling each other. No language either.

"Moving on in the Dark like Loaded Boats at Night, though there is no Course, there is Boundlessness."
—Emily Dickinson[10]

It is the "though" in this sentence that comes to the rescue. It marks a leap. Boundlessness is in another dimension from "no Course." Allowing ourselves to be lost, we dive into the infinite of language.

A train of thought departs. Spokes of the mind wheeling backward. Exhausted, the light. Erased, the fine line of the horizon.

Then desperate attempts to swim in this ocean, reaching for bits of words, phrases, to cover the emptiness, to create myself out of the tension between words and at the same time lose myself. And the uncanny moment when language takes over, when I am "the one who writes and the one who is written" (Jabès's formulation again).

Like the invention of God, that of language transcends the inventor. It is not by accident that most cultures have myths of a god giving language and writing to humankind.

> "Am Ende hängen wir doch ab
> von Kreaturen, die wir machten."
> —Goethe[11]

The infinite of language. Boundless in its potential, almost boundless in its actuality. Reaching down to the beginnings of humanity, throwing bridges between all human beings. For some, a direct connection with the Godhead. For some, another name for it.

> "In the beginning, there is language. God is a circle of luminous letters. He is each of the letters of His Name. He is also the middle, the void of the circle where man and the woman about to be mother stand."[12]

Snow drifted in under the door. The iron stove glowed red. The lilies spread their lush, insolent incense. All receding, toys drawn on a string.

I asked Edmond Jabès why he kept writing about God when he did not believe. He said it was a word his culture had given him.

> "To write as if addressing God. But what to expect from nothingness where any word is disarmed?"[13]

Roma quadrata. Inaccessible, he says. The embryo cannot be proved from adult lips blue with cold. Memory not regenerated in the marrow.

Silence. Nothingness. The boundless. Hosts of words trying to encircle it. Vertigo. Not *the* Logos, but *hosts* of words. Heavenly? Partaking of the emptiness with the empty spaces between them, the spaces that separate and connect them, that make meaning possible. As Charles Olson puts it in *Human Universe:*

> At root (or stump) what *is*, is no longer THINGS but what happens BETWEEN.[14]

Rising from the grass, the trees, the park, many obscure modifications of the spiritual life. Tumbled garments, faded photographs. The bodily forms of light can't be looked at face on. Nobody is that strong. The snow continues to fall.

A Key into the Key

My book *A Key into the Language of America* (New York: New Directions, 1994) takes its title, chapter sequence, and many quotations from Roger Williams's book of 1643 with the same title.

I live in the former territory of the Narragansett Indians, in Rhode Island, the colony Williams founded as a haven of religious freedom after he was banished from the theocratic Massachusetts Bay Colony for his nonconformist opinions. I was not born here. Like the first settlers, I came from Europe. I came expecting strangeness, expecting to be disoriented, but was shocked, rather, by my lack of culture shock. Nothing seemed too different from my native Germany—except for the Indian place-names. I was at first irritated by them: my ears could not quite take them in, my eyes were disoriented by their spelling:

Aquidneck
Chepachet
Cocumscussock
Misquamicut
Pascoag
Pawtucket
Pawcatuck
Quonochontaug
Woonasquatucket

Then, gradually, I became fascinated with the irritant, the otherness of these names, the strangeness of their music, which alone inscribes the Indian past in the present space. The Narragansett language, not written down, existed only in time and vanished with it.

I turned to Williams's book for a look at this language, for some context around these place-names. For a bit more Indian subsoil—or perhaps groundwater—under the soil of American English. I found something much richer than a primer or phrasebook, though Williams's book is that also: the first extensive vocabulary and study of an Indian language printed in English. Williams had not only

> a constant zealous desire to dive into the Indian language . . . , but a painful Patient spirit to lodge with them, in their filthy smoke holes (even while I lived at Plymouth and Salem) to gain their tongue . . . and could debate with them in a great measure in their own Language.[1]

The book is, besides, a sympathetic presentation of Indian customs— again, the first I know of. Williams recognized a culture where his compatriots saw only savage otherness.

Roger Williams was a preacher and initially approached the natives as a missionary, undertaking what the Massachusetts Bay and Plymouth colonists had professed as a goal but had not put into practice: the conversion of the native population to Christianity. "I am no Elder in any church . . . nor ever shall be, if the Lord please to grant my desires that I may intend what I long after, the Natives Soules," he wrote to Governor John Winthrop, in mid-1632.[2] Williams's Christianity proved perhaps the only hindrance to his anthropological observations; for the Indians' religion disturbed him deeply. He writes:

> I confess to have most of these their [religious] customs by their owne Relation, for after once being in their Houses and beholding what their Worship was, I durst never bee an eye witnesse, Spectatour, or looker on, least I should have been partaker of Sathans Inventions and Worships, contrary to *Ephes.* 5.11.[3]

Williams was all the more impressed with the Indians' conduct, which seemed to put the Christians to shame—and without the help of divine grace. For if he was uneasy about the Indian religion, he was indignant about much of what the colonists were doing. *The Key* is written for them, for his compatriots—who immediately misunderstood its intention. They regarded it as a factual handbook, of great practical use to traders, missionaries and settlers. As John J. Teunissen and Evelyn J. Hinz say in the introduction to their 1973 reprint edition:

> Since the conversion of the Indian and trade with him were the ostensible reasons for colonization advanced by all parties and since the granting of the charter [for the Providence Plantations] coincided with the publication of A Key, it was only natural for both Williams's supporters and opponents to treat the book as evidence of his success as a colonial agent.[4]

But the original book was not written as a handbook for successful colonization. It was not written only to teach a language, but also to teach a lesson.

Each chapter moves through three stages: through phrase lists and anthropological observations (which often contain ironical comments on the supposedly superior Europeans) to a final moralizing poem. The poem is always introduced with the words "More particular:" thus marking the importance of the lesson over the factual information preceding it. In these poems, the Indians serve as a mirror held up to the Christians:

> The courteous *Pagan* shall condemne
> *Uncourteous Englishmen,*
> Who live like Foxes, Beares and Wolves,
> Or Lyon in his Den.

> Let none sing *blessing* to their soules,
> For that they Courteous are:
> The wild *Barbarians* with no more
> Than Nature, goe so farre:

> If Nature's Sons both *wild* and *tame,*
> Humane and Courteous be:
> How ill becomes it Sonnes of God
> To want Humanity?
> —*A Key,* chapter I

Williams, the Christian, is amazed that the Indians tended to behave better than their Christian counterparts—and that with only "Nature's teaching." One could draw different conclusions from this. But Roger Williams saw the opportunity for a lesson. The lesson was moral and spiritual. It was also political.

> The Natives are very exact and punctuall in the bounds of their Lands . . . And I have knowne them make bargaine and sale amongst themselves for a small piece, or quantity of Ground: notwithstanding a sinfull opinion among many that Christians have right to *Heathens* Lands: but of the delusion of that phrase, I have spoke in a discourse. (*A Key*, chapter XVI)

The discourse referred to was a treatise written in 1632, which argued that a royal patent did not entitle English colonists to Indian land, that such land had to be purchased from the natives themselves, that it was in fact sinful of both the Crown and the colonists to usurp land from the natives.

One argument of particular interest (reported by the Puritan clergyman John Cotton) is Williams's attack on the doctrine of *vacuum domicilium,* the doctrine that the colonists were entitled to the land because the Indians were not making full use of it. Williams observed that while it was true that the natives cultivated only a small portion of their land, they used all of it for hunting and, for this purpose, regularly burned the underbrush. As Neal Salisbury points out in his book *Manitou and Providence,* this is an argument based not on some abstractions of international law but on direct ethnographic observation. Williams recognized that Indian hunting and burning were not random activities, but systematic, rational uses of land in the same sense that cultivation was for Europeans.[5]

Williams's recognition that the Indians were making rational and full use of the land was a most unwelcome idea. It challenged the colonists' right to the land they were occupying. It is not surprising that the Boston magistrates had the tract burned—nor that they considered Williams a dangerous man.

Roger Williams had already attacked the basis of the Puritan theocracy of Massachusetts Bay Colony by advocating the separation of church and state. He held that the civil power of a state could properly have no jurisdiction over the consciences of men, and that an oath could not be tendered to an unregenerate man, oaths being a form of worship. Challenging the colonists' title to the land was the last straw. Moreover, as Perry Miller states, he "thus threatened the very bases of the society at a moment when the possibility of an Anglican invasion to revoke the [Massachusetts] charter and to reduce Massachusetts to conformity with England was real," so that Williams seemed to be playing into the hands of the enemy. Hence, Miller continues, "the state dealt with him as any state must deal with such agitators. The statesmen who exiled him never repented."[6]

In July 1635 Roger Williams was formally tried for his political heresies by the Massachusetts General Court and, when he did not recant, was banished from Massachusetts for three hundred years. An attempt was made to deport him to England, but he was forewarned and fled to an Indian settlement on the east bank of the Seekonk River, where he bought land from the Indians and founded the settlement he called Providence, "in grateful remembrance of God's merciful providence to him in his distress." He lived by farming and trade with the Indians.

The mirror Roger Williams held up to the colonists in *A Key into the Language of America* was not welcome. Even a hundred years later, when the Massachusetts Historical Society reprinted extracts from *A Key* in 1794 and 1798, the poems and the passages critical of the New English were omitted, as well as phrases expressing Roger Williams's admiration for the Indians. For instance, "omitted from the observation of the Edenic nature of native clothing is the phrase, 'after the patterne of their and our first Parents.'"[7] What was reprinted was a utilitarian guide to customs and vocabulary.

I live in Roger Williams's territory. I was born in 1935, the year Williams's three-hundred-year banishment officially ended. I was born "on the other side," in Germany, which was then Nazi Germany. I am not Jewish. I was born on the side of the (then) winners. I was still a child when World War II ended with the defeat of the Nazis. I immigrated to the United States, the country of the winners, as a white, educated European who did not find it too difficult to get jobs, an advanced degree, and a university position. I can see myself, to some extent, in parallel to the European settlers/colonists of Roger Williams's time (though I did not think God or destiny had set the country aside for me as a virgin garden). Like Williams, I am ambivalent about my position among the privileged, the "conquerors."

But am I among them? I am white and educated. I am also a poet and a woman. A poet, in our days, is regarded as rather a marginal member of society, whose social usefulness is in doubt. As a woman, I do not figure as conqueror in the shell game of archetypes, but as conquered—a "war bride." As a woman, I also have no illusions about the Indian societies. They were far from ideal.

I live in Roger Williams's territory. By coincidence and marriage I share his initials. I share his ambivalence. In the shell game of archetypes, the conquered (people or land) is always female:

No more had Columbus landed, the flower once ravished . . . [8]

The colonization of America put the very "male" Indian culture in the position of the conquered female, part of the land that was considered there to be "taken." I can identify with both sides of the conflict and am ambivalent about each side.

In 1635 Roger Williams found the Narragansetts at the height of their power, in a strong, if not dominant, intertribal position. They had not been decimated by the great smallpox epidemic of 1616–1619 and, according to estimates, numbered some thirty thousand. For a while, Williams was able to arbitrate between them and the colonists. He was able to induce the Narragansetts to ally themselves with the English against the Pequots. But he was traveling to England (ironically, to secure a charter for Rhode Island) when the Narragansetts lost their fight with the Mohegans. The Narragansett sachem Miantonomi, who had called for the tribes to unite in common cause against the English, was captured, turned over to the Commissioners of the United Colonies, and executed at their behest by the Mohegan chief Uncas.

Williams was there but unable to arbitrate when another Narragansett sachem, Metacomet or King Philip, rose up against the English in 1675. Williams saw the Narragansetts defeated in the Great Swamp Fight, King Philip's head hung up as a public display in Boston, and the Narragansett tribe devastated, most of them indentured into service in colonial homes.

Indenture was better than being sold into slavery, but it helped erode Indian customs. By the middle of the eighteenth century, the Indians were dressing in European style. By 1800 the Narragansett language was dead. Except in place-names:

Conimicut
Matunuck
Meshanticut
Namquit
Poppasquash
Saugatucket
Usquepaug
Weekapaug

And what is left of the Narragansetts in our time? Grave sites on Conanicut Island, skeletons buried in the fetal position, facing southwest, in the direction of their paradise. Narragansett stonemasons, carpenters, and factory workers. A few owners of restaurants or gift shops, managers, or masonry contractors. "Achievement in professional employment has reached the level of the master's degree in nursing. Yet, most Narragansett do not go beyond high school in education, and many have dropped out of high school."[9]

But there has been much restoration of Indian practices. In 1934 only one of the elected tribal officials listed in *The Narragansett Dawn*, a local Indian monthly, has an Indian name; by 1950 all of them do. However, with the Narragansett language dead, "the Indians who wanted to have Indian names had the choice of picking names out of Roger Williams's 1643 volume or creating English word-names that conveyed something of the personality of the person."[10]

We have come full circle. Now, Roger Williams's book is for the Indians.

And for me. Besides giving me a glimpse of the vanished language and culture, Williams's *Key* has given me the form of my own *Key into the Language of America*. In parallel to Roger Williams's anthropological passages, the initial prose section of each of my chapters tries to get at the clash of Indian and European cultures by a violent collage of phrases from Williams with elements from anywhere in my Western heritage. I try to enact the confrontation of the two cultures by juxtapositions, often within a single sentence. Roger Williams's voice can be recognized by its archaic syntax and vocabulary printed in boldface. There is also an additional tension between the values of the seventeenth-century settlers, "Saints," "Pilgrims," and my own, which are not only secular but are also informed by twentieth-century hindsight as to the long-range destruction inherent in the settlers' struggle to survive. To reinforce the theme of conquest and gender, every chapter adds a narrative section in italics, in the voice of a young woman, ambivalent about her sex and position among the conquerors.

Every chapter also has its word list and final poem. These play across both themes. Unlike those of Roger Williams, my word lists are not of practical use, but they explore the language context (rather than cultural context) of the chapter titles. The words in the lists may be suggested by the sound of a title word (e.g., "fission" in the chapter on fishing) or may play across its semantic field ("interlacing" and "contagion" in the chapter on "Relations of Consanguinity"). Many lists explore compounds of title words (busy[body], [body]guard, [body]snatcher in chapter 7) or grammatical elements like suffixes ([season]able, [season]ing in chapter 10). There are also some Narragansett phrases.

All in all, my book could be called an immigrant's take on the heritage and complex early history of my adopted country. Or perhaps a dive into the waters of the Moosup and Pawtuxet Rivers, of Mishnock, Ninigret, Pasquiset, Watchaug, Wesquage, and Yawgoog Ponds.

Form and Discontent

In July 1995, I taught for a week at the Naropa Institute in Boulder or, more precisely, at the Jack Kerouac School of Disembodied Poetics. The theme of the week was "Wild Forms."

In the workshops, I naturally focused on procedures that combine "method and madness," processes that short-circuit logical and commonsensical thinking in order to get the muse interested: collage, crossings, all the techniques of Oulipo, forms based on mathematics (like permutations or Jackson Mac Low's diastics), and explorations of sound and space.

In my lecture during that week, I tried to present a theoretical, linguistic framework that had long preoccupied me, as well as a brief historical background.

———————

1. COMPOSITION AS EXPLANATION

In the beginning there is Gertrude Stein, for whom composition is explanation. I could also say, in the beginning is Aristotle: "the fable is simply this, the combination of the incidents."[1]

2. A LOOK AROUND

The forms that have been striking me as "wild" have tended to be Steinian in this sense of stressing the horizontal, the axis of composition. I'm most struck by three tendencies: one is literally spatial composition, for example, Susan Howe's work. Another is emphasis on discontinuity, leaps on the level of syntax, of logic, of grammar. Breaks that do not immediately fold back into a smooth unity and may occur in mid-sentence:

> I was on my way from Carthage, it was night. It is not wax I am scorching was dead about her with knots. (Norma Cole)

> I hide behind a category by misbehaving. (Carla Harryman)

> Loop conceived in a line, the spine with its regions, reasons. On another, sweaters hang by the wrist to dry. The list is sweet. You lie. The eye is met by the season. (Ron Silliman)

> The proportion of accident in my picture of the world falls with the rain. (Rosmarie Waldrop)

> Went out so I'd take the car and a whole system of banking and money is based on a hierarchy. (Leslie Scalapino)

> "ROAST POTATOES Roast Potatoes for. (Gertrude Stein)[2]

Or a subtler example, Mei-mei Berssenbrugge's almost unnoticeable shifts from one grammatical structure into another:

> Never mind if he calls, the places you get
> through inwardness take time, and to drift
> down to the shore of the island, you know
> by the sand moving, even the coarse sand here
> It's hard to say if you can even stand up, there[3]

The third tendency is mathematical. There is a lot of counting. Not stresses, not even syllables—I am not considering that most unimaginative bunch, the new formalists—but words per line, sentences per paragraph. You all know about Ron Silliman's (or Inger Christensen's) love for the Fibonacci number series, or Lyn Hejinian's *My Life*, which began with thirty-seven sections of thirty-seven sentences each. When she published a second edition at age forty-five, she added eight sentences to each section plus eight new sections.

Jacques Roubaud: "No ideas but in numbers."[4]

Then, in a somewhat more remote way, a number of people use ideas of permutation—for example, Jackson Mac Low's *4 Trains*, of which I will quote the first two stanzas:

Train rule atom intricate nitrogen.
Rule unusual leotard entropy.
Atom train ostrich might.
Intricate nitrogen train rule intricate casual atom train entropy.
Nitrogen intricate train rule ostrich genealogy entropy nitrogen.

Rule unusual leotard entropy.
Unusual nitrogen unusual social unusual atom leotard.
Leotard entropy ostrich train atom rule dies.
Entropy nitrogen train rule ostrich pope yearly.[5]

As Zukofsky puts it: "[Thus] poetry may be defined as an order of words that as movement and tone (rhythm and pitch) approaches in varying degrees the wordless art of music as a kind of mathematical limit."[6]

All of these examples draw attention to arrangement, composition. They all listen to language. I once wrote:

I don't even have thoughts, I say, I have methods that make language think, take over and me by the hand. Into sense or offense, syntax stretched across rules, relations of force, fluid the dip of the plumb line, the pull of eyes. . . . No beginnings. All unrepentant middle.[7]

And none of these forms are "organic form." None rely primarily on metaphor, though from the Romantics on poetry has been more or less identified with it.

3. FRAMEWORK

A. HISTORICAL

Let me step back for a moment to the beginnings of the concept of organic form and look at what *it* reacted against.

When Goethe started to make a splash writing free verse, around

1770, the dominant aesthetic was neoclassical. An aesthetic that— most clearly articulated in French classical drama—defined form in terms of unity, symmetry, continuity, and regularity: all concepts based on mathematics, especially geometry, relation in space. Goethe had to defend himself against the charge of formlessness, which he did by enlisting Gothic cathedrals as allies. The Strasbourg Cathedral, he writes, is "beautiful like God's trees."[8] A tree does not need to be symmetrical to have form. Its branches do not have to be regular to combine into a *whole* (a recurrent value word) that has balance and beauty. This image led naturally to the idea that as the form of the plant is already contained in the seed, the form of a work of art is determined by its conception, is an "inner" form, which lies behind the surface of the actual work and must be felt rather than measured. This was a most significant change of emphasis—which we are now in the process of reversing.

The neoclassical aesthetic had laid its stress on how the elements were combined on the surface, how they sat next to each other on the page, how they followed each other in the theater, that is, on metonymy, on composition and syntax.

But the moment poets started to think in terms of organisms, the relation of seed to tree, the focus shifted to the relation of inner to outer. The poem became an epiphany in the poet's mind, which is then expressed. Originality became a value that more than replaced elegance of composition (Alexander Pope's "what oft was thought, but never so well expressed"), which became suspect. The cluster of conception/content/meaning became primary and determined the form, the expression. (Remember Charles Olson/Robert Creeley: "Form is never more than an extension of content," though both their work and other theoretical statements contradict this.[9]) And the expression was considered an image, a metaphor for an internal "deeper meaning." Metaphor (in the large sense: any relation by similarity) became the dominant rhetorical device. Metaphor also became the way to see the relation between poem and world (the world is given, but can be represented, pictured), and, in a replay of Platonic and medieval ideas, to see the relation between physical and spiritual world. The world is God's book. Or Baudelaire's "Correspondences":

La nature est un temple où de vivants piliers
laissent parfois sortir de confuses paroles;

L'homme y passe à travers des forêts de symboles
Qui l'observent avec des regards familiers.[10]

[literal translation:
Nature is a temple where live pillars
Sometimes let escape confused words;
Man walks there through forests of symbols
That watch him with familiar eyes.]

Olson has called this vertical tendency of metaphor "the suck of symbol."[11] Metaphor as hotline to transcendence, to divine meaning, which casts the poet in the role of a special being, a priest or prophet. We know these ideas very well. They have dominated the thinking about poetry from Romanticism to the present.

B. LINGUISTIC

Now it happens that these two emphases, on metaphor or on metonymy, are not simply differences between two styles, but coincide with the two dimensions of every speech act, selection and combination (Ferdinand de Saussure, Roman Jakobson). Words always have a double reference: (1) to the code and (2) to the context. The code gives us a vertical axis with substitution sets where the elements are linked by similarity. We choose from them whether to say "the man," "the guy," "the fellow," whether to say "walked," "ran," "ambled," "sauntered," and so forth. Then we combine the selected words on a horizontal axis to say: "the man ran around the corner." This is a relation by contiguity, by syntax.

This model is based on ordinary language. Poetry tends to project a whole slue from the vertical axis into the horizontal, it tends to overdetermine (Robert Scholes, Michael Riffaterre).[12] Nevertheless, Jakobson is right that literary language tends to divide according to an emphasis on one axis or the other. In rhetorical terms, an emphasis on metaphor or an emphasis on metonymy (also in the large sense: any relation by contiguity). Some writers are more concerned with finding "*the* right word," *the* perfect metaphor; others are more concerned with what "happens between" the words,[13] with composition, exploring the sentence and its boundaries, slidings, the gaps between fragments, the shadow zone of silence, of margins.

Susan Howe has a funny send-up of the metaphoric emphasis, along with clichés, in a multiple-choice pattern:

as wise as an (earwig, owl, eel).
as sober as a (knight, minstrel, judge).
as crafty as a (fox, cuckoo, kitten).
as smooth as (sandpaper, velvet, wood).
as slippery as an (accident, eel, engine).
as straight as an (angle, angel, arrow).[14]

I say "more" concerned because it's a matter of emphasis. Of course we are always concerned with both. And what makes our moment *now* so interesting is that we seem in a period of tension between the two emphases.

For instance, everybody uses literary allusions. But look at the way Barbara Guest does it:

Thinking of You Prokofief

The steam settled into the atmosphere
        steam in atmosphere
it was cold; so the steam did not move
        it became lonely as a field of daffodils
on the earth we kept looking up
on the horizon there was admiration
                        those waltzes.

And the ivory of our lids felt vaporous
as if crevices were gained in the shell
where our eyes kept their hoods

        Thinking of you Prokofief
that tricky snow outside makes a steam indoors
and the china tea we brew keeps us quick
        as Prokofief
whose doors slam.

        Steam never lessens its latitude
in the sky

> like Prokofief
> while many cars creep over the bridge sweating
> finally equipped
> with their Mahler treads.[15]

We are lured into an image of cold, steam, and inertia when suddenly we are with Wordsworth. But the allusion is not used in the way we expect. It was very likely the analogy of "cloud" and "steam" that brought up Wordsworth's:

> I wandered lonely as a cloud
> That floats on high o'er vales and hills
> When all at once I saw a crowd
> A host of golden daffodils

However, Guest does not put "lonely as a cloud," which would have reinforced the image, but stayed as inert as it began. Instead, the term of similarity is skipped, the "as" shifts to a later term in Wordsworth's poem. This pokes fun at our expectations and at Wordsworth's poem, where the daffodils seem jolly rather than lonely. It jolts logic, for how lonely can a whole field of daffodils be? And, most important, it directs our attention outward and introduces motion into the poem. We look outward, forward in time from the cold of winter to summer, then upward and toward the horizon, into the mental/metaphorical realm with "admiration," and into the violent motion of "those waltzes." When an "as" or "like" appears in the other stanzas, it never produces the parallel we expect, but leads us inevitably to Prokofief. And just when we think we have done with these scurrilous musical references and regained the opening perspective of looking out of the window on a winter day, another composer, Gustav Mahler, creeps up in the most unlikely manner—not as a musical rival of Prokofief, but as the name of snow tread on cars.

4. COMPOSITION AS PROCESS; OR, SHALL WE ESCAPE ANALOGY

A. IMPLICATIONS

If we now look at the current pull away from organic form that began with Stein, toward an emphasis on combination, the implications are very different:

(1) Nothing is given. (Though all the elements are: there is nothing new under the sun.) Everything remains to be constructed.

Creeley: "a world that's constantly coming into being . . . [the poetry is] *in* the activity" (in analogy to action painting).[16]

(2) The poet does not know beforehand what the poem is going to say, where the poem is going to take her.

Barbara Guest: "The dark identity of the poem."[17]

John Cage: "The importance of being perplexed."[18]

The poem is not so much "expression" as a cognitive process that, to some extent, changes even the poet.

So the poem is not so much a mirror as "a window, opposite direction, lean out, not thrown back on yourself. A window, a lens gathering language [as the Objectivists meant it], a focus to burn. Conjunction and connotation."[19]

Form/composition is not an extension of content (Olson/Creeley), but is, on the contrary, primary. It is the form that generates the content.

(3) The aim is not unifying (the one right word, the one perfect metaphor), but to open the form to the multiplicity of contexts.

(4) The transcendence is not upward, but horizontal, contextual. It is the transcendence of language with its infinite possibilities, infinite connections, and its charge of the past. In other words, no split between spirit and matter.

B. PRACTICE

As I begin working, I have only a vague nucleus of energy, which is sometimes located in a rhythm, an observation, but more often in a phrase, a cluster of words. This means the energy has a semantic field. But the poem starts to happen as the energy encounters a formal pattern, an obstacle. This may be predetermined or may simply arise out of *listening* to the *sound*, the "body," of the starter words, which reveals their own vectors and affinities. These pull the poem in unforeseen directions, away from the semantic field of the original impulse. Hence there is tension, which creates more energy.

Duncan: "His intellect intent upon the ratios and movements of the poem, he is almost unaware of depths that may be stirred in his own psyche. What he feels is the depth and excitement of the poem. The poem takes over."[20]

Guest: "The poem enters its own rhythmical waters."[21]

Oppen: "When the man [writing] is frightened by a word, he may have started."[22]

C. PALIMPSEST

But it is obviously not true that "nothing is given:" language comes not only with an infinite potential for new combinations, but also with a long history contained in it.

The blank page is not blank. No text has one single author. Whether we are conscious of it or not, we always write on top of a palimpsest.

This is not a question of linear "influence" and not just of tradition, but of writing as a multiple dialog with a whole web of previous and concurrent texts, with tradition, the culture and language we breathe and move in, and that conditions us even while we help to construct it.

Historians speak of "the conditions of occurrence;" Duncan, of the "grand collage."

Mary Kelly, a British conceptual artist, speaks in *Post-Partum Document* of the mother censoring the child's sexual researches, the child's look at her body. She uses the phrase: "the mother wipes the slate clean." I don't want to take this very far, but the phrase intrigues me with its suggestion that innocence is not a primary state, but the result of suppressing a prior intuition. The slate is never clean.

Many of us have foregrounded this awareness of the palimpsest as a method, using, transforming, "translating" parts of other works.

CODA

One last remark. Most of our century's radical explorations have been in the direction of spontaneity, the unconscious, drugs, automatic writing, whereas I think the "wildest form" is to walk the interface of conscious and unconscious, a line much too thin for our feet, whether metrical, metaphorical, or physical. I suppose we are here, at the "School of Disembodied Poetics," to find something like "disembodied feet," which can walk in both realms at the same time.

Thoreau: "Nothing is worth saying, nothing is worth doing except as a foil for the waves of silence to break against."[23]

Thinking of Follows

This statement of poetics was written for Peter Baker's *Onward: Contemporary Poetry and Poetics,* an anthology of contemporary poetics of what Marjorie Perloff calls "the other tradition" (as opposed to the "mainstream").

I had on occasion made brief statements about particular texts or techniques, always well after completion of the project, when distance and hindsight clarified what had been going on. Mostly I had been content to let the poems stand on their own and show their implicit—or explicit—poetics. Here was an opportunity to pull together scattered remarks and think more explicitly about what I was doing.

If I were writing this now I would use Michael Davidson's term "palimtext" rather than "palimpsest." He defines it, in *Ghostlier Demarcations,* as "writing that displays its formations in other writings . . . an arrested moment in an ongoing process of signifying, scripting, and typing, . . . palimtext is a vehicle for circumventing generic categories and period styles by describing writing in its collaborative, quotidian, and intertextual forms."

The beginning paragraphs are a condensation of the preceding essay. Thereafter it continues with more personal matters.

I. COMPOSITION AS EXPLANATION

In the beginning there is Stein: "Everything is the same except composition and as the composition is different and always going to be different everything is not the same."

FRAMEWORK

Linguistic

Every speech act (every use of signs) consists of selection and combination (Saussure, Jakobson). This means words always have a double reference: to the code and to the context. The code gives us a vertical axis with substitution-sets where the elements are linked by similarity. We choose from them whether to say "the flower," "the rose," "the lily," whether to say "red," "beautiful," "radiant," and so forth. Then we combine the selected words on a horizontal axis to say: "the rose was beautiful against the window." We put them in a relation by syntax, by contiguity.

Literary language tends to divide according to an emphasis on one axis or the other. Some are more concerned with le mot juste, with *the* perfect metaphor, others, with what "happens between" the words (Olson).

Historical

For the long stretch from Romanticism through Modernism (and on?), poetry has been more or less identified with the axis of selection, relation by similarity, metaphor. This has large implications:

- that the "world" is given, but can be "pictured" in language (Baudelaire: "Man walks through a forest of symbols");
- that the poem is an epiphany inside the poet's mind, which is then "expressed" by choice of the right words;
- that content (and "meaning") is primary and determines its ("organic") form; (Creeley/Olson: "Form is never more than an extension of content");
- finally, that the vertical tendency of metaphor (Olson: "the suck of symbol") is our hotline to transcendence, to divine meaning, hence the poet as priest and prophet.

"SHALL WE ESCAPE ANALOGY" (CLAUDE ROYET-JOURNOUD); OR, COMPOSITION AS PROCESS

Nothing is given. Everything remains to be constructed.

I do not know beforehand what the poem is going to say, where the poem is going to take me. The poem is not "expression," but a cognitive process that, to some extent, changes me. Cage: "Poetry is having nothing to say and saying it: we possess nothing."[1]

As I begin working, far from having an "epiphany" to express, I have only a vague nucleus of energy running to words. As soon as I start listening to the words, they reveal their own vectors and affinities, they pull the poem into their own field of force, often in unforeseen directions, away from the semantic charge of the original impulse.

Valéry: "When the poets enter the forest of language it is with the express purpose of getting lost."[2]

Jabès: "The pages of the book are doors. Words go through them, driven by their impatience to regroup . . . Light is in these lovers' strength of desire."[3]

PALIMPSEST

But it is not true that "nothing is given:" language comes not only with an infinite potential for new combinations, but also with a long history contained in it.

The blank page is not blank. Words are always secondhand, says Dominique Noguez. No text has one single author. Whether we are conscious of it or not, we always write on top of a palimpsest (cf. Duncan's "grand collage").

This is not a question of linear "influence," but of writing as dialog with a whole web of previous and concurrent texts, with tradition, with the culture and language we breathe and move in and that conditions us even while we help to construct it.

Many of us have foregrounded this awareness as technique, transforming, "translating" parts of other works.

I, A WOMAN

This fact clearly shapes my writing—thematically, in attitude, in awareness of social conditioning, marginality—but does not determine it exclusively.

Lacan is preposterous in imposing his phallic cult on the signifier. And he is in bad faith when he claims gender neutrality.

Conversely, I don't see much point in labeling certain forms as "feminine." (Though I like some of the suggestions; e.g., Joan Retallack's and Luce Irigarai's that the feminine is "plural," comprising all forms that conspire against monolithic, monotonal, monolinear universes.)

I don't really see "female language," "female style or technique." Because the writer, male or female, is only one partner in the process of writing. Language, in its full range, is the other. And it is not a language women have to "steal back" (Ostriker). The language in which the poets move belongs as much to the mothers as to the fathers.

COMMUNICATION

In crossing the Atlantic my phonemes settled somewhere between German and English. I speak either language with an accent. This has saved me the illusion of being the master of language. I enter it at a skewed angle, through the fissures, the slight difference.

I do not "use" the language. I interact with it. I do not communicate via language, but with it. Language is not a tool for me, but a medium infinitely larger than my intention.

What will find resonance is out of my hands. If the poem works (and gets the chance to be read), it will set off vibrations in the reader, an experience with language—with the way it defines us as human beings.

Walter Benjamin: "Art posits man's physical and spiritual existence, but in none of its works is it concerned with his response. No poem is intended for the reader, no picture for the beholder, no symphony for the listener."[4]

MEANING, ESPECIALLY DEEPER

All I am saying here is on the surface, which is all we can work on. I like the image in Don Quixote that compares translation to working on a tapestry: you sit behind the canvas, with a mess of threads and a pattern for each color. You follow out patterns but have no idea what image will appear on the other side.

This holds for writing as well. We work on technical aspects, on the craft. We make a pattern that coheres. Our obsessions and preoccupations find their way into it no matter what we do.

What will appear "on the other side," what the text will "mean," is another matter. I can only hope that it gives a glimpse of that unreachable goal (which, paradoxically, is also its matrix), the concentration, the stillness of those moments when it seems we are taken out of our-selves and out of time.

II. PRACTICE

I don't even have thoughts, I have methods that make language think, take over and me by the hand. Into sense or offense, syntax stretched across rules, relations of force, fluid the dip of the plumb line, the pull of eyes. (*A Form/Of Taking/It All*)

1. EXPLORING THE SENTENCE

The tension of line and sentence. But especially the sentences. Erosion of their borders. Sliding them together, toward a larger (total?) connectedness.

Both in *The Aggressive Ways of the Casual Stranger* and in *The Road Is Everywhere or Stop This Body* I worked on making the object of one phrase flip over into being the subject of the next phrase without being repeated:

weightless inside a density
about to burn
the air
won't take the imprint we
talk
doubles the frequencies
brought up short

Consciously I was pushing at the boundaries of the sentence. I was interested in having a flow of a quasi-unending sentence play against the short lines that determine the rhythm. So on one level, I was simply exacerbating the tension between sentence and line that is there in all verse. And since the thematic field is cars and other circulation systems (blood, breath, sex, economics, language, a set of metaphors never stated, but made structural), I liked the effect of hurtling down main-clause highway at breakneck speed.

It was only later that I realized that this challenge to a rigid subject-object relation has feminist implications. Woman in our culture has been treated as object par excellence, to be looked at rather than looking, to be done to rather than doing. Instead, these poems propose a grammar in which subject and object function are not fixed, but reversible roles, where there is no hierarchy of main and subordinate clauses, but a fluid and constant alternation.

After a while, though, I began to long for subordinate clauses, complex sentences. So I turned to writing prose poems. I became fascinated by Wittgenstein and by the form of the proposition because of its extreme closure. This was a challenge after working toward opening the boundaries of the sentence by sliding sentences together or by fragmentation. I accepted the complete sentence (most of the time) and tried to subvert its closure and logic from the inside, by constantly sliding between frames of reference. I especially brought the female body in and set into play the old gender archetypes of logic and mind being "male," whereas "female" designates the illogical: emotion, body, matter. Again, I hope that the constant sliding challenges these categories.

> You took my temperature which I had meant to save for
> a more difficult day (*The Reproduction of Profiles*)

2. FRAGMENTS

> Isogrammatical lines connecting the mean incidence of comparable parts of speech map the discourses of the world, I say. Against their average, extremes of sense and absence create the pleasure of fragments. Break the silence and pick up the pieces to find a cluster of shards which catches light on the cut and the next day too. (*A Form/Of Taking/It All*)

This glint of light on the cut is what I am after. Juxtaposing, rather than isolating, minimal units of meaning.

And the break of linearity. When the smooth horizontal travel of eye/mind is impeded, when the connection is broken, there is a kind of orchestral meaning that comes about in the break, a vertical dimension made up of the energy field between the two lines (or phrases or sentences). A meaning that both connects and illuminates the gap, so that the shadow zone of silence between the elements gains weight, becomes an element of the structure.

> puberty: he
> and I know I

puff of smoke
insults
the future

. . .

centers unlimited
mirrors
a not yet open door
precisely: an occasion
—(*When They Have Senses*)

Jabès, like the German Romantics, holds that the fragment is our only access to the infinite. I tend to think it is our way of apprehending anything. Our inclusive pictures are mosaics.

3. COLLAGE OR THE SPLICE OF LIFE

I turned to collage early, to get away from writing poems about my overwhelming mother. I felt I needed to do something "objective" that would get me out of myself. But when I looked at the collage poems awhile later: they were still about my mother. This was a revelation— and a liberation. It made me realize that subject matter is not something to worry about. Our concerns and obsessions will surface no matter what we do. This frees us to work on form, which is what one can work on. For the rest, all we can do is try to keep our mind alive, our curiosity and ability to see.

Even more important was the second revelation: that any constraint stretches the imagination, pulls us into semantic fields different from the one we started with. For though the poems were still about my mother, something else was also beginning to happen.

Georges Braque: "You must always have two ideas, one to destroy the other. The painting is finished when the concept is obliterated."[5]

Guest would qualify that the constraints must be such that they stretch the imagination without disabling it.

Collage, like fragmentation, allows you to frustrate the expectation of continuity, of step-by-step linearity. And if the fields you juxtapose are different enough, there are sparks from the edges. Here is a paragraph from *A Key into the Language* of America that tries to get at the clash of Indian and European cultures by juxtaposing phrases from Roger Williams's 1743 treatise with contemporary elements from anywhere in my Western heritage.

OF MARRIAGE
Flesh, considered as cognitive region, as opposed to undifferen-
tiated warmth, is called woman or wife. **The number not stinted,
yet the Narragansett (generally) have but one.** While diminu-
tives are coined with reckless freedom, the deep structure of the
marriage bed is universally esteemed even in translation. **If the
woman be false** to bedlock, **the offended husband will be sol-
emnly avenged,** arid and eroded. He may remove her clothes at
any angle between horizontal planes.

4. "TRANSLATION"

By this I mean taking one aspect of an existing work and translating
it into something else. For instance, *When They Have Senses* uses the
grammatical structure of Anne-Marie Albiach's *État* as a matrix, much
in the way poets used to use a metrical scheme. It was an additional
challenge that *État* is written in French, so that the grammatical pat-
terns did not work very well in English and thus had a built-in push
beyond themselves.

An example closer to home is *Differences for Four Hands*. This se-
quence began with following the sentence structure of Lyn Hejinian's
prose poem *Gesualdo* and "translating" it into an invocation of Clara
and Robert Schumann.

In the finished version this is not always easy to trace anymore.
Hejinian's sentence is much quirkier than what I ended up with, be-
cause I needed something closer to the tension between fluidity and
stillness that is characteristic of Schumann's music. Also, a passage
about the increasing number of children—"Run. Three children
through the house" "Run. Five children through the house"—became
a kind of refrain or ostinato that changes the structural feel. But here
is a passage that has remained quite close:

Lyn Hejinian, *Gesualdo:*
Two are extremes. You place on noble souls. The most important
was an extraordinary degree. What has been chosen from this,
but a regular process of communication, shortly implored for
long life and forgiveness. You are a target of my persuasion. I
am overlooking the city. At times I am most devout and at others
most serene, and both pleasure and displeasure haunt me. My
heart is not above the rooftops.

Differences for Four Hands:
Any two are opposite. You walk on sound. The coldest wind blows from the edges of fear. Which has been written down. Passion's not natural. But body and soul are bruised by melancholy, fruit of dry, twisted riverbeds. Loss discolors the skin. At times you devour apples, at others bite into your hand.

5. RHYTHM

Rhythm is the elusive quality without which there is no poem, without which the most interesting words remain mere words on paper, remain at best verse. "Upper limit music, lower limit speech," said Zukofsky. Rhythm, I mean, not meter. It is difficult to talk about, impossible to pin down. It is the truly physical essence of the poem, determined by the rhythms of my body, my breath, my pulse. But it is also the alternation of sense and absence, sound and silence. It articulates the between, the difference in repetition.

6. REVISIONS

I think on paper and revise endlessly. I am envious of a poet like Duncan who has such absolute confidence that anything that comes to him is right. "Speaking in the God-Voice" I heard him call it. "Of course," he added, "if you speak in the God-Voice you say an awful lot of stupid things!" More important to me: he considered new poems his revisions (re-visions) of the old ones—this is beautiful.

But I feel closer to what John Ashbery said in conversation with Kenneth Koch, that he feels any line could have been written some other way, that it does not necessarily have to sound as it does.

I am slow and need to think about things for a long time, need to hold on to the trace on paper. Thinking is adventure. Does adventure need to be speedy? Perhaps revising is a way of refusing closure? Not wanting to come to rest?

The Ground Is the Only Figure

Notebook Spring 1996

In winter 1995–1996, Iselin Herman of Brondum publishers in Denmark conceived her "Connect the Dots" project. She planned to publish a series of notebooks written by a large international assortment of poets during spring 1996. These were the "dots," which readers then could connect into a picture. In the end, the series was more limited than planned. Only seven volumes were published, by Stefano Benni (Italy), Suzanne Brogger (Denmark), Marcel Cohen (France), Paal-Helge Haugen (Norway), Nuno Judice (Portugal), and, from the United States, Michael Palmer and me.

The English text was published in "The Impercipient Lecture Series," edited by Steve Evans and Jennifer Moxley, in April 1997. The present version is very slightly abridged.

I am fascinated with notebooks that record aspects of everything a person is reading, thinking, and doing. I once saw one of Norma Cole's, where poem fragments were interspersed with drawings, ticket stubs, reading notes, and newspaper clippings. It was beautiful. But for myself, I have always kept different notebooks for different things. Potential lines for poems kept separate from reading notes. Theater programs in a special box. My occasional, short-lived attempts at a diary again in a separate book. I have been more concerned with the possibility of retrieving particular items than with chronicling my mind and experience. So I found myself writing a notebook in a way I had not done before (or have since). What I had always considered "ground" became figure, temporarily the only one.

It was not so much like Max Ernst's finding figures in the grain of wood as like Mondrian's "Compositions" in which, as Rosalind Krauss has pointed out, the ground has risen to the surface of the work to the point that it coincides with it. The ground becomes foreground, becomes figure.[1] Or like John Cage accepting "noise" as part of the composition.

It was a valuable experience precisely in raising the question of what is figure, what is ground, and what is their relation. The "Annales" historians have long been saying that it is the quotidian that defines us, not the moments of crisis. It also made me wonder about my tendency to categorize my notes when, generally, I am so interested in crossing boundaries, for example, between genres.

The fragments under the working title "2 Voices?" are the beginnings of the book *Reluctant Gravities*. Other sketches became poems collected in *Split Infinites*. As the captions show, my reading and thinking at the time was focused on space and spatial metaphors for form.

THRESHOLD

Jabès begins the first *Book of Questions* "At the Threshold of the Book." He has already declared that he is building his dwelling: *Je bâtis ma demeure*. The Arabic in his ear tells him *bayt* is both house and verse. Dante built his *stanze*, that is, his rooms.

Kafka, though he did not write in stanzas, carried a room inside him. When he walked fast he could hear a mirror, poorly fastened, shifting on the wall.

The promise of the threshold: this is a place your feelings can inhabit.

The threat of the threshold: "this book is not for you." Threshing floor, beating the grain from the chaff. Worn unevenly. Thinking follows footsteps, grooves.

The threshold of morning. Less promising now, reefs and shallows, a pain in the stomach, a fluttering like a flock of birds, scattered notes, scraps of paper.

Hesitation before encounter, terror of the unknown, the blank page. Threshold of consciousness, pain.

When Jabès comes to write *The Book of Resemblances,* he is no longer sure of the threshold. He now begins (the third volume) "In Search of the Threshold" and makes his way there slowly, across "Ante-" and "Ante-Ante-Thresholds."

"The threshold is perhaps death."[2] Like any beginning.

THE SPACE OF A HOUSE

clapboard, shingles, brick, brownstone, steel, glass, wall, roof, gate, door, window, window sill

a day ajar
wind on the sill

The cat on the sill. The sun lights up the tips of his fur. Undisturbed by the blue jay cussing, the glare of the window.

Through it, a flat garage roof littered with plastic swords. 3 roofs with TV antennae, 2 bare maples sliced by telephone wires. A woman walks by holding her coat shut.

Moltkestrasse 5, the house of my dreams though hardly of happiness, was covered with dirty greyish-brown stucco, crumbling in places. I made it my job to enlarge those wherever I could, digging down to the brick with fingers or sticks.

As if Moltke weren't bad enough, the house stood at the corner of Moltke- and Bismarckstrasse. But if I leaned out from the balcony, I could see the "hat" of the *Schiefe Turm,* the "leaning tower" of Kitzingen. It was built in a time of drought, the story goes, so, lacking water, the masons mixed their cement with the local Frankenwein.

A mind building around it room after room? House? Tower? Leaning a little, I would hope.

Thus my body builds around it room after room . . . (Proust, *Contre Sainte-Beuve*)

I remember extending my body
premenstrual geometry equating horizon and hollow
add up cobble stones against more unguessable events
Mother sat elsewhere in the body

My nose level with the table of my mother's sewing machine.

What shall I do:	*Was soll ich machen?*
Mother:	*Tanzen und lachen.*

I wanted a suggestion more specific than "dance and laugh." But she gave me a perfect little couplet.

THE OPENING OF THE FIELD

> The Source of Snow
> the nearness of Poetry
> —(Susan Howe, "Thorow")

The room/house metaphor may be right in an existential sense. The writer has no other home. And how precarious: "*le site du poème s'éva-nouit à peine le poème écrit*" (Dominique Fourcade).[3] One can come into a poem (if not into language) as into a room.

But it's wrong as a working notion. A space too like a box, a container, a concept of form that isn't mine. I would have my form/house be open. "A book is only a book when open" (Jabès).

> The way into the form,
> the way out of the room—
> The door, the hat,
> the chair, the fact.
> —(Robert Creeley, *Pieces*)[4]

Dig holes in the stucco. Let air blow through. Porch, portico, canopy, arcade? Lyn Hejinian has funnier containers:

> I carry my thoughts in
>   an ocular bucket
> Space accumulates in a far
>   larger tub[5]

Gottfried Benn's "Orangenstil:" the parts of the work are gathered, like the sections of an orange, around a center.[6]

The next step: de-center, multiply the centers. As in a Merce Cunningham dance: Centers unlimited. An orange in every word.

A grid, a net of city streets opening outward in all directions and yet bounded at every intersection. A field, "high energy-construct," "of Action," electromagnetic, a balance of forces, projective verse: "what *is*, is no longer THINGS but what happens BETWEEN" (Olson).[7]

PARADIGM SHIFTS

organism → field
opposition (thesis-antithesis, etc.) → difference

LITTLE WORDS

"The little word *and* is a nest of ambiguity" (Whitehead).[8] So wrong: it's the words with "meaning" that are the nests of ambiguity. The connectives are the only words that are absolutely clear! Pure relation. What happens if the connectives proliferate, the hinges take over? Michael Donhauser does this in *Dich noch und*. Let me try:

> The and sun's light and is compounded, casts and long and shadows a and look on the and face and of a and girl turns and to. And a schedule and of approximated pleasure and changing and seasons

The mathematical pattern doesn't work except that it breaks up the syntax. If I play intuitively, the repeated "and" becomes a rhythmic device:

> The sun's light and
> is compounded
> and casts long and shadows
> and a look and on
> the and face
> of a girl

THE OPENING OF THE FIELD

Open as avoiding premature definition of the work as of myself. Not a mirror on the inside of the lid, to discover things about myself; rather a window, opposite direction, room with a view, lean out, into the next moment, the unknown. Naked to what cuts. Open to the "world."

AND ITS HORRORS

Growing up in Germany after the Nazi years, my friends and I clung to the idea that at least the holocaust had been so horrible that nothing like it could ever happen again anywhere. And that we could not distance ourselves from it, that we didn't have the luxury of saying "they."

We swapped knives to peel off childhood like so many skins.

The Hanky of Pippin's Daughter tries to get at the Nazi time, obliquely. Not the ambition of a map, at best a small periplus along an edge. But still reference to a given "reality." And foregrounding a mapmaker's concern with scale, with the foreshortening inherent in representation, which can reduce a woman's whole life to the one gesture of dropping her handkerchief. Not my usual way.

Jasper Johns: "representative art is a tragedy, I much prefer the real fork."

Small memories surface.

My first schoolday, September 1941, a cool day. Time did not pass, but was conducted to the brain. I was taught. The Nazi salute, the flute. How firmly entrenched, the ancient theories. Already using paper, pen and ink. Yes, I said, I'm here.

I was six or seven dwarfs, the snow was white, the prince at war. Hitler on the radio, followed by Le'har. I had learned to ride a bike.

All hands in the field. Women and prisoners. War internalized as everything. Grammar aligned according to race. Too bitterly other. Surplus of privation. Polish. Yiddish. Prisoners in the field.

SPACE OF A LENS, WITH SOUNDTRACK

Again, window is not the right metaphor. Not even a window on memories. Never that transparent. A lens, rather, Zukofsky's objective, gathering details of seeing and thinking, of language, a focus to burn. With a frame wide enough for conjunctions and connotations. And the music of words, with its constant vanishing, to fill in the distance.

Tones approach us, come to us, surround us. . . . When a film is shown without music, the pictures appear remote, marionette-like and lifeless. We lack contact with what is being represented. We are spectators at, and not participants in, what is occurring. As soon as the music starts, contact is re-established. It is not even necessary for the music to be appropriate to the images. (Erwin W. Straus)[9]

Detachment, too, has its bridges. (Jabès)[10]

After watching "absolute dance," a trend after World War I to free dance from "the tyranny of music," Straus concludes that music creates the space for dance. "In its absolute form, dance had not lost the ground from under its feet, to be sure, but it had lost the space produced by the music."

Merce Cunningham's moving against the beat of the music decenters this space without destroying it. Even Cage telling stories creates a space of sound.

THE SPACE OF THE ACTUAL

Chernobyl, 3-Mile Island, Love Canal, Bhopal, Exxon Valdez. Now: oilspill off the coast of Rhode Island.

speechless tissue / black / even in light, black

THE SPACE OF SMELL

Smell, like sound, comes to us, envelops us. The oil sickening. Whereas the mere mention of jasmine takes me back to a leafy cave, the very ground heavy with the scent. Glowworms glimpsed between leaves. Evening as if there were no other time of day.

THE SPACE OF MUSIC

Nathaniel Mackey's *Djbot Baghostus's Run*. As in the *Hornbook*, amazing how the description/discussion of music actually moves the narrative, is what matters, rather than ornament or texture. Novalis's *Heinrich von Ofterdingen* uses interspersed poems this way, but they remain a much smaller part of the narrative.

THE SPACE OF REFLECTION

Emmanuel Hocquard opens up the house metaphor:

> In book after book, I build glass houses with reflecting facades where the images fade into different surroundings.[11]

(You'd think he'd be more careful throwing stones at metaphor!)

Reflections on a framed photograph or print are to the picture what noise is to music. If we are with Cage, we accept it as a way of letting the environment in. The way goes through things, the outside.

> That this is I,
> Not mine, which wakes
> To where the present
> Sun pours in the present
> —(Oppen, "The Hills")

Reflection, broken light, broken identity, broken line of thought, death/life.

> *Erst in dem Doppelbereich*
> *werden die Stimmen*
> *ewig und mild*
> —(Rilke, "Sonette an Orpheus," IX)

SPACE

extension, expanse, stretch; distance, interval, gap, abyss, void, vacuum; capacity, room; country, region, wilderness; field, area, scope, compass, range; infinity, boundlessness; duration, time

A space of time before the rain. The pigeons scream their heads off. Figures swept toward doorways by force of wind or habit, bluish shadows before rain, blue like the stripes of my blouse run out in the wash.

Clouds the color of earth. The wind whips the maples, the spiderweb, the depth of shadow.

THE SPACE OF A LENS

on certain vowels a color like calico was pasted
—(Barbara Guest)[12]

I leave it to natural philosophers . . . if the image (idolum) is made to appear before the soul or tribunal of the faculty of vision by a spirit within the cerebral cavities or if the faculty of vision, like a magistrate sent by the soul, goes out from the council chamber of the brain to meet an image in the optic nerves and retina, as it were descending to a lower court. (Johannes Kepler, "How Vision Takes Place")[13]

Color does not inhabit. Lies on top. The skin of the visible. A yellow tugboat, in wait. Subtract color: grisaille, limp, soft, drunk, minor key.
   The octave in the eye, the white of the mind, all the hues in the cry. The middle of the cornea introduces an erotic quality.

Of bodies
of various
sizes of
vibrations

of blue excite
of never except
in his early
in childhood has he touched

of the space of
between of
to allow
of for impact

now of that color
has slowed
its pitch
or of skin

of but light
no deep foundation
nor of leans into
the blue

THE SPACE OF LANGUAGE

Between English with a German accent and "for an American your German is excellent." Between bed and breakfast, kitchen and table, desk and drawer, pencil and laptop, analogies and suppositions, memory and conjecture.

Phonemes float in mid-Atlantic. No illusion of "mastery." I enter at a skewed angle, through the fissures, the slight difference.

as when 2 tongues claim
a single mouth
difficult
as over-
lapping a limit

Enigmatic French-English in Dominique Fourcade's *IL:* "le s de neige."[14]

The first foreign languages I heard were "enemy languages." Two Polish prisoners of war worked on my uncle's farm. Soft sounds. A song that sounded to my ears like "Bee bee bee bradgee bee." Another, French, worked for our hairdresser. She tried to learn some French from him and was indignant, later, to find he had taught her obscenities. I got my ears boxed for laughing.

Beautiful books are written in a kind of foreign language. (Proust)[15]

The writer is a secret criminal . . . it's as if he or she were a foreigner in his or her own country. (Hélène Cixous)[16]

new pleasures of the tongue
now only half
belongs to mother
a stammer a stutter a gasp an almost

THE SPACE OF POETRY

A refuge "where the fear of speaking in strange ways could be left behind" is what poetry offered second-generation immigrant Laura Riding.[17]

> *native speakers come true as extreme points of overtones touch the ear*
> *fear overtones*

That Riding, with her background, would want literalism, would want to *fix* the meanings of words! Of course, *A Dictionary of Related Meaning* ["belated meaning," I had typed] was never finished. (Nor did Flaubert write his "beautiful book about nothing." To want beauty as much an error as to want certainty.)

On Riding's side, opting for stability and centrality, J. L. Austin, *A Plea for Excuses:*

> Our common stock of words embodies all the distinctions men have found worth drawing, and the connexions they have found worth marking, in the lifetimes of many generations.[18]

—beautifully demolished by Joan Retallack.

On the contrary: Poetry as "site of the heretical imagination . . . as what Robert Duncan referred to as a 'place of first permission'" (Michael Palmer).[19]

Larry Eigner died February 3.

THE SPACE OF A HOUSE

71 Elmgrove Avenue is nearly a century old. Old for this country. There are no elms left on Elmgrove Avenue. Maples. Water seeps into the basement. The wind sets the wood creaking, the walls crack where they've been forced to meet. When I roll a marble along the floor for the cat, its path maps the most unpredictable slopes and valleys.

THE MATTER OF WORDS

Giorgio Agamben: "where language stops the matter of words begins . . . its woody substance."[20]

She writes as if leafing through forms of wood she knows, trees, books,
in an improbable quest of bloom. But her lack of discipline exaggerates,
even with outstretched arms, the distance to cover.

More interesting to me: the matter *between* words. The nothing that defines. Tangible emptiness. Not a divine void grafted on human intersections, but tracing the beat of silence.

the silence that is the matter between parts of speech
the silence that molds my words
now I am dark matter that does not emit or reflect radiation

Printed matter.

ELECTRONIC SPACE

A space of phantasms, of dreams marked by the tides of my emotions, desires. A space of reality marked out by my commerce with the world. An electronic space that confuses the distinction, where wars are present as if they were phantasms. All of our poems become "Poems within a Matrix for War:"

The images effected a hole
in the approximate center of my body.
I experienced no discomfort
to my somewhat surprise.
                    —(Michael Palmer)[21]

THE GROUND

base, basis, foundation, earth, soil, land, footing, substratum, reason, cause. See BASE, LAND, MOTIVE

Though Jabès never gives up the house metaphor altogether, he too seems to get doubtful about it, uncertain of the threshold. In *Elya* the sections are called "Approaching the Ground of the Book" and "The Ground of the Book." Something altogether vaguer, less circumscribed, less clearly shaped than threshold and house, not even manmade. The givens of experience? The self-evident?

Notebook: literal ground of books? Soil to be tilled? From which nothing follows. And fresh sheets. Priming canvas. Gathering what comes always before: the "dark, invisible precursor" that maps the path of lightning as if in a mold (Deleuze).[22]

But not only the threshold, the ground too has become uncertain, matter too porous for us to put our feet on. Space no longer Aristotle's solid "container of all," but a "manifestation upon occasion" (Michael Whiteman).[23] So much for continuity, unity. And Maurice Merleau-Ponty:

> L'espace n'est pas le *milieu dans lequel* se disposent les choses, mais le *moyen par lequel* la position des choses devient possible.[24]

A kind of *natura naturans?* Earlier he has defined "form" in exactly the same terms, not as "the *space in which,* but the *means through which.*" What Pound's idea of form as a "center around which, not a box within which" began to adumbrate,[25] though a crucial step away, the step from space to instrumentality.

THE SPACE OF THE ACTUAL

Wendy Steiner, in *The Scandal of Pleasure,* thinks it is not surprising that Senator Jesse Helms and his ilk mistake Robert Mapplethorpe's representation of sadomasochism for advocating sadomasochism: A photo in their world (the "real world") always advertises a product.

the water of life
is all in bottles & ready for invoice
—(J. H. Prynne, *Kitchen Poems*)

THE SPACE OF A SYSTEM

Works that try to establish a system of the universe: Yeats's *A Vision,* Riding's *The Telling,* Pound's *Cantos.* I take refuge—and pleasure—in fragments. Against the average incidence of comparable parts of speech. Extremes of sense and absence.

THE SPACE OF A GAP, A FRAGMENT

Interruption is one of the fundamental devices of all structuring. (Benjamin)[26]

"The splice of life," I have called it. The spark given off by the edges is the stronger the more disparate the sources. This has of course been said about the two elements in a metaphor (by Pierre Reverdy, for instance).

> Dissonance
> (if you are interested)
> leads to discovery
> —(W. C. Williams)[27]

When eye and mind are interrupted in their travel, a vertical dimension opens out from the horizontal lines. Suddenly we're reading an orchestral score as it were. No longer one single voice. A multiple meaning. The shadow zone becomes an element of structure. Blanchot's "other kind of interruption," which:

> introduces waiting, which measures the distance between two speakers, not the reducible distance, but the irreducible . . . Now what is at stake is the strangeness between us.[28]

Jabès, following the German Romantics, holds that the fragment is our only access to the infinite.

"Wir suchen überall das Unbedingte, und finden immer nur Dinge" (Novalis).[29]

And, simpler, maybe the essence of the fragment is that it cuts out explanation, an essential act of poetry (and of philosophy, Wittgenstein would say).

THE GROUND

Not taking shelter, not "going to ground" like a fox—nor falling in battle, I hope—but preparing an "occasion."

Of course I may "strike ground" and drown. In the sea of possibles. "Some phrase will fall here; hence all are signaling" (Roubaud).[30] John Ashbery wants reading his long poems to be like "reading the fine print of the Encyclopaedia Britannica . . . one feels as if one is drowning in a sea of unintelligible print—and yet this is one's favorite ocean, just as drowning is said to be delicious when one stops struggling."[31]

THE SPACE OF THE ACTUAL

Bosnia, Chechnya, Rwanda, Israel, Palestine, Lebanon, Ireland

Jabès sees the basis of intolerance in our craving for unity, for One Truth, One religion, One identical image of ourselves: "as if the soul vibrated to only one single sound, as if the mind could get excited only once." Whereas, "when we say 'I' we already say *difference*."[32]

"This war came out of a terrible lack of imagination." (Kafka)

"2 VOICES"?

My mother, she says, always spread, irresistibly, across the entire room, her features flooding me with familiarity to breed content. I did my best to sponge it up. Often I asked to open the window onto more water, eyes level with its surface. And lower, till the words "I am here" lost their point with the vanishing air. Just as it's only in use that a proposition finds its sense.

THE GROUND

Publishing a notebook. What should be mere ground is declared figure. Of course, the distinctions have long been broken down: Ponge, Coolidge, Benjamin . . .

Keith Waldrop describes his book *A Ceremony Somewhere Else* as "poems of the ground rather than of the figure. They point to transitions, those *edges* from which we infer things. . . . (The ground referred to is not the invisible, merely the unseen.)"[33]

> At the ridge, a change
> of reflection. The clear
> line of coast does not
> know its own boundary,
> facing, as it
> does, wave after wave of
> wash
> —(Keith Waldrop, *A Ceremony Somewhere Else*, 23)

THE SPACE OF THE ACTUAL

The drama of the California coastline. Wall after wall, the tide moves in on sheer cliffs, event into light. With a noise as white as traffic, as sleep.

Surfers, strange unearthly creatures gliding between the elements. "Mermen," says Peter Gizzi. And takes us to the ultimate parody, the monument TO THE UNKNOWN SURFER. A bronze of a muscular man in bathing trunks, style rather socialist realism, with a surfboard as mandorla behind him.

It's almost as much a parody, though, that it took over 10 years to find an Unknown Soldier to represent the 58,012 servicemen killed in the Vietnam War. Advanced medical technology can identify the dead from even small fragments of bodies, so only in 1985 was the United States able to honor and bury an Unknown Soldier in Arlington National Cemetery.

THE SPACE OF A GAP, A FRAGMENT

The fragment we have left after history gets through with Sappho's or Archilochus's manuscript; after Claude Royet-Journoud and Anne-Marie Albiach get through with the discursive prose they begin with; after Reznikoff gets through with the court records; Anthony Barnett, with *Terminology of Forest Science;* after Ronald Johnson reduces *Paradise Lost* to *RadiOs;* after Tom Phillips paints *A Human Document* into *A Humument.*

Or, on the contrary, a beginning. Notes toward, "Denkübungen" (Novalis). Pascal, Chamfort, Joubert, Novalis, Schlegel, Leopardi. Goethe's "Fragments of a Great Confession." Duncan's "Fragments of a Disordered Devotion."

The fragment as answer to system-building (Romantics), with, however, the system, or the infinite, remaining a challenge in the background (Nietzsche, Pound, Eliot, Jabès).

Questions of closure and genre: fragment, aphorism, pensée, epigram, maxim, anecdote, "character." Friedrich Schlegel surprisingly wanted the individual fragment to be complete in itself: "A fragment must, like a work of art, be completely separate from the surrounding world, complete in itself like a hedgehog," which Novalis seconds with: "Der Igel—ein Ideal"![34]

THE GROUND

Clear, conscious discrimination is an accident of human existence. In our analysis of detail we are presupposing a background which supplies a meaning. These vivid accidents accentuate something which is already there. That factor in our experience, being a matter of course, does not enter prominently into conversation. There is no need to mention it. [But] if we forget the background, the result is triviality. (Whitehead)[35]

"2 VOICES"?

A frame supports what would, on its own, collapse, he says. And our focus can make the ground turn figure in retrospect. Like a German sentence that comes clear only once you reach the verb at its end. By a strong effort of will. Time divides us into dust, but also binds our bodies forward. Though the exhaustion will not be squared. When I say "book" you think of pages sewn, or glued now, into a cover, not clay tablets or Japanese silk scrolls. Or palm leaves strung together.

THE SPACE OF THE ACTUAL

The Inuit have twenty-seven words for snow. The United States now has more for getting fired, most of them atrocious euphemisms: axed, canned, fumigated, riffed (from RIF = Reduction in Force), sacked, decruited, downsized, excessed, outplaced, redirected, terminated, transitioned, pink-slipped, indefinite idling, career transition, chemistry change, workforce imbalance correction, etc.

FREEDOM TO WRITE

The poet must be able to say anything, in complete freedom. Well, try it, my friends, you'll see that you are not free. (Robert Desnos, in Roubaud, *Poésie, etcetera: ménage*, 93)

I am typesetting Paul Auster's "Prayer for Salman Rushdie"—and here is Rushdie, in teleconference, patiently repositioning the question "why do what you know will offend?" He is not interested in writing what would be acceptable to fundamentalists, but in ending fundamentalism. True, with the long-standing separation of church and state, the evil of church power is not real to Americans. But will *The Satanic Verses* end (help end) fundamentalism? Or will it function as blasphemy, as negative confirmation?

THE SPACE OF THE "I"

The house, the single-family house, still seems to speak of the I as a whole, of our body as a center of the world, of the self in possession of its representation. The book a much less assured dwelling, the fractures part of the structure.

I, a mere grammatical proposition.

I am turning into metal. . . . I have the strange impression that I do not belong to the human race. (Clarice Lispector)[36]

Writing is the destruction of every voice, of every point of origin . . . the negative where all identity is lost, starting with the very identity of the body writing. (Roland Barthes)[37]

At least in this country, the literary "mainstream" does not seem to have heard of this idea. "Identity" and "voice" are all that's talked about. Do we have to get rid of houses to get rid of it?

Collage as a way of getting out of myself. Into what? An interaction with language and other writings. Relation rather than substance. Whitehead's "occurrences," Olson's "between." But the collages are still about my mother!!

The fragmentary, "torn" nature of the elements is important to my way of using them. A lessening of distinctness, of "identity." Not "quoting," not a reference to the other work.

Find the Benjamin passage that has quotation return the quoted words to a kind of "original," free, noncontextual state.[38]

THE SPACE OF THE ACTUAL

Republican doubletalk: "Raising the minimum wage will not benefit the poor. Cuts in welfare will. A flat tax is good for everybody!"

THE SPACE OF THE "I"

"Place there is none. We go forward and backward, and there is no place," says Saint Augustine. We go forward and backward like a boat, which, according to Olson, is the first recorded sign for *self*. Royet-Journoud, who is proud of not using the pronoun "I" in an entire book of poetry, wants his words to be boats: "mots-bateaux."[39] Relation. Movement. Between.

> *Travels along the border of norm and experience. So that the meaning changes back and forth.*

Erwin Straus notes that the "I" of the awake, active person is felt at the base of the nose, between the eyes, but that in dance it descends into the trunk.[40] Where is it felt when we are writing? I have claimed:

> *A poem*
> *like trying*
> *to remember, is a movement*
> *of the whole body.*[41]

A kind of oscillation, another going forward and backward, between head and gut? The poem, in any case, moves *within* language the way a dancer moves within music. Not moving *through* it to some destination or message. Moving within the constant disappearing and coming-into-being. With a new, fluid definition of figure and ground the way the hierarchy of the body turns fluid in dance. Left, for the poem, is neither clumsy nor sinister, but the beginning to which each line returns.

THE SPACE OF WRITING

I love zeugma. It seems I want my concepts to have extension, take up space, become bodies with the weight of particulars, form a land-scape, a ground of movement. And vice versa? Do I want particulars, objects to become abstract? No, on the contrary.

> *as if a space of time, too, could only be filled by one body*

Even a poem that works with juxtaposition (if it works) is not felt as an assemblage of lines juxtaposed in space, no more than a body as an assemblage of organs. Or than a person as an anthology of characteristics. Those are our most impersonal traits, being what is "sounded," reinforced by other people (cf. Robert Musil's *The Man without Qualities*). Just as a poem's phrases or lines may come from elsewhere. It's the movement between them, the "dizzying succession across a vacancy relentlessly refusing a whole world and racing behind it" (Charles Bernstein).[42]

such organs
obscure, out of sight

Adjective under skin. House sealed in sensation. Whereas a transparent medium creates years under water.

THE SPACE OF AFFINITY

The strange closeness when I read Mei-mei Berssenbrugge. At least partly because we both use Wittgenstein, write on a common ground. But what shimmering spaces she takes him into:

I is not the name of a person, nor "here" of a place, and "his" is not a name. But they are connected with names. . . . It is also true that it is characteristic of physics not to use these words. (*Philosophical Investigations* #410)

She is not the name of a person, nor *there* of a place, but they are
    connected with names. . . .
Why science does not use a word like she or there, is why the
    hand cannot make a sharp edge in the sand.
The hollow his hand would make in bright sun, micaed, was
    the place where the wing of the person
would fold into itself, almost a shadow in skin. The fold is the
    object or resemblance
between the head turning over a shoulder, and the wing folding
                                    —("Honeymoon," *Empathy*)

PALIMPSEST

The blank page is never blank. No text has one single author. Whether we are conscious of it or not, we always write on top of a palimpsest.

> Ventriloquy
> is the mother tongue
> —(Rae Armantrout, "Attention")[43]

JE EST UN AUTRE

If I wanted to render precisely the perceptual experience, I ought to say that one perceives in me, and not that I perceive. Every sensation carries within it the germ of a dream or depersonalization such as we experience in that quasi-stupor to which we are reduced when we really try to live at the level of sensation. . . . Each time I experience a sensation, I feel that it concerns not my own being, the one for which I am responsible and for which I make decisions, but another self which has already sided with the world. (Merlau-Ponty)[44]

another self which has already sided with the world

In back of thought there are no words: *on s'est [é-se]. Je me suis [sou-me]. Tu t'es [tu te és].* (Lispector)[45]

Impossible in English. It would come out as "I am me, I am myself!" The reflexive, which I suspect is as strange and unorthodox in Portuguese as in the French translation, seems to suggest a kind of active, transitive being. I bring myself into being? I give birth to myself? Then, later: "But there is also the mystery of the impersonal which is the *it*." In English in the Portuguese text!

THE SPACE OF THE ACTUAL

Elizabeth Willis takes me to the eucalyptus grove just outside Santa Cruz where millions of monarch butterflies come to hibernate. They cling to each other, forming long orange-brown strings hanging down from the leaves. Then the sun hits them, and all around us the air is soft, fluttering wings.

INAUGURAL SPACE

The act of inauguration refers to the rectangular field of observation that the augur traces in the sky with his curved staff, where he will note the passage of birds.

[It is] the setting for a particular path traced in the sky, not for some general and lasting form of organization. And the whole point about this path is that it is random, governed by chance. As much as to say by nothing. . . . "This space, impossible to locate or quantify, is the narrative space of writing, beyond the bounds of representation."

The narrative *is the ground* of its own legibility. (Hocquard)[46]

THE DISTANCE OF HEALTH

Erwin Straus, *The Primary World of Senses:* A schizophrenic no longer goes out into geographical space, "he remains in the space of landscape."[47]

What keeps a person safe from delirium or hallucination is the structure of her space: objects stay in front, keep their distance, touch her only "respectfully." In hallucination, or myth, the lived space shrinks, so that objects invade the body.

An infant's space?

Artaud: "Les cieux s'entrechoquent." But in the correspondence with Jacques Rivière, Artaud speaks rather of not being able to hold on to thoughts or things. Hence, "once I *can seize a form,* no matter how imperfect, I fix it for fear of losing all thought." He sees his whole era suffering from this "inapplication à l'objet" (e.g., Tzara, Breton, Reverdy!), but with him it becomes "une inapplication à la vie."[48]

W. G. Sebald has taken this inability to hold on to "reality" as his theme. The vertigo we feel in moments when "fact" clashes with memory; or perception, with the complex layering of knowledge and expectation. Vertigo. *Schwindel. Gefühle.*

THE SPACE OF UP AND DOWN

Up, the heroic dimension! I know it every morning. (A baby, at bottom!) André Leroi-Gourhan thinks upright posture came before higher brain capacity, made it possible by freeing the hand from locomotion, which in turn freed the "facial mask" from foraging tasks and thus stimulated speaking and brain growth.

It is not only that my body allows me to move among things, but, says Merleau-Ponty, "it's through my body that I understand another person. . . . The body is our means to have a world."[49] And a sense of space. I struggle to stand upright, head atop spine. Head in a spin. The world opens up in front and closes behind. But balance is difficult. I tip my chair on its hind legs and sometimes over.

With what effort the vines grew erect on the valley slopes. Desperately hugging each ray of sun.

We step up to the front door of a house, an image of upright posture. In back, "the attention, with all the anal implications, is to service, trash removal, privacy" (Kent C. Bloomer/Charles W. Moore).[50]

And, oh, "the suck of symbol" (Olson)![51]

"2 VOICES"?

We must decipher our lives, he says, forward and backward, down through cracks in the wall, back into the formation of crystals. And up. The way a lark at the end of night trills vertically out of the rustling leaves which I know only too vaguely—so many of them and hardly darker for the passing of anxiety. Up into anemic heights, the stand-still of time. Could we call this god? or meaning?

An inflection of the voice, rather, she says. My shadow lies quietly. It's real enough and outside myself, and maybe I should grant the rest. That light may flood and blot me out completely. But it won't come walking in flowing robes and take me by the hand with the assurance of a stranger from a more rational country. Nor does my body slope toward airbags as it does toward you, no matter how level the ground.

Should the voices stand in for "characters," be consistent in what they say, gendered? I don't think so. I'd like it floating, so that the 2 voices could also be 2 voices within one person, the "zwei Seelen, ach." I've gotten to like working with "he said"/"she said" as a rhythmic marker, the question being where to put it in the sentence. Other ways of coding? Vaslaw Nijinski coded social standing in "Till Eulenspiegel" by the way the feet were turned: turned in for the poor, turned out for aristocrats, parallel for servants, functionaries.

THE SPACE OF UP AND DOWN

Not as evident as it seems. If you wear glasses that reverse the retinal inversion, things look upside down and unreal. On the second day, things seem normal, but the body feels upside down.

The scene in Djuna Barnes's *Nightwood* where the Doctor prays with bowed head, and his tears fall straight to the floor rather than run down his cheeks. A ninety-degree displacement only, but eerie.

When I first entered the space of English, the feeling that my body was not there, was lost in the intersection.

Gradually the body regains its position, adapts to the new image.

the body inhabits the spectacle
energy relocates and there is a large area for the hand and upper limbs

THE SPACE OF WRITING

Not so much unreal as dark. I am in my light. I cast my shadow over what I would see. I am my own obstacle. How move in such a space? And where? Night without clear outlines, without profiles, let alone their reproduction. No words. None at all. Or few, thin like my hair. Slow, out-of-breath climbing the stairs. Leaden legs. Start, break off, out of it, always. Then, in the good moments: a sudden streaming. Grass bending in the wind.

"2 VOICES"?

She tries to draw a strength she dimly feels out of the weakness she knows,
as if predicting an element in the periodic table, a word on the next page.
He wants to make a flat pebble skim across the water inside her body.

THE SPACE OF IN AND OUT

Moebius strip.

THE SPACE OF A HOUSE

Moltkestrasse 5. 615 Turner Park Court. Creamery Road. 69 rue des Saints Pères. 71 Elmgrove Avenue. 11 Boulevard Beaumarchais. 11 Lordship Park. Schlüterstrasse 52. 14 rue de l'Abbé de l'Epée.

THE SPACE OF POETRY

Forrest Gander quotes one of my lines back to me and asks: Do you really feel that way? I must have, when I wrote it. But maybe the opposite also. I'm not elaborating a body of doctrine.

> La poésie ne pense pas
> La poésie ne dit rien
> La poésie dit ce qu'elle dit en le disant
> —(Roubaud)[52]

A poem, even though it is composed in the language of information, is not used in the language game of giving information. (Wittgenstein)[53]

God is a word my culture has given me. (Jabès)[54]

"Negative capability." Possibilities and contradictions held in balance, without "irritable reaching" for certainties.[55]

A bit like the dream state. Heinrich von Kleist was fascinated by the fact that in dreams we are everything: the dreamer and all that is dreamed—persons, things, surroundings, events.

THE SPACE OF A HOUSE

Roofs mediate with the sky. Ours is so steep it brings you back down to the earth in no time. The snow too. The sun distant, diffuse, a shimmering yellow without body, without strength.

Will future archeologists think our century extremely religious because of the skyscrapers?

WALLS

Claude Royet-Journoud thinks of his work as a tetralogy (in three volumes, so far!). His idea of completion is four walls. He gestures at the room. Keith asks: what about a ceiling, a roof? He dismisses the question. Is it that he wants boundaries like the yard, the garden, enclosures open to the sky, but has the image of room/house stuck in his mind?

> A *picture* held us captive. And we could not get outside it, for it lay in our language and language seemed to repeat it to us inexorably. (Wittgenstein, *Philosophical Investigations* §115)

German and English both show this bias. We say "within my four walls." Would the idea of roof destroy the equilibrium, demand a "crowning achievement"? Or is it rather geometrical? Four walls, like four lines, transform pure potential extension into a space, an empty space. The walls to lean on ("écrire le dos au mur")[56] as you face the emptiness within.

behavior, a balance of alphabet and straight walls

THE SPACE OF THE ACTUAL

Then there's THE WALL. Its fall. And rise. In the heads. (What did the Iron Curtain do? tear? melt? come down? rust away?)

> *All that is never said. In one reunited language. All the rays intersect in the pupil and left becomes right. Without subtitles. In walls we trust. Overstated chemicals in the folds of history. Excited, to the detriment of uncushioned flesh. The relation to memory a blind corridor. Footnotes absorbed into blood.*

I imagine a museum of monumental Soviet statues in the form of an open field. Like the actual field full of old printing presses that rust away in the rain, in Taunton, Massachusetts. A surreal landscape. But what *has* happened to all the statues taken down? Keith wonders: how would a monumental Stalin look in our front yard?! But only succumbs to buying a small piece of The Wall, a Baby Lenin medal, a fur hat with hammer-and-sickle.

In foreign parts. Of speech.

THE SPACE OF WRITING

Adrift on my table. All landmarks disappear. Sleeves rolled up to indicate hard work, avert my own suspicion of imposture. Am I a real writer? Wouldn't it have to come easier? Not this despair as I suck the pen, the pencil, words on loan, charged, not enough, too many, too used. Can I use them over again? Ideas in the air. Nouns by the hour. The sun invades, a blinding glare. Car horns. Cackling blue jay. The cat not interested.

Barbara Guest quotes Picasso: you must have an idea, but it must be vague. So that in the end it becomes something else.[57]

OCCASIONS OF WILDERNESS

The world is irregularly strewn with regular dispositions. Crystals, flowers, leaves. . . . If all were irregular or all regular, there would be no thought, for it is an attempt to pass from disorder to order, and it needs occasions of the former and models of the latter. (Valéry)[58]

Yes, except that thought doesn't go just one way from disorder to order. It needs to go back and forth, mess with "Mr. In-between" to find "a form that accommodates the mess" (Beckett),[59] preserve the energy of disorder, the tension between the two:

Breathway to confusion keeps the pass it makes to the spark inside. (Charles Bernstein)[60]

Cependant, je retournais, le plus sciemment du monde, au désordre. (Breton)[61]

QUOTATION

Interrupts the context of the original as well as that of the new text.
Unlike the smaller collage element, it brings the original with it.

For echo is the soul of the voice exciting itself in hollow places.
(Christopher Smart)[62]

Constant quotation marks in Alice Notley: a carnival of voices? Every-
thing is overheard? A general distancing? In Claire Needell's "Season
One," on the other hand: a difficulty with naming, with saying. A seis-
mic threat she cannot separate from the word? Experience attached
to strings.

THE SPACE OF MOVEMENT

One can always go farther. This does not mean one can always
go farther, step by step. (Roubaud)[63]

All winter the little footpath across the empty lot at the corner of
Elmgrove and Angell was frozen as hard as the sidewalk. Now it again
has that bit of springiness underfoot—when not downright soggy—
that makes me feel my steps all the way up to the head. Not that brittle
disappearance of foot into cold hurry.

Perception of movement as a relation of figure and ground. Of two
luminous points moving in the dark, the one we focus on seems the
one in motion. But words are in perpetual motion, a multitude of
impulses, a twittering inside the skull. And focus, on the contrary,
slows them, stops them—before beginning the movement that mat-
ters, sweating it out in a million small adjustments to the plumb line.

Zen aims at "movement of the mind," at a "liquid state of the capi-
tal of libido" (Christoph Kellerer).[64]

Der Geist, flüssig,
angesammelt, wie Wasser,
in den Bechern am Weltrand
　　　　　—(Celan)[65]

Implications for collage: the connection of disparate elements shakes up the fixed relations in the mind, activates the dynamics, the speed against the weight of habit.

Pam Rehm: "the unbedding of the always"[66]

WINGSPACE

The bird that soars in my dream does not soar in a physical space but on the pulse of my desire, breath cut loose from the body. On waking, sexuality returns to the genitals.

wind-folded
this side of the air

THE SPACE OF THE ACTUAL

peculiar motion, superclusters, standard candles, the Great Attractor, the Wall, galactic honeycomb, antimatter, red shift, white dwarf, black hole, dark matter, big bang, steady state

THE POWER OF WORDS

John Boslough (*Masters of Time*) wonders if the "big bang" theory was so successful because it is so consistent with the biblical creation mythology.

But also: Hoyle coined the phrase "big bang" to lampoon a theory he didn't believe. But it was a livelier phrase than the "steady state universe" he championed.

"2 VOICES"?

Deciphering, he says, is not a horizontal motion. Though the way a sentence is meant can be expressed by an expansion that becomes part of it. As a smile may wide-open the case of a stranger. I struggle uphill, my body so perfectly suspended between my father's push and gravity's pull that no progress can be made. But if you try to sound feelings with words, the stone drops into reaches beyond recognition, without ground.

THE SPACE OF TOUCH

more complex than hands between thighs

only on skin and muscles can we, without harming ourselves, build a symbolic system

closely savored power line

James J. Gibson (*The Senses Considered as Perceptual Systems*) defines touch as the "haptic sense," which involves not just hands, skin, but the entire body. As does his "sense of postural orientation," which, with the help of gravity, establishes our knowledge of the ground plane. A hunter sensing danger will turn his head and focus his eyes and ears symmetrically on the source. This mobilized orientation, again, involves balance of the whole body.[67] (My "Ambition of Ghosts" revisited!)

Sitting for my portrait drawing with Irving Petlin confirmed my belief that we bring the whole body to such tasks as writing, painting, composing. It was odd having to sit still while he was practically *dancing* in his chair.

Petlin also tried to draw Jabès, but kept erasing and, at the end of the session, had two sheets of paper with smudged eraser lines. He was upset: "but I know how to draw." Jabès said: "this is like my own way of working." They agreed on another date, a few weeks later, which turned out to be the day of Jabès's funeral.

Meanwhile Petlin had done a portrait from memory, which is what we saw. From the ears down, the face gets absorbed into a network of roots. As I am writing this, I am looking at the photo by Maxime Godard, also taken a few weeks before Jabès's death. He stands between the shutters on the shallow balcony and looks at me and through me. At his roots in the Non-Place.

THE SPACE OF LANGUAGE

Whitehead: "Our understanding outruns the ordinary usages of words."[68] I suppose this is a mandate for literary innovation. As if a net of language were thrown over "reality" without quite fitting it. The poets stretch the net so that it fits—for a moment.

But I so often feel that, on the contrary, the words outrun my understanding, take over and me by the hand.

THE SPACE OF TOUCH

Aristotle saw it as a problem that touch had no organ like the eye, ear, nose, or mouth. Skin did not fit his idea.

IT IS A QUESTION

Whether touch has a stone. And what its organ. A woman with a peacock feather studies the migration of carp. Shirts on a clothesline. How vulnerable the order of civilized achievement. Modes of transport undone in fog. We are not prepared for. The sound of pain, a strident, high-pitched, syncopated melody.

Whether the flesh extends to Iowa. Five senses in the city. In the country, seven. Years itching. Eddies of leaves, color awakened in shuttered light. Even though there is little happiness. And has to be learned like a language.

Whether Adam and Eve could talk, not having clothes. Lips intent only on kiss. No shirts drying from one identity to another. While in respect to the other senses we fall below many species of animals. Though touch is neither good nor evil, its exact discriminations separate real from world, foreign from body, pleasure from principle.

Whether thought is in danger of. Disappearing inside itself. A smithy in the ear. Categories in the retina. A flapping shirt, a snowfall of face value pointless to fight. Likewise the more genuine part of my life goes by, impossible to define. Flow of breath, the unfolding of a minute, the low notes of pain.

THE SPACE OF THE ACTUAL

Robert Doisneau's photograph "Le baiser de l'Hôtel de Ville" captured the mood of post-Liberation Paris so perfectly that several couples wrote to Doisneau, convinced they were the couple kissing in the photo. It was only when one couple sued him that he admitted having

used actors, that it was all posed. Once again, the artifice of sponta-
neity.

THE SPACE OF MOVEMENT

I read that children who skip the crawling stage have trouble learning
to read. This seems less obvious than the relation of walking and
thinking, the movement of the body setting thought in motion. Rim-
baud composed many of his poems while walking. So did Jabès. Walk-
ing the space of a line, a phrase. As if finding it. A grammar of motion.

"As If We Didn't Have to Talk" was me walking through Paris; *The
Road Is Everywhere or Stop This Body*, driving between Providence and
Middletown, Connecticut. Flying next? No chance. Walking again, in
Washington, trying to keep a log of my steps, downbeat of the body,
weight rolling from heel to toes, as they carried me outward from the
centers of power to where the buildings sized down to warmer brick,
a foghorn from the river, a dog lifting its leg against the curb, women
with shopping bags . . .

Now I sit at my desk, think on paper rather than with my feet. Sit
on the page and chew my pencil down to the lead. Chew my words.
Because I have few. Eat them? Have had to. And the journey may lead
nowhere, may end where it started. Cursor stuck. But there is no way
not to move.

THE SPACE OF THE ACTUAL

Was it Tom Ahern who told me how his father took him hiking to a
hill from which he could see their house, then to a mountain from
which he could see the hill, then to a higher mountain from which
he could see the first mountain and so on?

This must create a lovely sense of connectedness.

I was immediately taken to the Everests: Bach, Beethoven, Mo-
zart, Goethe. There seemed no connection between them and my
scratchings.

THE SPACE OF A HOUSE

The basement is the dark space of the id (Bachelard).[69] It does seem
to presuppose narrative and a past, though not necessarily as far back

as Freud would have it. It is the printing presses that take me back, the smell of ink and solvents. Behind Moltkestrasse 5 there was Kummor's print shop. Next to it a bit of untended yard I was allowed to play in, among the slabs of limestone leaning upright against the wall. Each slab still showed the negative of the wine labels that had been printed from it. In bright colors. *Iphöfer Kronsberg, Nordheimer Vögelein, Würzburger Stein, Escherndorfer Lump*.

It was part of local history that Franconia is the source of limestone. If Alois Senefelder, the inventor of lithography, had tried his experiment elsewhere, with any other kind of stone, it would not have worked.

What I found out recently is that Senefelder (1771–1834), son of an actor at the Munich Royal Theater, tried to support himself as a performer and author. He turned printer in order to publish his own works.

THE SPACE OF THE ACTUAL

pulsars, quasars, quarks: up, down, strange, charmed, top (or truth), bottom (or beauty)

THE SPACE OF WRITING, OF SILENCE

When Jabès's defines writing as a translation from silence ("the silence which has shaped the word") into more silence ("the silence of the book: a page being read"), he allows that it takes words to make the silence visible. "Writing is an act of silence that makes it legible to us in its entirety."[70]

> Er, der Schweigende, steht in der Atempause
>   —(Rilke, "Sonette an Orpheus," 2, XIX)

> till a drift of snow
> slides from a branch,
> then, silence more intense
>   —(H. D., "Winter Love")[71]

[The pause] carries the mystery of language itself: pause between phrases, pause from one speaker to the other, pause of attention, of understanding . . . pause which, alone, makes speech

into conversation. . . . The gap, the discontinuity, assures conti-
nuity of understanding . . . It is the breathing of discourse. . . .

But there is another kind of interruption. It introduces wait-
ing, which measures the distance between two speakers, not the
reducible distance, but the irreducible. . . . Now what is at stake
is the strangeness between us.

[This is the ultimate form of interruption, the one where]
idleness shows (and perhaps thought). (Blanchot)[72]

"Out of great need"
"Out of our great misery"
Out of Africa

CLINAMEN

Ian Hamilton Finlay on making "Little Sparta": you can embark on
making a garden with a vision, but never with a plan. I would accept
this as a poetics. Whereas Jackson Mac Low chooses a procedure and
follows it to the letter. "I am a pedant," he declares proudly! But if I
make the rule I can also break it if the text changes course. Even
Oulipo allows for "clinamen," the swerve in the fall of the atoms.

Revision: from seeing only one possibility I pass to seeing at least
one other. What a relief.

Whenever I read a sentence, including a line of my own poetry,
I am beset by the idea that it could have been written any other
way. When you are conscious of this while writing, it can be very
exciting. I respond to works of art which express this idea, such
as the music of Busoni, the main element of whose style is that
it didn't necessarily have to sound this way. (Ashbery) [73]

Then there is Duncan's way: my new poems are revisions of my earlier
ones.

THE SPACE OF THE ACTUAL

Three crucial Supreme Court cases: "Brown vs. Board of Education"
(desegregation), "Roe vs. Wade" (abortion rights), "Romer vs. Evans"
(May 96, the Court strikes down Colorado's anti-gay amendment).

Satyr play: "State of Connecticut vs. Waldrop." "Books weigh a ton," people say. Seven and a half tons in our case. More than our U-Haul truck was licensed for when we moved to Rhode Island. The people at the weigh station couldn't believe it. Made us get out of the cabin, as if our bodies were responsible. We paid a thirty-dollar fine, but our check was not cashed. Instead we received: "State of Connecticut vs. Waldrop: Officer X made a mistake. The minimum bond in this offense is $300. If you do not intend to pay this fine you must immediately return your Connecticut driver's license." We had already changed to a Rhode Island license, so did nothing except write them that they should cash our check because we would close out our Connecticut bank account by a certain date. We closed the account, our check still uncashed. A few weeks later we got a check for thirty dollars from the State of Connecticut!

THE SPACE OF MOVEMENT

Travel. Originally the same word as "travail." The hard labor of travel. Meister Eckhart traveled on foot between Erfurt, Strasbourg, and Paris. Goes out expecting trouble, goes out prepared. The foot falters on unfamiliar terrain. Gives birth to distance. To heresy, said the Archbishop of Cologne.

Breton wants poetry to have the speed and urgency of thought.

"Wo denken Sie hin?" I love the directionality of thinking in this idiom. Where, to what lengths, are your thoughts taking you? Thread of thought, thread through the labyrinth of words, literal thread that goes—used to go—through the book.

But, in art, he who takes but one step,
in any direction, is already lost.
                    —(Clark Coolidge) [74]

THE SPACE OF CHILDHOOD

Climbing trees, swaying with the branches, running till the blood pumped in my ears, grass and wildflowers up to my chest, wheat over my head, wind, the feel of the cat's fur, smell of inks and solvents. Kicking with rage. Later, a book, and fingers in my ears.

THE SPACE OF THE ACTUAL

Save the Bay. Civil Liberties. Amnesty International. No Nukes. Green-
peace. A Mind Is a Terrible Thing to Waste. Doctors Without Borders.
AIDS Research. Planned Parenthood. NOW.

THE SPACE OF THE BODY

We may be building our rooms, our dwellings, and in the process
undo our bodies. I don't mean ascetic or mystical practices, as de-
picted in "2 Jinas removing themselves from their physicality," a lovely
Jain sculpture of two men, arms straight down without touching the
body. "Kayot sarga," or, "body-abandonment posture."

In *L'île des morts,* Jean Frémon's narrator works at not having a
body, no proprioception, by trying not to make any gesture, not pro-
duce any sound that might betray emotion.

Body = emotion?

"2 VOICES"?

*When you grope for feelings with words, she says, the feelings don't even
seem to be there yet, not yet feelings, but something different, below the
surface, weeds combed by the current, a mere tip rising here or there, a
ripple from a pebble.*

THE SPACE OF THE BODY

Children (all?) draw the house as a face. Our houses resemble us.
Roof on my shoulders. So do our books. Jabès, who always felt rejected
by his books, has now been absorbed into them. With all his body.

To write, now, only to make known that one day I ceased to exist;
that everything around me turned blue, an immense empty space
for the flight of an eagle whose powerful wings forever beat
goodbye to the world.[75]

grief-muscles (Darwin)

THE SPACE OF EMPTINESS

The photo shows me in front of a wall covered with graffiti. My sister: don't you mind, everything smeared over? But I have the same impulse to cover white surfaces. Waldrop, like nature, abhors (yet is fascinated by) a vacuum. Most of all, the emptiness inside me. I am everything I have ever read or written or thought. Language has no limits.

(Surprise: graffiti in Berlin exactly the same style of lettering as the graffiti in New York City. The new "international style!")

> Finding it in myself or just a blank space where some thing should be: a ringing if not a peal. (Charles Bernstein)[76]

My obsession with empty centers: womb, resonance body, "I," God. God as void, infinite, nothingness, silence, death, desert. As ultimate otherness. As metaphor for all that calls us into question. Our primal opponent. The center we long for, which, we think, would give meaning to our lives. The center that all of Jabès's books circle and circle, but that remains unreachable. Of course. Because it is empty. There is nothing there.

> *The longing for the father is incontestable. You feel a splinter and you don't know where it came from.*

> *When we say infinite we have no conception but our own inability. Therefore the name of God is used. The I has no sharp boundaries inward.*

> each Gott—die Götter! Feuchtigkeit und Schauer!
> —(Benn, "In einer Nacht")[77]

PAUSE AND EFFECT

Another empty center: the caesura. For Agamben, "the element that arrests the metrical impetus of the voice, the caesura of verse, is thought."[78]

> Blanchot: interruption *where idleness shows and perhaps thought.*

> Poetry is having nothing to say and saying it. (Cage)[79]

THE NOBLE RIDER AND THE SOUND OF WORDS

Agamben, in the same essay, turns to the poet Sandro Penna for con-
firmation of "caesura = thought:"

> Io vado verse il fiume su un cavallo
> che quando io penso un poco un poco egli si ferma.
>   [I go toward the river on a horse
> which when I think a little a little stops.]

Commenting on Apoc. 19.11, in which logos is described as a
faithful and honest knight astride a white horse, Origen explains
that the horse is the voice, the word as utterance.

Here he is again, "The Noble Rider." Only, Stevens derived the image
from the *Phaedrus*.

But the image is so wrong, with its implication that the body/
horse/language obeys thought. A centaur image would be more ac-
curate for the fusion of sound-thought in a poem. (Valéry always
seems contemptuous of Descartes for his neat division *esprit de géo-
metrie* vs. *esprit de finesse*—clearly Descartes had no sense of poetry.)[80]

If anything dominates, it would seem to be the sound/body. Guil-
laume IX's rider needs to be asleep, unconscious, to let the horse
(language) take over:

> Sheer nothing's all I'm singing of:
> Not me and no one else of course;
> There's not one word on youth and love
>   Nor anything;
> I thought this up, once, on my horse,
>   While slumbering.
>   —(trans. W. D. Snodgrass)[81]

"I thought this up" seems not right. Too conscious, though one could
argue for the paradox. Guillaume says, "This was found."

In psychology, too, the mind-body gap seems to be closing in favor
of the body: grounding all thought in images, body-representing neu-
ral structures, "somatic markers." So that there is no "pure" thought

(Antonio Damasio, *Descartes's Error,* passim). No such thing as: a thought that does not need my body. Unless, of course, it is dead.

> Torn apart by my hands
> so the mind is physical
> This soul is a whipping boy
> held fast in his delicate purse
> —(Elizabeth Willis, "Songs for A")[82]

THE SPACE OF THE ACTUAL

A photo of the BANCO DI SANTO SPIRITO in Rome. Well, we have IN GOD WE TRUST on our coins. "Money is pure spirit," says Keith Waldrop.

THE SPACE OF EMPTINESS

John Golding on the importance of "negative space" in Japanese art, where the empty areas are as highly calculated and as important as the ones painted. So that emptiness can yield a particular sensation of space. Degas was very aware of this, whereas Whistler concentrated on the decorative aspects.

In poetry, there is nobody keener in the art of leaving out, of holding a mirror to absence, than Royet-Journoud and Albiach. With a precision that makes Olson's typewriter space as measure seem both vague and mechanical.

But what if the negative space takes over, if what lies behind a poem (the ground) is erased completely? As are the events behind Royet-Journoud's "Error in Localization of Events in Time" (see "From White Page to Natural Gaits" in this volume).

THE SPACE OF EMPTINESS: DESCORT

"Descort de tous plans," Roubaud says in "Idée de la forme,"[83] which I make "*Descort* of any blueprint" in order to keep both the reference to the medieval poetic genre and the sense of lack that the context gives.

All definitions of *descort* run toward "irregular form." The Fayard *Dictionnaire des lettres francaises:*

> To show his sadness or anger to see his love unshared, the trou-
> badour composes a poem where everything is in disorder, the
> text as well as the melody. . . . Raimbaut de Vaqueiras wrote one
> where every stanza is in a different language.

But Agamben: "the Provencal poets recognized a poetic genre—the *descort*—which testified to the reality of a unique, absent language, but only through the babel of multiple idioms."[84] This is parallel to Chernoff's "phantom beat," the absent beat that holds the multiple rhythms of African music together. And perhaps Benjamin's "pure language," which makes translation possible.

Meister Eckhart on the empty center as receptive/creative:

> In the very essence of the soul there is the silent "middle," for
> no creature ever entered there and no image, nor has the soul
> there either activity or understanding . . .
> For the powers she works with emanate from the ground of
> being, yet in that ground is the silent "middle:" here nothing but
> rest and celebration for this birth, this act, that God the Father
> may speak His word there. (Sermon 1, trans. M. O'C. Walshe)

FREEDOM TO WRITE

At the "Freedom to Write" conference, a documentary on Tiananmen Square 1989, *The Gate of Heavenly Peace*. Heartrending to see the moment of possible negotiation pass. Then all leads inexorably to the point where bodies are pitched against tanks, where soldiers shoot to kill.

Xue Di fighting tears, reliving it all.

(I am reminded of Kent State, the four students shot by the National Guard. And the yet greater shock to see a student of mine grab the mike: "I'm going to join the National Guard. Next time we meet I'll be on the other side.")

Curious: The Chinese student leaders were sentenced to three to four years in prison. But a man who afterward, in the street, called it an outrage to send tanks against one's own people: ten years. The telling, the myth more important than the event?

THE POWER OF WORDS

This goes toward confirming Emile Cioran:

> All orthodoxy, whether religious or political, postulates the usual expression. In the name of a sclerotic word, the stakes, the pyres were erected.[85]

It's the form that the heretic's ideas take rather than the ideas themselves that cause the scandal. (But can they be separated?) Which Michael Palmer takes as witness to poetry's power to affect society *through its language, its form.* Adorno says the same, less elegantly:

> The unresolved antagonisms of reality reappear in art in the guise of immanent problems of artistic form. This, and not the deliberate injection of objective moments or social content, defines art's relation to society.[86]

THE SPACE OF A HOUSE

The Other House. A House and Its Head. Sleep Has No House. The House of Mirth. The Fall of the House of Usher. House of Breath. The House of Illnesses. The House Seen from Nowhere.

THE SPACE OF A HORIZON

Open form as inclusiveness, as in the change from classical harmony to twelve-tone music. Do we still need a "horizon note," as the drone in Indian music is called? Euclid's "horizon sphere" as limit of visibility? At least in hyperbolic geometry, "visual space has no edge or periphery" (Patrick A. Heelan).[87]

> *event without horizon*
> *my body now expands horizontally, stretching the distance between my breasts to incomprehension*

THE SPACE OF THE ACTUAL

The State of Rhode Island, replaying the national scenario, cuts arts funding by 36 percent.

"Wozu Dichter in dürftiger Zeit?" Why indeed: we can't afford poets! And what piddly sums are saved by these cuts. In a year, for the whole United States, the NEA spent:

less than the *city* of Paris;
what the Pentagon spends in 5 hours 26 minutes and 12 seconds;
what costs each taxpayer $.64, i.e., 2 postage stamps.

CITY SPACE

New Orleans is below water level. In the early days, coffins buried European-style came floating up with the first rain. Now, in "The City of the Dead," burial is above ground. In brick tombs that act as natural crematoria in the Louisiana summer, with the brick absorbing—almost—the smell of decomposition.

If our language can be seen as an old city (Wittgenstein), it is one where the dead come floating back and welcome. Sunk metaphors, an old writer's phrases.

I also like to think of it
of language, as a form of
light continuing beyond the shadow
of the city limits

Downtown Providence. Torn-up streets. A cityscape of cranes and holes in the ground. Just like Berlin. Well, not quite! It also lacks the faint smell of sewer that hovers over East Berlin.

Even with The Wall no longer there, you know when you're in the East. A shock to see so many buildings still in the bombed-out state they were in at the end of the war. Especially in the "Scheunenviertel," poor quarters where Jews freshly arrived from the East used to live.

Hannah Möckel-Rieke and I searched in vain for the building where, at the beginning of the deportations, the names of the disappeared had been scratched into the walls. But we came by the old synagogue, which is being repaired and has acquired a shiny gold dome. Which surprised me because I had thought it was being kept a ruin as a memorial of the Kristallnacht. It was closed. A close-lipped policeman on guard. While Hannah asked him various questions, I wondered what he thought of his assignment, and whether he took us for foreign Jews wanting to worship or for neo-Nazis planning an attack.

Another synagogue very near our apartment, in Pestalozzi-Strasse, so unobtrusive I had walked by without noticing. Heinz Ickstadt points it out as we walk through the first snow. One knows it by the guard in front.

NO, BOTH

Both the precise Cartesian coordinates (how else to navigate the too-much from all sides) and the rhythm of the body: breath, blood. I used to think maybe even the rhythm of the earth's rotation up through the sole of the foot (not metrical!). But that's crazy. What kind of contact do we have with the earth: concrete, cars, trains, airplanes!

Columns of words. Arching into bridges, colonnades. Once we reach the border it gets dark, wintery.

But: alternation of sense and absence, sound and silence. The between, the difference in repetition. "Upper limit music," as Zukofsky says ("A," 138).

only as long as he moves from left to right does he have this feeling of mystery

SPACE OF THE ACTUAL

Toni Warren tells me of her anger, in the late forties in Switzerland, when any dumb yokel could vote, but she, a medical doctor, could not.

Women's suffrage: Finland 1906. Germany, USA, Britain 1918. Sweden, Austria, Luxembourg 1919. France 1944.

Odd for France to be this late, since the fight for women's rights there goes back to the Revolution. (Olympe de Gouge "eut l'audace de rédiger une déclaration des droits de la femme et de la citoyenne" and was guillotined in 1793.)

In 1936 Senator Duplantier declares:

Vous allez accorder le droit de vote à toutes les femmes qui se livrent à la prostitution. . . . Ces dames voudraient être députés. Eh bien non! Qu'elles restent ce qu'elles sont: des putains!

[You are going to grant the right to vote to all the women who practice prostitution. . . . These ladies would like to be represen-tatives. Well no! Let them remain what they are: whores!]

But then, as late as 1992:

Mr. Robertson warned that a proposed equal rights amendment to the Iowa state constitution was part of a "feminist agenda" that he described as "a socialist, anti-family political movement that encourages women to leave their husbands, kill their chil-dren, practice witchcraft, destroy capitalism and become lesbi-ans." (*New York Times*, August 30, 1992)

THE DEPTH OF SPACE

deer started up from
deep started up from
deep thicket of words. Aroused.
          —(Duncan)[88]

Bloomer and Moore: the dimensions of setback from the street signal the importance of a building, the town hall farther back than a pri-vate house. The most important things sit far back in memory or the unconscious. Not easily approached with words. But, like silence, needing more words to be—almost—reached? So that the unsayable gets its charge from our attempts at saying. Or do we have to try for something like saying and unsaying at the same time?

Collage to the rescue. For Roubaud, too. I was stunned to discover that the lines in *Quelque chose noir* (Some Thing Black) that I had taken to be the most direct reference to his finding his wife dead: "I knew there was a hand. Who could from now on grant me the rest?" are from Wittgenstein's *On Certainty*.[89]

I need a book to say "I love you," the distance of another's words to say what touches me most. Or is it that it needs to remain masked?

Hugo von Hofmannsthal says somewhere: "We must hide what is deep. Where? On the surface."

THE SPACE OF THE ACTUAL

A boy sails by on a skateboard. The Japanese cherry cascades with purple. Across the street, white blossoms on a tree whose name I don't know. Finally things are growing—other than hair and fingernails.

Maybe even the "peace process." It is a great step that Arafat got the destruction-of-Israel clause *voted* out. Now if they could stop throwing bombs. Both sides.

But: In the last 17 months, 28 black churches across the South of the U.S. have been burned. (*New York Times*, May 26, 1996).

THE DEPTH OF SPACE

> The problems arising through a misinterpretation of our forms of language have the character of *depth*. They are deep disquietudes; their roots are as deep in us as the forms of our language and their significance is as great as the importance of our language. Why do we feel a grammatical joke to be *deep*? (And that is what the depth of philosophy is.) (Wittgenstein, *Philosophical Investigations* §111)

> *The rustlings of language give us the illusion of a deep dimension. But our equations don't net the unknown quantity. We're only as good as our words.*

Both Empiricists and Rationalists assimilated depth of space to size of objects seen in profile. Merleau-Ponty points out that this is no human experience: the subject would have to leave his point of view and imagine himself more or less ubiquitous. In other words, *depth is not a human experience, but rather God's perspective* on it![90] I love this!

THE DEPTH OF THE BODY

"Thought-diver" (John Taggart).[91] But I don't have thoughts. I have ways that make language think, take over and me by the hand.

Valéry places depth in the body: the "deep organic life" of the body carries "the superficial life we call mind [*esprit*]."[92] Deep-tissue diver.

"We have a lovely
      finite parentage
            mineral
      vegetable
            animal"
Nearby dark wood—
—(Lorine Niedecker, "Wintergreen Ridge")

Why Do I Write Prose Poems

When My True Love Is Verse

This brief essay began as notes on the form of the prose poem. A bit later there was a question of writing an introduction for the reprint of the French *Reproduction of Profiles,* which made me expand these notes. The reprint did not happen, thus, in its present form, the essay is unpublished.

———————

I love the way verse refuses to fill up all of the available space of the page so that each line acknowledges what is *not*.

> [Poetry] is the very art of turnings, toward the white frame of the page, toward the unsung, toward the vacancy made visible, that worldlessness in which our words are couched. (Heather McHugh)[1]

And I love the way poetry's rhythm, maybe its very essence, arises from the tension, the mismatch between line and sentence, between the halt at the "turn" that interrupts the syntactic connection and the meaning's push forward toward completing the sentence.

> Contrary to the received opinion that sees in poetry the locus of an accomplished and perfect fit between sound and meaning, poetry lives, instead, only in their inner disagreement. (Giorgio Agamben)[2]

For a fraction of a moment, this void stops everything. It suspends the assurance of statement to reintroduce uncertainty, possibility, and potential. According to Friedrich Hölderlin, the gap of the caesura, metrical poetry's additional locus of disjunction, blocks the hypnotic enchantment of rhythm and images:

> the caesura (the counter-rhythmic interruption) becomes necessary to block the torrential succession of representations . . . in such a way as to make manifest . . . representation itself.[3]

A void that shows representation itself. (I would say: language itself.) The silence that makes possible the music.
Or perhaps:

> the shape of thought, the impersonal music of silence hovering over every page like a ghost emptied from a land of shadows. (Russell Edson)[4]

In addition, a bit more tangibly, it lets us feel the magnetic field between the two dimensions, energy's horizontal push becomes dammed up, vertical, orchestral. An aura.

I pursued this void, this numinous showing of language. I tried to exacerbate the tension and disjunction between sentence and line by keeping the lines very short while opening the confines of the sentence into one quasi-unending flow.

> *In order not to*
> *disperse*
> *I think each movement of*
> *my hand*
> *turns*
> *the page*
> *the interval has all the rights*[5]

But I began to long for complex sentences, for the possibility of digression, for space. The space of a different, less linear movement: a dance of syntax.

The comma stands quite independently in the place where the edges of bodies touch. (Vera Linhartová)[6]

The prose paragraph seemed the right kind of space where form could prove "a center around which, not a box within which" (Ezra Pound).[7]

To write as if leafing through forms of wood I know, trees, books, in an improbable quest of bloom.

I gave up stress for distress, as Charles Bernstein says, the distress of lacking coordinates, of the unstructured space of prose, the uncharted territory of the page. The excitement and terror of the open. Versus the challenge of closure: in the complete sentence and, extreme, in the proposition.

He wrestled with Sleep like a man reading a strong sentence. (Robert Duncan)[8]

No. This was not enough tension. Not enough to compensate for the absence of *turning*, of margin. I must try to move the vacancy and the mismatch from the margin inward.

the empty space I place at the center of each poem to allow penetration (*Lawn of Excluded Middle*, 11)

I must cultivate the cuts, discontinuities, ruptures, cracks, fissures, holes, hitches, snags, leaps, shifts of reference, and emptiness *inside* the semantic dimension. *Inside* the sentence. Explode its snakelike beauty of movement.

Again speed. A different one. An energy that knots and unknots constellations before they can freeze into a map.

"Gap gardening," I have called it. My main gardening tool is collage. And it is perhaps just another way of talking about poetry as concentrated language. (As Pound and the German language know, *dichten = condensare*.) Making dense, cutting out steps.

In *The Reproduction of Profiles*,[9] all of my poems started out from Wittgenstein phrases. Some other phrases come from Mei-mei Berssenbrugge, many from Kafka.

I had mistaken the Tower of Babel for Noah in his Drunkenness.[10]

Displacement, dialog, transformation. We write on a palimpsest. The quotation left intact carries the whole "Description of a Struggle," along with a whiff of the destruction that is the Beatrice of creation.

In [quotation] is mirrored the angelic tongue in which all words, startled from the idyllic context of meaning, have become mottoes in the book of Creation. (Walter Benjamin)[11]

With a stronger whiff, Wittgenstein's rejection of "the deepest questions" comes to prove "that the deepest rivers are, in fact, no rivers at all."

The displacement matters less to me than the glint of light on the cut, the edges radiating energy. The fragmentary, "torn" nature of the elements. A full quote like the sentence on the Tower of Babel is the exception and functions as a signpost.

Fascination of logical syntax. "If—then." "Because." But I try to undermine the certainty and authority of logic by sliding between frames of reference, especially pitting logic against the body.

The body is, after all, our means to have a world—even to have logic.

The rhetorical theater: a woman addresses her lover?

A dialogue between two sides of one mind?

Dialogue cultivates gaps by definition, by the constant shift of perspective. *Lawn of Excluded Middle* continues to use the rhetorical "you."[12] But in the third volume of the trilogy, *Reluctant Gravities,*[13] I decided to give the second person equal time and weight. This led to the question: do I want the voices to be distinct? Do I, for instance, give the scientific vocabulary to the male voice, to the female voice the statements about language? But I'm not interested in characters, psychology, or in poetry's traditional "persona" or mask. The voices do not "represent," but frame the synaptic space between them. Except for this constant crossing of this gap they could have been one single voice. This is also why the voices do not always engage with what the other has said, but veer off, pursue their own train of thought and thus enlarge the gap, the tension, mark the cut.

But what has become of sound? When "free verse" took a step away from meter, it was a step away from the oral. The prose poem moves yet farther in this direction. Its sound and rhythm are subtler, less immediate, less "memorable." If it counts, it counts words or sentences rather than stresses or syllables.

Valéry's definition of the poem as "a prolonged hesitation between sound and sense" does not work here—not the way I think he meant it. My beloved clash of these two (still present in the wordplay) has been displaced. The fissure is now more between sense and sense, sense and syntax, density and intensity.

But there are many kinds of music. Syntax is rhythm, sound in motion. Even if sound does not seem to be in the foreground, it is the body, the materiality of poem. What carries the surface we call mind. It is (mostly) the sound that short-circuits the word's transparency for the signified, which some consider its advantage:

A symbol which interests us also as an object is distracting. (Susanne Langer)[14]

This "distraction" is exactly what poetry worth the name gives us: the word as a thing, palpable, a sensuous, sounding body. The word made flesh. The flesh of a bird, so it can also take wing. Toward the kind of mathematic limit where, to vary Zukofsky, the word approaches both the wordless art of music and the soundless music of silence.

Between, Always

I feel a strong affinity to this word, "between." It is the title of one my earliest poems in English. When I felt still very much between my native Germany and my newly adopted country. Between "not all here / or there / a creature with gills and lungs."

> BETWEEN, ALWAYS. Between father and mother. Between memory and conjecture. Between English with a German accent and "For an American your German is excellent." (The Hanky of Pippin's Daughter)

Of course, it is not just a matter of my personal situation between countries and cultures. Our reality is no longer substances, but systems of relations, "no longer things, but what happens BETWEEN things," as Charles Olson paraphrases Alfred North Whitehead.[1] And for art and literature we have long known this, but perhaps not expressed it as succinctly as Viktor Shklovsky:

> A literary work . . . is neither thing nor material, but a relationship of materials.[2]

The two novels in this volume are the matter between two phases in my writing. Hinges. On which things turned.

Why did I, who see myself as a poet, turn to prose? to the novel?

My verse lines had gotten shorter and shorter. I was paring them down to a point where I was feeling almost claustrophobic. Worse, I was using a syntax in which the object almost always topples into being the subject of the next sentence.

> *two pairs of eyes*
> *see*
> *two different initial*
> *questions too*
> *disappear . . .*
> —(*The Aggressive Ways of the Casual Stranger*)

There was—is—much I like in this. The speed. The tension between the flow of an almost unending sentence and its constantly being brought up short by the irregular grammar. It subverts the hierarchy of subject and object, which, I realized later, has definite feminist implications. And again, the speed. But it took me down the middle of the road. Main-clause highway. It did not allow any paths off to the side. I began to hanker for subordinate clauses, for digressions, meanders, space to amble.

The idea of a novel, of a "loose and baggy monster," became attractive. It would be spacious. It would, at least theoretically, have room for anything.

But I knew that this was too simple-minded an idea of the novel—of any form. It was at about this time that my concept of form began to be challenged. There are better definitions of space than the Aristotelian model of the container.

Merleau-Ponty defines both "space" and "form" in exactly the same terms: not as "the *medium in which*," but "the *means through which*."[3]

And with even greater emphasis on discontinuity, Michael Whiteman tells us that the special theory of relativity "requires a principle of 'manifestation upon occasion' instead of the 'container theory' in which shapes and durations are absolute."[4]

Ezra Pound already knew this in regard to verse. As he told Robert Creeley:

> "Verse consists of a constant and a variant . . . " His point was that any element might be made the stable, recurrent event, and that any other might be let to go "hog wild," as he put it, and such a form could prove "a center around which, not a box within which."[5]

Clearly, this is not just a matter of verse, but a large paradigm shift, if we can spot it in areas as divergent as science, philosophy, and the arts. It also puts some precision into the notion of "open form," with which I had been grappling.

The sentence seemed an area where I could explore this. Even without placing it in tension with the line. The tensions could happen inside it, between one sentence and the next, between it and grammatical norms.

⌒

In 1975–1976 I spent a year in Berlin. Back in the medium of German—my mother's Northern variety, not the softer *Fränkisch* I had grown up with—memories flooded. I realized if I wrote about my childhood, I would in some way have to address the Nazi Germany into which I was born. A subject so overwhelming, a knot of connections so complex I knew it would be impossible to treat head-on. I would need room to approach it indirectly, via detours, from various angles, from the margins.

So the idea of a novel began to go beyond being an idea. I almost said began to "take on flesh," but that would be an exaggeration. Writing this novel was a very difficult process. During the eight years I worked on it, I often despaired, put it away, turned to other projects. But I kept coming back to it—for yet another false start. The beginning was perhaps doomed because I began with the not very congenial idea that I would have to tell things "straight," try to write a more or less realistic novel, open a Jamesian "window."

(I think I felt it was material that maybe shouldn't—couldn't— be monkeyed with. As if "realism" were not also "monkeying," as much of an artifice as any other form.)

At the same time I wanted to use the structure of Wittgenstein's *Tractatus*: there were to be seven central sentences, ("centers, around which") with all the rest in a logical (?) relation to them. Johannes Bobrowski has done something like this in his great novel *Levin's Mill: 34 Sentences about My Grandfather*.

I could not do either. The *Tractatus* structure proved much too closed a form. Unable to do plain narrative, I came away with great respect for it, but knew I had to find other ways.

The window metaphor, like Stendhal's mirror traveling along a road, assumes there is something there to be seen or mirrored. But I was struck by how little I knew, even about my parents. I did not "have" a story. In spite of memories flooding, it seemed there was nothing outside my window. And yet:

> Impossible to doubt the world; it can be seen
> and because it is irrevocable
> It cannot be understood, and I believe that fact is lethal
> —(George Oppen, "Five Poems about Poetry")

Becoming aware of this paradoxical void, this lack of story—and certainly of understanding—seemed to dislocate me from my own childhood, move me—where? Toward possibility? Toward absence taking the center of the stage, with presence mere ground to its figure? The way John Cage's attention transforms noise into music? Toward an inclusiveness before selection? Could the lack of knowledge allow certain elements to come forward, the way dim light makes short wavelengths prevail and blues the world?

> To find a form that expresses the mess, this is now the task of the artist. (Samuel Beckett)[6]

Could it be what Joan Retallack calls "poethical form"?

> a rash and presumptuous affirmation and assertion—affirmation of form, assertion of meaning withheld, affirmation and assertion of silent unintelledge*a*bilities—a strangely potent agency. ("Blue Notes on the Know Ledge")[7]

My novel would have to stake its progress on not knowing where it was going. It would have to be an imagining and testing of models, of possible situations, an exploration, a search. It would have to do and undo, "pluralize and pulverize," as Julia Kristeva recommends, and take its finding "to the point of laughter."[8] It would have to move along the blurred borders of fact, fabrication, experience, empathy, memory, tradition, possibility, imagination, and changes of weather.

(The way the two narratives and two generations interact parallels the reading/writing processes. On the one hand, the narrator is trying to understand her own story while trying to "read" that of her parents. The way we glance off into our own meditations and bring them into the text we are reading, as we always do. On the other hand, the sisters' knowledge is spotty so that there is constant conjecture, inventing and imagining what went on in the past. The narrator uses her own life as a model to project onto the past. So that the past becomes a text alternately read and written.)

The gaps would have to remain gaps rather than be filled in. To point at negative space, at what eludes the grip of language. On the other hand, they could allow a sense of possibility:

The sky is blue. Is the sky blue? Yes. The "Yes" does in no way reestablish the simplicity of the plain affirmation. In the question, the blue of the sky has given way to the void. The blue has, however, not dispersed, on the contrary it has risen dramatically to its POSSIBILITY, above its actual being. It unfolds in the intensity of this new space, bluer than it has ever been before. (Maurice Blanchot)[9]

And, after all, discontinuity is the natural state. "Ruins and fragments," Joan Retallack reminds us, "are not accidents or anomalies, but the most reliable constructs of Western Civ."[10] And it is by glimpses that we come to know anything that has any complexity.

(Discontinuity has been my experience from childhood.

There was the war, the air raids, the bombing of my hometown in 1943, when I was eight. When we climbed out of the cellar there were no streets, no rows of houses. Instead: craters, heaps of rubble, mortar, stones, walls broken off, a craggy desert, air thick with dust. A few houses were left standing. They seemed out of place, incongruous with their insistence on boundaries, definite lines. Then came two years of being shifted from village to village, from parents to acquaintances to relatives.

It was the first drastic change of my world. A second followed in 1945, a not exactly Nietzschean revaluation of all values. "Our leader" turned into "the criminal," "the enemy" into "Amis" [short for Americans], "surrender" into "liberation." This went deeper. And took years to understand.)

Most importantly, perhaps, I reverted to the habits I had acquired in poetry: to think less about representation or character, setting, plot (the enemies of the novel, says John Hawkes!) than about creating a surface, a textual reality. I would put my trust in language, its ability to gather the force of thinking. I would concentrate on the words and sentences themselves and trust in their built-in thrust (to signify? represent? symbolize? denote? connote? define? reveal? name? express? tie together? separate?) to take care of the rest.

And here it was again, the tension between the impulses toward flow and toward fragmentation, the same tension I had worked with in poems. Small, fragmentary glimpses. Then try to weave them into a flow, with recurrences for rhythm. And do not worry whether this is proper narration or not.

(I knew I was on the road when the writing began to subvert my system. The titles of the short sections were to stress the discontinuity. But now and again they pulled toward continuity, their opposite: a sentence might stretch across the section boundary, including the title, into the next section.)

Still, I hoped that the gaps would function like Brecht's interruptions, that they would be jolts into consciousness, reminders that we are among words and representations. A narrative rhythm of alternating empathy and stepping back rather than a rhythm that might become one-directional and mesmerizing.

"To form is necessarily to 'inform,'" says Marcel Cohen.[11] Here, in finding a form, lay my hope of "information," of gaining some understanding of my early experiences, family, the Nazi period—if not of how it *was*, at least of how it *could have* been.

By the time I began work on *The Hanky of Pippin's Daughter*, I had translated the first volume of Jabès's *Book of Questions*. And though I was very conscious about "defending myself" against this powerful writer, his work has definitely changed my thinking. Certain ideas in particular helped shape the form my book would finally take. For instance, that the question rather than the answer is the important mode of writing (and living, for that matter). That our questions always lastly intend something unknowable, a void (in Jabès's case called God). But in contrast to Oppen, who (at least in the poem I cited) believes the combination of irrevocable and incomprehensible is lethal, Jabès suggests that our questions' energy (and our own vitality?) may be fed by this very frustration. And that a book that refuses a single line of discourse, that "explodes" it into fragments and facets, thereby opens it to multiple perspectives, difference, ambiguity, and multivalence—and is more likely to encircle what eludes our grasp than any coherent "system."

Earlier, as a student in Germany, I had discovered Musil's *The Man without Qualities* and the way his narrative calls itself into question, both thematically and by always pitting a grid or web of details against the famous "narrative thread."

In the sixties, in Ann Arbor, Michigan, I encountered the music of Gordon Mumma, Robert Ashley, John Cage, and Merce Cunningham's choreography. An aleatory grammar, a decentering, an out-of-phase syntax.

And there was Djuna Barnes's *Nightwood*, which I read and reread. Its spatial arrangements, circularities, discontinuities.

Creation is destruction. This came home to me once again in the process of writing *The Hanky of Pippin's Daughter*. It was not so much that I became very aggressive in setting up test situations, in imagining "the worst." It was more that I became very conscious of how much violence there is inherent both in the drive to know and in telling—how it distorts/disintegrates the "world." There is always, at the very least, a drastic foreshortening. This is why my title refers to the legend of how my hometown, Kitzingen am Main, was founded. Around 750, the time of the Merovingians. The daughter of Pippin the Short dropped a handkerchief from the castle window. The wind carried it down the mountainside to the Main River, where shepherd Kitz found it. The town of Kitzingen was built on the spot. All of this is a bit unlikely. But what interests me in this story is that a whole life is reduced to one single gesture. Nothing else is told about this woman. Not even her name: "Pippin's daughter."

The first reactions to *The Hanky* were not exactly encouraging: not really a novel, a "poet's novel," too ornate, too metaphorical.

(When I returned to Germany for the first time, seven years after coming to the States, I was in for a shock. My little nieces laughed whenever I opened my mouth. I "talked funny." I had an American accent in my native language! I spoke nothing "right" anymore. Even my speech marked my place between languages, between countries. My non-place.)

Now I found myself in another non-place. A place between genres. Between poem and novel. Between verse and prose.

Between two stools. A bad spot. Supposedly. Close to the middle excluded by the law. But does a door have to be open or closed? All words are ajar. Could I not settle in the between? Like most truly contemporary writing? And could I not, like Luce Irigaray, make it not only a third term between the binaries, but a locus of desire as well?[12] Of encounter? Dynamic and dynamite?

I went on to another novel—which, if we count the title, begins and ends in verse. And from there to poems in prose that would take up residence on the *Lawn of Excluded Middle,* cultivating this fruitful and "female" emptiness.

~

The germ of *A Form/Of Taking/It All* goes back to 1970–1971, when Keith Waldrop and I both received fellowships. We settled in Paris, though I spent part of the year in Munich, doing research on German poetry. There were many jokes on the "mystical marriage" of Amy Lowell and Alexander von Humboldt, in whose name we were brought there, but it was only twelve years later that I actually "married" these two figures.

What my two "characters" had in common was more or less suppressed homosexuality. Their differences, aside from the century between them, required that the thematic range span poetry, natural science, and exploration. The latter quickly widened to include history, especially the conquest of America.

(The enormous migration from Europe to America, wave after wave of explorers, conquerors, immigrants. Being part of this has marked me. It was my third change of world. It surfaces again and again in my writing.)

Writing began with the second part, "A Form of Memory," which imitates the structure of *The Head of Vitus Bering,* a collage-prose by the Austrian Konrad Bayer. Though I flatter myself that I pushed the juxtaposition of heterogeneous materials further than he had, even into the sentence.

Collage, juxtaposition, is the heart of this book. "Between sentence and sewn, between two words at just the right distance that the spark flies. Or two bodies. A matter of betweens." And not only formally. Out of the encounter of elements from divergent fields came the overarching theme: the encounter with otherness. Encounter with another being, the discovery of America, and the new physics so disturbing to me because of the absence of images.

The idea of juxtaposition also led to each part of the book taking a different formal approach, countering aesthetic expectations and moving, as our image of the world has done, from the concrete and personal toward the more abstract. So that in the end it seemed right that after the stream of consciousness, the collage, and the first-person meditation on writing, love, and politics, the last section should be a poem. A poem that sets into parallel the "new worlds" of Columbus's America and the new physics, letting Columbus discover the "Unpredicted Particles" of the latter.

~

I had used collage before. But since *A Form/Of Taking/It All,* it has become my main procedure. The splice of life. "Cluster of shards which catches light on the cut and the next day too."

(No text has one single author. To foreground this awareness as technique. Writing as dialog with previous and concurrent texts. A desire to see what happens at the edge: dimensions contained, but hidden in the original contexts may shine.)

An art of separation and fusion, of displacement and connection. For without our connecting them into a picture, the dots are not even visible.

An art of betweens.

Human. Between hum and humbug.

Nothing to Say and Saying It

After the terrorist attack on the World Trade Center on September 11, 2001, Anna Rabinowitz, the editor of *American Letters & Commentary*, invited responses to the following.

> After WWII Theodor Adorno famously declared that to write poetry after Auschwitz is barbaric, to which Edmond Jabès less famously replied: "I say that after Auschwitz we must write poetry but with wounded words." We want to ask the following questions:
> 1. What do we as writers do at times when our modes of speech and even language itself seem incapable of making meaning?
> 2. How can we adapt our defeated, exhausted language to something fresh and clear-sighted, to something that can carry the human narration/commentary forward when conditions themselves are unspeakable?
> 3. What wellsprings can we draw upon to refresh the always living, always dying word?
> 4. Do we need to explore or develop new ways of reading as well as writing?

———————

I.

"Poetry is having nothing to say and saying it." (John Cage)
"The word poet is synonymous with truth-teller." (Joy Harjo)[1]

Harjo is seconded by Kafka, who believes (I quote from memory) that literature makes true speech possible between man and man.

I identify with Cage's position. The first part of his statement is my constant experience. I've felt it when I tried to write a poem "about" 9/11. "And saying it" always seems impossible, yet sometimes, by the grace of language, it happens.

Truth, on the other hand, is a difficult word. When it parades as Truth, with a capital *T*, it makes me as uneasy as it did Pilate. "The Truth" is unavailable to us, is not on a human scale. It is by definition too complex to be fully grasped. We have to make do with lowercase truths. In the plural. Because there are many. All partial. All contradicting one another.

I won't try to sort out the many truths of September 11. In any case, the truths of the terrorists remain guesswork. (It is likely that the history of U.S. policy in the Middle East and our unquestioning support of Israel have more to do with it than hatred of U.S. "values.")

(And elsewhere: Isabel Allende was asked what September 11 meant to her. She replied: "September 11, 1973, when Allende was murdered and the military junta took over Chile." [*New York Times*, December 9, 2001]

The *Times* added a line about the "amazing coincidence that two major American tragedies" would take place on the same date, but did not mention the part we, the United States, played in that assassination.)

(As for my own lowercase truth: I can't imagine not grieving for the victims. I can't imagine not being deeply shocked by this crime. But I also consider it criminal that our government uses the grief and anger of its people to retaliate against terrorism with more terrorism, worse because it is carried out with the arsenal of a superpower; that we are fighting a "war" that has not been declared and whose definition, like that of "terrorist," can change from one day to the next as it suits President Bush.)

To come back to my initial quotations: maybe they are *not* opposites. If the Truth is unavailable, it joins—*is*—the nothing we have to say.

"Truth is the void," replied Reb Mendel. (Edmond Jabès)[2]

And if poetry *can* perhaps come closer to saying it than other forms, it is because it is not a linear discourse, but can by indirection, in the process of "saying It," set into play multiple ways of knowing

II.

"*I can't go on, I'll go on.*" (Samuel Beckett)[3]

I have tried to write a poem with 9/11 in it. I have not succeeded. Words fail us in shock, in horror, in the face of death. And yet we turn to words. It is language, with its possibility of lies, of fiction, that allows us to perceive—and to live. Language, consciousness projected outward and shared, is fundamental to our being human. So are the language arts, poetry in particular, for their "attending" to language. We turn to words, not so much to "express" our experiences as to question, reflect, and, above all, make them real.

Only what we manage to give form to exists. And we ourselves exist only insofar as we manage to give form to our existence, regardless of whether we write or not. This is why saying one has nothing to say is still saying something. (Marcel Cohen)[4]

So what can we do in practice? On the one hand, we can speak out like any citizen, argue, analyze, read, yes, with double attention—especially the statements of our government, examine euphemisms ("collateral damage") and hypocrisies.

We [the United States] complained to the Emir of Qatar that al-Jazeera, the Qatar-based TV station that has carried many of bin Laden's statements and which has a huge popular audience in the Arab world, was providing terrorism with a platform and should be curtailed. The unelected Emir duly reminded the representatives of one of the world's oldest democracies that a free press is essential to democratic life. (BBC Web site of October 12, 2001, quoted in Tony Judt, "Americans and the War," *New York Review of Books*, November 15, 2001)

A positive attitude implies looking also at the dark side.
But as writers? How can we turn emergency into emergence, as Andrew Joron puts it?

A kind of topological fold or failure (called a "catastrophe" in mathematics) precedes the emergence—constitutes the emergency—of the New. If poetry makes language new then it must be defined as *the translation of emergency*. The abyssal language of poetry represents (translates) the *motion* of social change more than it does the *facts* of social change.[5]

To work toward such emergence, toward language that makes it new, that "surpasses itself" (Joron's term) we must work on form. What concerns us deeply will always get into what we write.

"To form is to inform." (Marcel Cohen)[6]

III.

"The shipwreck of the singular" (George Oppen)[7]

I don't know that there are "wellsprings" we can draw on. If there are, I can only imagine them in our common humanity.

On 9/11 our country joined the rest of the world in experiencing aggression and destruction on home ground. We have now experienced vulnerability. For many—though too few—this has been an occasion for thinking. Especially about our relation to other countries.

Perhaps the most important word is "and."

Agamben points a way toward encounter rather than domination or confrontation:

We can communicate with others only through what in us—as much as in others—has remained potential, and any communication is first of all communication not of something but of communicability itself. After all, if there existed one and only one being, it would be absolutely impotent. . . . And where I am capable, we are always already many.[8]

I read this as an imperative to guard against our thinking becoming fixed in ideologies and -isms (including patriotism), to cultivate our potential, our openness. It resonates strongly with George Oppen:

Obsessed, bewildered

By the shipwreck
Of the singular

We have chosen the meaning
Of being numerous.

Have we?

Notes

INTRODUCTORY NOTE

1. T. S. Eliot, *Selected Prose*, ed. Frank Kermode (New York: Farrar, Straus, and Giroux, 1975), 64.
2. "Aeschylos Agamemnon metrisch übersetzt" (trans. Sharon Sloan) in *Theories of Translation*, ed. Rainer Schulte and John Biguenet (Chicago: University of Chicago Press, 1992), 58.

I. APPRENTICESHIP AND AFFINITIES

THE URGE TO ABSTRACTION

1. Hélène Cixous, *Three Steps on the Ladder of Writing*, trans. Sarah Cornell and Susan Sellers (New York: Columbia UP, 1993), 32.
2. André Malraux, *Les Noyers de l'Altenburg* (Paris: Gallimard, 1948), 88.
3. Wilhelm Worringer, *Abstraction and Empathy*, trans. Michael Bullock (New York: International Universities Press, 1953), 37, 18.
4. Page references for *Monsieur Teste* and *Der Ptolemäer* are to Paul Valéry, *Oeuvres*, vol. 2 (Paris: Gallimard, 1960), and Gottfried Benn, *Gesammelte Werke*, vol. 2 (Wiesbaden: Limes, 1958). "K/W" after the page reference indicates that I used the chapter translated by Ernst Kaiser and Eithne Wilkins in Gottfried Benn, *Primal Vision*, ed. E. B. Ashton (New York: New Directions, n.d. [1960]); otherwise all translations are mine. Both titles are significant: *Teste* is the Old French form of *tête*, "head"; Valéry also suggests derivation from Latin *testis*, "witness" (64). The *Ptolemäer* is literally a follower of the Ptolemaic system, but Benn uses the term also in the sense of solipsist: not only the earth but the ego is the center of the universe.
5. Cf. Valéry's comment on M. Teste's language: "a large number of words were banned from his speech" (18).
6. Reported by Edmond Jaloux in 1922, in Valéry, *Oeuvres*, vol. 2, 1384.

7. Worringer, *Abstraction and Empathy*, 17.
8. Valéry, *Oeuvres*, vol. 1, 1225.
9. It is a nice irony that the German term for the old stand-up collar is *Vatermörder*, "parricide."
10. Cf. Valéry's remark on M. Teste: "the existence of a type of this kind in reality could not be prolonged beyond a few quarters of an hour" (13).
11. In *Weinhaus Wolf* and *Roman des Phänotyps*, Benn calls art lethal too, and art is his only value.
12. Benn, "Answer to the Literary Emigrants" (1933), *Gesammelte Werke*, vol. 4, 245.
13. Evelyn Underhill, *Mysticism: A Study in the Nature and Development of Man's Spiritual Consciousness* (New York: Noonday Press, 1955), 71.

HELMUT HEISSENBÜTTEL, *POET OF CONTEXTS*

1. Helmut Heissenbüttel, *Über Literatur* (Olten: Walter, 1966), 219.
2. Helmut Heissenbüttel, *Textbuch I* (Olten: Walter, 1960), reprinted in *Textbücher 1–6* (Stuttgart: Klett-Cotta, 1980), 7:

das Sagbare sagen
das Erfahrbare erfahren
das Entscheidbare entscheiden
das Erreichbare erreichen
das Wiederholbare wiederholen
das Beendbare beenden

das nicht Sagbare
das nicht Erfahrbare
das nicht Entscheidbare
das nicht Erreichbare
das nicht Wiederholbare
das nicht Beendbare

das nicht Beendbare nicht beenden

3. P. K. Kurz, in *Stimmen der Zeit* (February 1967).
4. Heissenbüttel, *Über Literatur*, 223.
5. Heissenbüttel, *Textbücher 1–6*, 99.
6. [J]emand geht dahin und macht das weil er da wo er hingeht was findet was sich machen lässt und er findet das weil das was sich machen lässt und was er macht was ist was da wo er hingeht und was macht ist.
7. Heissenbüttel, *Textbücher 1–6*, 143.
8. Bertold Brecht, *Gedichte*, vol. 7 (Frankfurt: Suhrkamp, 1964), 7:

Ich sitze am Strassenhang.
Der Fahrer wechselt das Rad.
ich bin nicht gern, wo ich herkomme.
Ich bin nicht gern, wo ich hinfahre.
Warum sehe ich den Radwechsel
Mit Ungeduld?

9. Roman Jakobson and Morris Halle, *Fundamentals of Language* (The Hague: Mouton, 1956), 61.

10. August Stramm, *Das Werk* (Wiesbaden: Limes, 1963), 98.

11. Heissenbüttel, *Über Literatur,* 223.

12. Heissenbüttel, *Textbücher 1–6,* 57. *Referat: Was ist Wirklichkeit? Wirklichkeit ist etwas das.*

13. Heissenbüttel, *Über Literatur,* 149–52.

14. Cf. Max Bense, *Programmierung des Schönen* (Baden-Baden: Agis, 1960), passim.

MARAT/SADE: A RITUAL OF THE INTELLECT

1. Claude Lévi-Strauss, quoted in Giorgio Agamben, *Image et Mémoire* (Paris: Editions Hoëbeke, 1998), 50.

2. See Donald Freed, "Peter Weiss and the Theatre of the Future," *Drama Survey* 6 (fall 1967), 110–73.

3. Weiss limits himself to remarks like: "Just as the aspects change constantly, so change the means of representation. In one case constructive criticism of the times is required; in another, Antonin Artaud's theses are valid." *Materialien zu Peter Weiss' Marat/Sade* (Frankfurt: Suhrkamp, 1967), 92.

4. I am using the revised version of Peter Weiss, *Die Verfolgung und Ermordung Jean Paul Marats dargestellt durch die Schauspielgruppe des Hopizes zu Charenton unter Anleitung des Herrn de Sade* (Frankfurt: Suhrkamp, 1965). This is version E in *Materialien.*

5. Weiss himself usually refers to the relation as such a confrontation. See *Materialien,* 8, 93, and others.

6. I disagree with Schneider, who thinks the strength of Sade's position is unintentional and weakens the play (*Materialien,* 132ff.). Karlheinz Braun sees Sade projecting one of his own possibilities in Marat. But he sees Sade as simply withdrawing from it (*Materialien,* 139).

7. Cf. *Materialien,* 11.

A BASIS OF CONCRETE POETRY

1. Augusto de Campos, Décio Pignatari, Haroldo de Campos, "Pilot Plan for Concrete Poetry," in *Concrete Poetry,* ed. Mary Ellen Solt, special issue of *Artes Hispanicas* 1, No. 3/4 (1968), 72.

2. Willard Van Orman Quine, *From a Logical Point of View* (New York: Harper, 1961), 9.

3. Eugen Gomringer, *Worte sind Schatten: Die Konstellationen, 1951–1968* (Hamburg: Rowohlt, 1969), 281. Emphasis mine.

4. Solt, ed., *Concrete Poetry,* 72.

5. Ibid., 13.

6. Siegfried Schmidt, *Ästhetische Prozesse* (Köln: Kiepenheuer and Witsch, 1971), 93.

7. Gomringer, *Worte sind Schatten,* 277.

8. Roman Jakobson, "Linguistics and Poetics," in *Style in Language,* ed. Thomas A. Sebeok (Cambridge, MA: MIT Press, 1960), 358ff.

9. Solt, *Concrete Poetry,* 49.

10. Samuel R. Levin, *Linguistic Structures in Poetry* (The Hague: Mouton, 1969).

11. Franz Mon, *Texte über Texte* (Neuwied: Luchterhand, 1970), esp. 44–47.

12. Ian Hamilton Finlay, *The Blue and the Brown Poems* (New York: Jargon, 1968).

13. Ibid.

14. Solt, *Concrete Poetry,* 108, fig. 15. Translation by Maria José de Queiroz and Mary Ellen Solt.

15. Gerhard Rühm, *Gesammelte Gedichte und visuelle Texte* (Hamburg: Rowohlt, 1970), 227.

16. Ibid., 270.

17. Renate Beyer, "Innovation oder traditioneller Rekurs," *Text und Kritik* 30 (April 1971), 23–33.

18. Ernst Jandl, *Sprechblasen* (Neuwied: Luchterhand, 1968), 95.

19. *Anthology of Concrete Poetry,* ed. Emmet Williams (New York: Something Else Press, 1967). This is a translation by the editor of the German original, which begins "*lesbares in unlesbares übersetzen.*"

20. Schmidt, *Ästhetische Prozesse,* 60, 91, and passim.

21. E. Williams, *Anthology of Concrete Poetry.*

CHARLES OLSON: PROCESS AND RELATIONSHIP

1. Charles Olson, *Human Universe and Other Essays,* ed. Donald Allen (New York: Grove Press, 1967), 51–63. Hereafter abbreviated *HU.*

2. Cf., for instance, André Spire, *Plaisir poétique et plaisir musculaire* (New York: Vanni, 1949).

3. Don Byrd, "The Possibility of Measure in Olson's Maximus," *Boundary2* 2, No. 1/2 (1973–1974), 50. The references are to *The Literary Essays of Ezra Pound,* ed. T. S. Eliot (Norfolk, CT: New Directions, 1954), 205, 154, and William Carlos Williams, *Selected Essays* (New York: New Directions, 1969), 280–91.

4. Robert von Hallberg, "Olson, Whitehead, and the Objectivists," *Boundary2* 2, No. 1/2 (1973–1974), 93.

5. Ibid., 95.

6. Ibid., 109.

7. Charles Olson, *The Maximus Poems* (New York: Jargon/Corinth Books, 1960).

8. Robert Duncan, "Ideas of the Meaning of Form," *Kulchur* 4 (1961), 73.

9. Paul Ricoeur, *La métaphore vive* (Paris: Editions du Seuil, 1975), 20.

10. Gérard Genette, *Figures*, vol. III (Paris: Editions du Seuil, 1972), 37.

11. W. B. Yeats, *A Vision* (1937; rpt. New York: Collier Books, 1966), 3–5.

12. Cf. Daniel D. Pearlman, *The Barb of Time: On the Unity of Ezra Pound's Cantos* (New York: Oxford UP, 1969).

13. Charles Olson, *The Special View of History* (Berkeley, CA: Oyez, 1970).

14. Frank Davey has examined the recurrence that seems to come closest to a Poundian use, Maximus of Gloucester and Maximus of Tyre, in his essay "Six Readings of Olson's Maximus," *Boundary2* 2, No. 1/2 (1973–1974), 291–323. But in spite of a few correspondences between the teachings of the Platonist and Olson (mostly advocating participation in the natural process), the parallel does not assume the structural importance that this kind of bridging has in *The Cantos*.

15. Charles Olson, *Maximus IV, V, VI* (London: Cape Goliard Press, 1968). No pagination.

16. Charles Olson, *Causal Mythology* (San Francisco: Four Seasons Foundation, 1969), 11.

17. Robert Duncan, "Towards an Open Universe," in *The Poetics of the New American Poetry*, ed. Donald Allen and Warren Tallman (New York: Grove Press, 1973), 224.

Mirrors and Paradoxes

1. Galileo Galilei, *Dialogue Concerning the Two Chief World Systems, Ptolemaic and Copernican*, trans. Stillman Drake (Berkeley: U of California P, 1953), 42.

2. Rosalie Colie, *Paradoxia Epidemica: The Renaissance Tradition of Paradox* (Princeton, NJ: Princeton UP, 1966). I am much indebted to this book for the discussion of self-reference.

3. Maurice Beebe, "Reflective and Reflexive Trends in Modern Fiction," *Bucknell Review* 22, No. 2 (1976), 14. This encompassing article also carries a list of other articles on the phenomenon of self-reference.

4. Colie, *Paradoxia Epidemica*, 483.

5. Edmond Jabès, *Le Livre des Questions*, 7 vols. (Paris: Gallimard, 1963–1974): *Le Livre des Questions*, 1963 (*LdQ*); *Le Livre de Yukel*, 1964 (*LdY*); *Le Retour au Livre*, 1965 (*R*); *Yaël*, 1967 (*Y*); *Elya*, 1969 (*E*); *Aely*, 1972 (*A*); and *El, ou le dernier livre*, 1974 (*El*). [In English: *The Book of Questions: Vol. I* (*The Book of Questions, The Book of Yukel, Return to the Book*), *The Book of Questions:*

Vol. II (*Yaël; Elya; Aely; and El, or the Last Book*), trans. Rosmarie Waldrop (Middletown, CT: Wesleyan UP, 1991); hereafter referred to as *BQI* and *BQII*.]

6. Giancarlo Carabelli, "L'esperienza della scrittura," *Tempo Presente* (June 1964), 41–48.

7. Jacques Derrida, "Edmond Jabès et la question du livre," in *L'Écriture et la différance* (Paris: Editions du Seuil, 1967), 114. Italics his, translation mine.

8. Cf. Joseph Guglielmi, "Edmond Jabès et la fascination du désert," *Critique* 296 (January 1972), 32–53, or my own "Edmond Jabès and the Impossible Circle," *Sub-Stance* 5/6 (spring 1973), 183–95.

9. Gershom G. Scholem, *Major Trends in Jewish Mysticism* (New York: Schocken, 1961), 27.

PALMER'S *FIRST FIGURE*

1. Michael Palmer, *First Figure* (Berkeley, CA: North Point Press, 1984), 9, 75.

CHINESE WINDMILLS TURN HORIZONTALLY

1. Lyn Hejinian, "The Rejection of Closure" ("RC"), *Poetics Journal* 4 (May 1984), 134–43; "Two Stein Talks," *Temblor* 3 (1986), 128–40. Not surprisingly, phrases from these essays also turn up in poems; cf. "The Person," *Temblor* 4 (1986).

2. Lyn Hejinian, *My Life* (Providence, RI: Burning Deck, 1980). My page references will be to this edition. The second edition, eight years later, has been augmented to forty-five paragraphs of forty-five sentences each (Los Angeles: Sun and Moon, 1988). It is curious, and at the same time logical, that mathematical conceptions of form, dominant in the neoclassical era and so violently fought by Goethe and other early proponents of organic form, are coming back.

3. L. S. Vygotsky, *Thought and Language* (Cambridge, MA: MIT Press, 1962), 146–47.

4. Lyn Hejinian, *The Guard* (Berkeley, CA: Tuumba, 1984), no pagination.

5. Hejinian, "The Person," *Temblor* 4 (1986), 33.

6. Stephen Ratcliffe, "Two Hejinian Talks," *Temblor* 6 (1987), 141–48.

SHALL WE ESCAPE ANALOGY

1. Some of the French poets in question would be Emmanuel Hocquard, Alain Veinstein, Jean Daive, Michel Couturier, Jacqueline Risset, Jacques Roubaud, and Joseph Guglielmi. In the United States we have witnessed a similar shift of emphasis from metaphor to metonymy, contiguity, and syntax in the work of Olson, Creeley, Zukofsky, Guest and, long before them, Gertrude Stein. *Siècle à mains* not only helped focus an attitude but was also seminal in a more general way. When it began in 1963, independent "little" magazines

without support of a publishing house or gallery were rare in France. Royet-Journoud was encouraged by the mushrooming magazines and small presses of England and the United States that he encountered in London. Paris bookstores now carry magazines like *Première Livraison, Verriers,* and *La Répétition,* as well as books published by "Orange Export, Inc.," "Le Collet de Buffle," and other small presses. And a surprising number of the editors will tell you that they have taken their cue from Royet-Journoud's initiative.

2. Cf. Jakobson, "Two Aspects of Language and Two Types of Aphasic Disturbances," in *Fundamentals of Language.*

3. Books by Claude Royet-Journoud are cited in the text according to the following abbreviations: *R: Le renversement* (Paris: Gallimard, 1972); *N: La notion d'obstacle* (Paris: Gallimard, 1978); *O: Les objets contiennent l'infini* (Paris: Gallimard, 1983). [In English: *Reversal,* trans. Keith Waldrop (Providence: Hellcoal, 1973); *The Notion of Obstacle,* trans. Keith Waldrop (Windsor, VT: Awede Press, 1985).] The translations throughout are by Keith Waldrop except where I needed an absolutely word-by-word version. The page numbers refer to the French originals.

4. Claude Royet-Journoud, interview with Mathieu Bénézet, *France Nouvelle* (November 27, 1978). Other interviews quoted are: Emmanuel Hocquard, *Action Poétique* 87 (1982) [trans. G. Young, in *Code of Signals: Recent Writings in Poetics,* ed. M. Palmer, Berkeley, CA: North Atlantic, 1983], hereafter cited as *H.* Natacha Michel, *Le Perroquet* 35 (February 13, 1984); hereafter cited as *M.*

5. For instance, in *Les objects* . . . : "La bête est dépecée sur-le-champ" (17); "quelque chose comme aiguiser un couteau" (20); "chaque pièce / comme une mutilation" (42); "du mort à la bête dépecée" (43); "avancer dans une région étourdissante où l'équarissage est règle quotidienne" (66). Cf. Françoise de Laroque, "La langue et l'équarrisseur," *Action Poétique* 87 (1982), 36ff.

6. Joseph Simas, "Entretien avec Anne-Marie Albiach," *Ex* 4 (1985), 54. [English version in *Acts* 4 (1986)]. Most of the other statements by Albiach are from the interview with Henri Deluy, Joseph Guglielmi, and Pierre Rotenberg, *Action Poétique* 74 (1978); hereafter cited as *AP.*

7. Emmanuel Hocquard, "Prenez-le vivant," *Critique* 347 (April 1976), 456.

8. Ibid.

9. Books by Anne-Marie Albiach are cited in the text according to the following abbreviations: *F: Flammigère: Poème* (London: Siècle à mains, 1967); *É: État* (Paris: Mercure de France, 1971; *MV: Mezza voce* (Paris: Flammarion, 1984). [In English: *État,* trans. Keith Waldrop (Windsor, VT: Awede Press, 1987).] Again, translations throughout are by Keith Waldrop except where I needed a strict word-by-word version. The page numbers refer to the French originals.

10. "Car il faut savoir" (*E* 11); "Car s'il est un thème" (*E* 17); "si elle subit" (*E* 45); "dans le cas où" (*E* 46); "Car un foyer" (*E* 51); "Car le profil sait" (*E* 52); "si ce n'est" (*E* 60), etc.

11. The author identified the *sa* as "her" in working with Keith Waldrop on the English translation.

12. I am grateful to Gary Gach for pointing to this. On the importance of "graphisms:" when asked about the significance of the italic *E* of her title *E*tat, Albiach said she wanted to introduce a distinction that would be purely written, purely graphic, that could not even be pronounced.

II. TRANSLATION

The Joy of the Demiurge

1. Leonard Forster, "Translation: An Introduction," in *Aspects of Translation,* ed. A. H. Smith (London: Secker and Warburg, 1958), 1.

2. Renato Poggioli, "The Added Artificer," in *On Translation,* ed. R. A. Brower (New York: Oxford UP, 1966), 139.

3. Jabès, *Book of Questions: Vol. I,* 362.

4. Walter Benjamin, "The Task of the Translator," in *Illuminations,* ed. Hannah Arendt, trans. Harry Zohn (1968; New York: Schocken Books, 1986).

5. Eugene A. Nida, *Toward a Science of Translating* (Leiden: E. J. Brill, 1964), 146.

6. Benjamin, "Task of the Translator," 81.

7. Celia Zukofsky and Louis Zukofsky, *Catullus* (London: Cape Goliard, 1969).

8. Nida, *Toward a Science,* 146.

9. Jabès, *Book of Questions: Vol. I,* 33.

10. Benjamin, "Task of the Translator," 79.

11. Richmond Lattimore, "Practical Notes on Translating Greek Poetry," in *On Translation,* ed. Reuben A. Brower (New York: Oxford UP, 1966), 54.

12. Michel Leiris, "Le Caput mortuum ou la femme de l'alchimiste," *Les Cahiers du double: Constat* 1 (fall 1977), 63ff.

Silence, the Devil, and Jabès

1. Benjamin, "Task of the Translator," esp. 75, 79, 81.

2. Haroldo de Campos, "Transluciferation," *Ex* 4 (1985), 10–14.

3. Keith Waldrop, *The Quest for Mount Misery* (Isla Vista, CA: Turkey Press, 1983). The psychoanalyst in question was John Rickman.

4. This statement is not quite as facetious as it sounds. Translation is never transparent. It will bear the mark of the translator and of his or her time. Stated in extreme terms, the destruction of the original, a "parricidal

impulse, is necessary to provide the immense energy necessary to re-create, reengender the work.

5. This makes it evident that the whole concept of "fidelity" in translation is simple-minded, especially (though not only) when it means fidelity to the "content."

6. Jabès, *Le Livre des questions*, 35 [*Book of Questions: Vol. I*, 33]. Other works of Jabès cited: *Aely* (*Le Livre des questions*, vol. 6), 1972 [*Book of Questions: Vol. II*]; *Le Livre du dialogue*, 1984 [*The Book of Dialogue*, trans. Rosmarie Waldrop (Middletown, CT: Wesleyan UP, 1987)]; *Le Livre du partage*, 1987 [*The Book of Shares*, trans. Rosmarie Waldrop (Chicago: U of Chicago P, 1989)]. On the closeness of writing and translating, cf. Paul Valéry, *Variations sur les Bucoliques:* "Ecrire quoi que ce soit . . . est un travail de traduction exactement comparable à celui qui opère la transmutation d'un texte d'une langue dans une autre." *Oeuvres*, vol. 1 (Paris: Gallimard, 1957), 211.

7. Hans-Georg Gadamer, *Philosophical Hermeneutics*, trans. David E. Linge (Berkeley: U of California P, 1976), 67–68.

8. Jabès, *Book of Dialogue*, 39. Phrases like this abound throughout Jabès's work.

9. Cf. the less abstract spatial metaphor of Wittgenstein: "Our language can be seen as an old city: a maze of little streets and squares, of old and new houses, and of houses with additions from various periods; and this surrounded by a multitude of new boroughs with straight regular streets and uniform houses." (*Philosophical Investigations*, trans. G. E. M. Anscombe (Oxford: Basil Blackwell, 1968), 83). Or compare with Walter Benjamin's forest: "Translation does not find itself in the center of the language forest but on the outside facing the wooded ridge; it calls into it without entering, aiming at that single spot where the echo is able to give, in its own language, the reverberation of the work in the alien one" (*Illuminations*, 76).

10. This is so basic it would hardly need to be mentioned if it were not for people like Robert Bly who presume that a smattering of grammar and a few consultations of a dictionary are ample preparation. The mutilation he has performed on Georg Trakl, for instance, has nothing to do with the necessary erosion I talked of, but only with ignorance, hubris, and contempt for the author he professes to admire.

11. If I had known about it at the time, I also would have consulted Arabic works like the *Wedding Nights* of 'Abd al-Rahmane al-Souyoûti, which has a similar structure of guests assembling on various occasions to tell stories, discuss, argue, and quote poems or philosophers. A French translation by René R. Khawam was published by Albin Michel in 1972.

12. Osip Mandelstam, *Selected Poems*, trans. Clarence Brown and W. S. Merwin (Atheneum, 1974).

IRREDUCIBLE STRANGENESS

1. Friedrich Schleiermacher, "Über die verschiedenen Methoden des Übersetzens" (1813), quoted in Lawrence Venuti, *The Translator's Invisibility* (London: Routledge, 1995), 19.
2. J. W. v. Goethe, "West-Östlicher Divan: Noten und Abhandlungen," *Werke: Hamburger Ausgabe,* vol. 2, ed. Erich Trunz (Hamburg: Christian Wegner, 1949).
3. Venuti, *Translator's Invisibility,* 5.
4. Goethe, "West-Östlicher Divan," 256.
5. Emmanuel Hocquard, "Blank Spots," trans. Stacy Doris, *Boundary2* 26, No. 1 (spring 1999).
6. Valéry, "Variations sur les Bucoliques," 215.
7. De Campos, "Transluciferation," 10–14.
8. Carl Dahlhaus, *Ludwig van Beethoven,* trans. Mary Whittall (Oxford: Clarendon Press, 1991), 4.
9. Justin O'Brien, "From French to English," in *On Translation,* ed. Reuben A. Brower (Cambridge, MA: Harvard UP, 1959).

III. POETICS

ALARMS AND EXCURSIONS

1. Edmond Jabès, "Repondre à repondre pour," unpublished except in English translation (*Acts* 10, 1989). Unless otherwise noted, all translations are mine.
2. Paul Valéry, *Aesthetics,* trans. Ralph Manheim, Bollingen Series, vol. 13 (New York: Pantheon Books, 1964), 129.
3. Bertold Brecht, *Schriften zur Literatur und Kunst,* vol. 2 (Frankfurt: Suhrkamp, 1967), 23.
4. There have been several convincing studies of how the little perverted phrases spread and reinforced anti-Semitism in Germany; e.g., Victor Klemperer, *Die unbewältigte Sprache* (München: dtv, 1969), or Sternberger/Storz/Suskind, *Aus dem Wörterbuch des Unmenschen* (Hamburg: Claassen, 1968).
5. Barthes quoted in Urs Jaeggi, *Literatur und Politik* (Frankfurt: Suhrkamp, 1972), 105.
6. Edmond Jabès, *Le petit livre de la subversion hors de soupcon* (Paris: Gallimard, 1982), 7; *The Little Book of Unsuspected Subversion,* trans. Rosmarie Waldrop (Stanford, CA: Stanford UP, 1996), 1.
7. Jabès, *Le petit livre,* back cover.
8. Theodor Adorno, *Noten zur Literatur,* vol. 2 (Frankfurt: Suhrkamp, 1961), 168.
9. Georges Bataille, "La part maudite," *Oeuvres Complètes,* vol. 7 (Paris:

Gallimard, 1976), 40, 9, 29. An English translation of *La Part Maudite* (1949) has been published as *The Accursed Share* (Cambridge, MA: Zone Books, 1988).

10. Jaeggi, *Literatur und Politik*, 21.

11. Roland Barthes, *Roland Barthes par Roland Barthes* (Paris: Seuil, 1975), 53.

12. Jaeggi, *Literatur und Politik*, 7.

13. Brecht, *Schriften zur Literatur und Kunst*, vol. 1, 115, 30.

14. Valéry, *Aesthetics*, 48–49.

15. Tristan Tzara, "7 Manifestes Dada," *Oeuvres*, vol. 1 (Paris: Flammarion, 1975), 382.

16. Jaeggi, *Literatur und Politik*, 52.

17. Adorno, *Noten zur Literatur* II, 163–64, 175.

18. Charles Reznikoff, *Testimony I: The United States, 1885–1890: Recitative* (Santa Barbara, CA: Black Sparrow, 1978), 30–33.

19. Heissenbüttel, *Textbücher 1–6*, 171.

20. Georges Bataille, "La Littérature et le mal," *Oeuvres Complètes*, vol. 9, 437.

21. Tzara, *Oeuvres*, vol. 1, 363.

22. Steve McCaffery, *North of Intention: Critical Writings, 1973–1986* (New York: Roof Books, 1986), 201–22.

23. Susanne Langer, *Philosophy in a New Key: A Study in the Symbolism of Reason, Rite, and Art* (New York: Mentor Books, 1948), 61.

24. Roman Jakobson, "Linguistics and Poetics," in *Style in Language*, ed. Thomas A. Sebeok (Cambridge, MA: MIT Press, 1960), 356.

25. Jean-Paul Sartre, *Situations*, vol. 2 (Paris: Gallimard, 1948), 64.

26. Rosmarie Waldrop, *The Road Is Everywhere or Stop This Body* (Columbia, MO: Open Places, 1978), 1.

SPLIT INFINITE

1. Edmond Jabès, *The Book of Margins*, trans. Rosmarie Waldrop (Chicago: U of Chicago P, 1993), 191.

2. Jabès, *Book of Questions: Vol. I*, 204.

3. Ibid.

4. Edmond Jabès, *Intimations, The Desert* (Middletown, CT: Wesleyan UP, 1991), 104; *Book of Questions: Vol. I*, 203.

5. Edmond Jabès, *The Book of Resemblances* (Middletown, CT: Wesleyan UP, 1990), 20.

6. Jabès, *Book of Questions: Vol. I*, 109.

7. Robert Duncan, "The Delirium of Meaning," in *The Sin of the Book, Edmond Jabès*, ed. Eric Gould (Lincoln: U of Nebraska P, 1985), 221.

8. John Taggart, in *Code of Signals*, ed. Michael Palmer (Berkeley, CA: North Atlantic Books, 1983), 34.

9. Clark Coolidge, "From Notebooks 1976–82," in *Code of Signals*, 173.

10. Emily Dickinson, Letter to Susan Gilbert Dickinson, *The Letters of Emily Dickinson,* ed. Thomas H. Johnson (Cambridge, MA: Harvard UP, 1958), letter number 871.

11. "In the end we depend / on creatures we created." Goethe, *Faust, Werke,* 214.

12. Jabès, *Book of Questions: Vol. I,* 78.

13. Jabès, *Book of Questions: Vol. II,* 153.

14. Olson, *Human Universe,* 123.

A KEY INTO THE KEY

1. Neal Salisbury, *Manitou and Providence: Indians, Europeans, and the Making of New England, 1500–1643* (New York: Oxford UP, 1982), 194.

2. Ibid.

3. John J. Teunissen and Evelyn J. Hinz, ed., *Roger Williams: A Key into the Language of America* (Detroit: Wayne State UP, 1973), chapter XXI.

4. Ibid., 24.

5. Salisbury, *Manitou and Providence,* 176–77.

6. Perry Miller, *Roger Williams: His Contribution to the American Tradition* (New York: Atheneum, 1966), 26.

7. Teunissen and Hinz, *Roger Williams: A Key,* 25.

8. William Carlos Williams, *In the American Grain* (New York: New Directions, 1966), 26.

9. Ethel Boissevain, *The Narragansett People* (Phoenix, AZ: Indian Tribal Series, 1975), 93.

10. Ibid., 92.

FORM AND DISCONTENT

1. "Poetics," chapter 6, quoted after *The Basic Works of Aristotle,* ed. Richard McKeon (New York: Random House, 1941), 1460.

2. Norma Cole, *Mars* (Berkeley: Listening Chamber, 1994), 70; Carla Harryman, *Under the Bridge* (San Francisco: This, 1980), 51; Ron Silliman, *Paradise* (Providence, RI: Burning Deck, 1985), 9; Rosmarie Waldrop, *The Reproduction of Profiles* (New York: New Directions, 1987), 7; Leslie Scalapino, *Considering How Exaggerated Music Is* (San Francisco: North Point Press, 1982), 73; and Gertrude Stein, *Selected Writings* (New York: Modern Library, 1962), 490.

3. Mei-mei Berssenbrugge, *The Heat Bird* (Providence, RI: Burning Deck, 1983), 13.

4. Jacques Roubaud, "Hypothèse du compact," in *Revue de littérature générale* 1 (1995), 291.

5. Jackson Mac Low, *4 Trains* (Providence, RI: Burning Deck, 1974), 7.

6. Louis Zukofsky, *Prepositions: The Collected Critical Essays of Louis Zukofsky* (New York: Horizon Press, 1967), 27.

7. Rosmarie Waldrop, *A Form/Of Taking/It All* (Barrytown, NY: Station Hill Press, 1990), 74.

8. J. W. v. Goethe, "Von deutscher Baukunst," *Werke: Hamburger Ausgabe,* vol. 12 (Hamburg: Christian Wegner, 1953), 7.

9. Charles Olson, "Projective Verse," in *Human Universe,* ed. Donald Allen (New York: Grove Press, 1967), 52.

10. Charles Baudelaire, *Oeuvres Complètes,* ed. Y.-G. Le Dantec (Paris: Gallimard, 1954), 87.

11. Olson, *Human Universe,* 10.

12. References are to Ferdinand de Saussure, *Cours de linguistique générale* (Paris: Payot, 1949); Roman Jakobson, "Two Aspects of Language and Two Types of Aphasic Disturbances," in *Fundamentals of Language* (The Hague: Mouton, 1956); Robert Scholes, *Structuralism in Literature* (New Haven, CT: Yale UP, 1974); and Michael Riffaterre, *Semiotics of Poetry* (Bloomington: Indiana UP, 1978).

13. Olson, *Human Universe,* 18.

14. Susan Howe, *The Western Borders* (Willits, CA: Tuumba Press, 1976), n.p.

15. Barbara Guest, *The Countess from Minneapolis* (Providence, RI: Burning Deck, 1974), 4.

16. Robert Creeley, *A Quick Graph: Collected Notes and Essays* (San Francisco: Four Seasons Foundation, 1970), 61, 21.

17. In a talk given at the Naropa Institute, July 1995.

18. Quoted in Paul Hoover, ed., *Postmodern American Poetry: A Norton Anthology* (New York: W. W. Norton, 1994), 624.

19. R. Waldrop, *A Form/Of Taking/It All,* 57.

20. Robert Duncan, *The Truth and Life of Myth: An Essay in Essential Autobiography* (Fremont, MI: Sumac Press, 1968), 28.

21. In a talk given at the Naropa Institute, July 1995.

22. George Oppen, "Notes on Prosody?" quoted in Paul Auster, "A Few Words in Praise of George Oppen," *Paideuma* 10, No. 1 (spring 1981), 49.

23. Quoted in Edward Foster, *The Space between Her Bed and Clock* (San Francisco: Norton Coker, 1993), 4.

THINKING OF FOLLOWS

1. John Cage, *Silence* (Middletown, CT: Wesleyan UP, 1961), 109.

2. Valéry, *Aesthetics,* 48–49.

3. Jabès, *Book of Questions: Vol. 1,* 25.

4. Benjamin, *Illuminations,* 69.

5. Braque, quoted in Eric Mottram, *Selected Poems* (Twickenham: North & South, 1989), 118.

The Ground Is the Only Figure: Notebook Spring 1996

1. Rosalind Krauss, *The Optical Unconscious* (Cambridge, MA: MIT Press, 1993), 16.

2. Jabès, *The Ineffaceable The Unperceived* (Middletown, CT: Wesleyan UP, 1992), 7.

3. Dominique Fourcade, *IL* (Paris: P.O.L., 1994), 82.

4. Robert Creeley, *Pieces* (New York: Scribner's, 1969), 7.

5. Lyn Hejinian, *The Cell* (Los Angeles: Sun and Moon, 1992), 22.

6. Benn, *Gesammelte Werke*, vol. 2, 482.

7. Olson, *Human Universe*, 123.

8. Alfred North Whitehead, *Modes of Thought* (New York: Free Press, 1968), 53.

9. Erwin W. Straus, *Phenomenological Psychology* (New York: Basic Books, 1966), 7, 19–20, 3.

10. Jabès, *Book of Margins*, 170.

11. Emmanuel Hocquard, "Les jardins de Salluste," *Un privé à Tanger* (Paris: P.O.L., 1987), 73.

12. Barbara Guest, *Stripped Tales* (Berkeley, CA: Kelsey St. Press, 1995), 20.

13. Quoted in David C. Lindberg, *Theories of Vision from Al-Kindi to Kepler* (Chicago: U of Chicago P, 1976), 203.

14. Fourcade, *IL*, 76.

15. Marcel Proust, *Contre Sainte-Beuve*, ed. Pierre Clarac (Paris: Gallimard, 1971), 305.

16. Cixous, *Three Steps*, 93.

17. Quoted in Deborah Baker, *In Extremis: The Life of Laura Riding* (London: Hamish Hamilton, 1993), 37.

18. Quoted in Joan Retallack, "Blue Notes on the Know Ledge," *Poetics Journal* 10 (1998), 47.

19. Michael Palmer, "The Site of the Poem," in *Exact Change Yearbook* 1 (1995), 191.

20. Giorgio Agamben, *Idea of Prose,* trans. Michael Sullivan and Sam Whitsitt (Albany: SUNY Press, 1995), 37.

21. Michael Palmer, *At Passages* (New York: New Directions, 1995), 15.

22. Gilles Deleuze, "Différence et répétition," quoted in Hocquard, *Un privé à Tanger,* 66.

23. Michael Whiteman, *Philosophy of Space and Time* (London: Allen and Unwin, 1967), 23.

24. Maurice Merleau-Ponty, *Phénoménologie de la perception* (Paris: Gallimard, 1945), 281.

25. Quoted in Robert Creeley, *The Collected Essays* (Berkeley: U of California P, 1989), 591.

26. Benjamin, *Illuminations*, 151.

27. William Carlos Williams, *Paterson*, Book IV, revised ed. prepared by Christopher MacGowan (New York: New Directions, 1992), 175.

28. Maurice Blanchot, "L'Interruption [comme sur une surface de Riemann]," *L'entretien infini* (Paris: Gallimard, 1969), 108.

29. Novalis, "Blütenstaub," *Schriften*, ed. Richard Samuel, vol. 2 (Darmstadt: Wissenschaftliche Buchgesellschaft, 1965), 413.

30. Jacques Roubaud, *The Plurality of Worlds of Lewis*, trans. Rosmarie Waldrop (Elmwood Park, IL: Dalkey Archive Press, 1990), 104.

31. Quoted in review of *Flow Chart* by Mark Ford, *Times Literary Supplement* (December 27, 1991).

32. Jabès, *A Foreigner Carrying in the Crook of His Arm a Tiny Book*, trans. Rosmarie Waldrop (Middletown, CT: Wesleyan UP, 1993), 12, and *Le Livre de l'Hospitalité* (Paris: Gallimard, 1991), 35.

33. Unpublished manuscript. Similar passages can be found in the Interview with Peter Gizzi, *The Germ* 5 (summer 2001), 270–319.

34. Friedrich Schlegel, "Athenaeums-Fragmente." *Kritische Schriften*, ed. Wolfdietrich Rasch (München: Carl Hanser, 1956), 45; Novalis, *Schriften*, vol. 2, 639.

35. Whitehead, *Modes of Thought*, 108.

36. Clarice Lispector, *Agua Viva*, trans. R. H. de Oliveira Machado (Paris: Des Femmes, 1981), 31, 65.

37. Roland Barthes, "The Death of the Author," *Image-Music-Text*, trans. Stephen Heath (New York: Hill and Wang, 1977), 145–46.

38. Walter Benjamin, *Reflections: Essays, Aphorisms, Autobiographical Writings*, trans. Edmund Jephcott, ed. Peter Demetz (New York: Harcourt Brace Jovanovich, 1978), 269.

39. Royet-Journoud, in conversation with the author. When he later saw this passage, he explained that I had misunderstood the expression "mots-bateaux," which means commonplaces, and that he had meant to say he wanted to write in an "unpoetical," flat language, a language of clichés and commonplaces: "je préfère le plat et, pour tout dire, la platitude."

40. Straus, *Phenomenological Psychology*, 26.

41. "The Ambition of Ghosts," in *Streets Enough to Welcome Snow* (Barrytown, NY: Station Hill, 1986).

42. Charles Bernstein, *Poetic Justice* (Baltimore, MD: Pod Books, 1979), 45.

43. Rae Armantrout, *Necromance* (Los Angeles: Sun and Moon, 1991), 39.

44. Merleau-Ponty, *Phénoménologie de la perception*, 215–16.

45. Lispector, *Agua Viva*, 67.

46. Hocquard, "Il rien," *Un privé à Tanger*, 54–56, trans. Mark Hutchinson.

47. Erwin Straus, *The Primary World of Senses*, trans. Jacob Needleman (London: Collier-Macmillan Ltd., 1963), 359–61.

48. Antonin Artaud, "Correspondance avec Jacques Rivière," *Oeuvres Complètes,* vol. 1 (Paris: Gallimard, 1956), 20, 28, 39.

49. Merleau-Ponty, *Phénoménologie de la perception,* 171.

50. Kent C. Bloomer and Charles W. Moore, *Body, Memory, and Architecture* (New Haven, CT: Yale UP, 1977), 47.

51. Olson, *Human Universe,* 10.

52. Jacques Roubaud, *L'Invention du fils de Leoprepes* (Saulxures: Editions Circé, 1993), 138–40.

53. Ludwig Wittgenstein, *Zettel,* trans. G. E. M. Anscombe (Berkeley: U of California P, 1970), 160.

54. Jabès, in conversation with the author.

55. John Keats, Letter to George and Tom Keats, December 21, 27[?] 1817.

56. Royet-Journoud, in conversation with the author.

57. Barbara Guest, in a talk at Naropa Institute, week of July 9, 1995.

58. Valéry, *Oeuvres,* vol. 1, 1172.

59. Charles Juliet, *Rencontre avec Samuel Beckett* (Montpellier: Fata Morgana, 1986).

60. Bernstein, *Poetic Justice,* 40.

61. André Breton, *Les vases communicantes, Oeuvres complètes,* vol. 2, ed. Marguerite Bonnet (Paris: Gallimard, 1992), 151.

62. Quoted in "Interview with Michael Palmer," *Exact Change Yearbook* 1, 162.

63. Roubaud, "Hypothèse du compact," 291.

64. Christoph Kellerer, *Object trouvé Surrealisme Zen* (Köln: DuMont, 1982), 86.

65. Paul Celan, *Eingedunkelt: und Gedichte aus dem Umkreis von Eingedunkelt* (Frankfurt: Suhrkamp, 1991), 42.

66. Pam Rehm, manuscript.

67. In Bloomer and Moore, *Body, Memory, and Architecture,* 34.

68. Whitehead, *Modes of Thought,* 49.

69. Gaston Bachelard, *La Poétique de l'espace* (Paris: Presses Universitaires de France, 1957), 35.

70. Jabès, *Book of Shares,* 31.

71. H. D., *Hermetic Definition* (New York: New Directions, 1972), 88.

72. Blanchot, "L'Interruption," 108.

73. John Ashbery and Kenneth Koch, *A Conversation* (New York: Interview Press, n.d. [1965]), 16–17.

74. In Palmer, ed., *Code of Signals,* 175.

75. Jabès, *Le Livre de l'Hospitalité,* 9.

76. Bernstein, *Poetic Justice,* 46.

77. Gottfried Benn, *Gedichte, Gesammelte Werke,* vol. 3 (Wiesbaden: Limes, 1960), 319.

78. Agamben, *Idea of Prose,* 43.

79. In Paul Hoover, ed., *Postmodern American Poetry*, 624.

80. Valéry, *Oeuvres*, vol. 1, 1172.

81. W. D. Snodgrass, *Six Troubadour Songs* (Providence, RI: Burning Deck, 1977), n.p.

82. Elizabeth Willis, *The Human Abstract* (New York: Penguin, 1995), 52.

83. Roubaud, *Plurality of Worlds of Lewis*, 69.

84. Agamben, *Idea of Prose*, 48.

85. Quoted by Michael Palmer in "Interview with Michael Palmer," *Exact Change Yearbook* 1, 163.

86. Adorno, *Aesthetic Theory*, quoted in Jaeggi, 47.

87. Patrick A. Heelan, *Space-Perception and the Philosophy of Science* (Berkeley: U of California P, 1983), 58–59.

88. Robert Duncan, "Pages from a Notebook," *Selected Prose* (New York: New Directions, 1995), 22.

89. Jacques Roubaud, *Some Thing Black*, trans. Rosmarie Waldrop (Elmwood Park, IL: Dalkey Archive Press, 1986), 11; Ludwig Wittgenstein, *On Certainty*, trans. Denis Paul and G. E. M. Anscombe (New York: Harper Torchbooks, 1969), 2e.

90. Merleau-Ponty, *Phénoménologie de la perception*, 295–96. My italics.

91. In Palmer, ed., *Code of Signals*, 34.

92. Valéry, *Oeuvres*, vol. 1, 1224.

Why Do I Write Prose Poems

1. Heather McHugh, quoted by Sharon Dolin, "Broken English," *AWP Chronicle* (December 1996), 11.

2. Agamben, *Idea of Prose*, 40.

3. Friedrich Hölderlin, "Anmerkungen zum Oedipus," *Sämtliche Werke*, vol. 5, ed. Friedrich Beissner (Stuttgart: Kohlhammer, 1954), 214.

4. Russell Edson, "Commentary on 'The Tunnel,'" *The Prose Poem* 7 (1998), 88.

5. Rosmarie Waldrop, *The Aggressive Ways of the Casual Stranger* (New York: Random House, 1971), 63.

6. Vera Linhartová, *Mehrstimmige Zerstreuung*, trans. from the Czech by Dorothea Neumärker (München: Deutscher Taschenbuch, Verlag, 1971), 142.

7. Quoted in Creeley, *Collected Essays*, 591.

8. Robert Duncan, "The Structure of Rime 1" in *The Opening of the Field* (New York: Grove Press, 1960), 12.

9. Rosmarie Waldrop, *The Reproduction of Profiles* (New York: New Directions, 1987).

10. Cf. R. Waldrop, *Reproduction of Profiles*, 6, and Franz Kafka, *Description of a Struggle* (New York: Schocken, 1958), 32.

11. Benjamin, *Reflections*, 269.

12. Rosmarie Waldrop, *Lawn of Excluded Middle* (New York: Tender Buttons, 1993).

13. Rosmarie Waldrop, *Reluctant Gravities* (New York: New Directions, 1998).

14. Langer, *Philosophy in a New Key*, 61.

Between, Always

1. Olson, *Human Universe*, 123.

2. Viktor Shklovsky, *Theory of Prose*, tr. Benjamin Sher (Elmwood Park, IL: Dalkey Archive Press, 1990), 189.

3. Merleau-Ponty, *Phénoménologie de la perception*, 281, 118.

4. Whiteman, *Philosophy of Space and Time*, 23.

5. Creeley, *Collected Essays*, 591.

6. Juliet, *Rencontre avec Samuel Beckett*.

7. Retallack, "Blue Notes on the Know Ledge," 46.

8. Julia Kristeva, *La révolution du langage poétique* (Paris: Editions du Seuil, 1974), 203.

9. Blanchot, *L'Entretien infini*, 14.

10. Joan Retallack, "Post-Scriptum—High-Modern," in *Postmodern Genres*, ed. Marjorie Perloff (Norman: U of Oklahoma P, 1989), 260.

11. Marcel Cohen, "Notes," *Le Travail de l'art* 2 (1998).

12. Cf. Carolyn Burke, "Translation Modified," in *Engaging with Irigaray*, eds. Carolyn Burke, Naomi Schor, Margaret Whitford (New York: Columbia UP, 1994).

Nothing to Say and Saying It

1. Cage, *Silence*, 109; Joy Harjo, *The Woman Who Fell from the Sky* (New York: Norton, 1994), 19; quoted in Jonathan Monroe, "Untranslatable Communities, Productive Translation, and Public Transport," *We Who Love to Be Astonished: Experimental Women's Writing and Performance Poetics*, ed. Laura Hinton and Cynthia Hogue (Tuscaloosa: U of Alabama P, 2002), 95.

2. Jabès, *Book of Questions: Vol. I*, 117.

3. Samuel Beckett, *The Unnamable* (New York: Grove Press, 1958), 179.

4. Cohen, "Notes."

5. Andrew Joron, *The Emergency of Poetry* (Berkeley, CA: Velocities Chapbook, 2002).

6. Cohen, "Notes."

7. George Oppen, *Collected Poems* (New York: New Directions, 1975), 151.

8. Giorgio Agamben, *Means without End*, trans. Vincenzo Binetti and Cesare Casarino (Minneapolis: U of Minnesota P, 2000), 9.

Bibliography

Adorno, Theodor. *Noten zur Literatur,* vol. 2. Frankfurt: Suhrkamp, 1961.

———. *Aesthetic Theory.* Trans. Robert Hullot-Kentor. Minneapolis: U of Minnesota P, 1997.

Agamben, Giorgio. *Idea of Prose.* Trans. Michael Sullivan and Sam Whitsitt. Albany: SUNY Press, 1995.

———. *Image et Mémoire.* Paris: Editions Hoëbeke, 1998.

———. *Means without End: Notes on Politics.* Trans. Vincenzo Binetti and Cesare Casarino. Minneapolis: U of Minnesota P, 2000.

Albiach, Anne-Marie. *Flammigère: Poème.* London: Siècle à mains, 1967.

———. "A9." *Siècle à main* 12 (spring 1970).

———. *Etat.* Paris: Mercure de France, 1971.

———. *Etat.* Trans. Keith Waldrop. Windsor, VT: Awede Press, 1987.

———. *Mezza voce.* Paris: Flammarion, 1984.

———. Interview with Joseph Simas. "Entretien avec Anne-Marie Albiach." *Ex* 4 (1985). [English version in *Acts* 4 (1986).]

———. Interviews with Henri Deluy, Joseph Guglielmi, and Pierre Rottenberg. *Action Poétique* 74 (1978).

Alferi, Pierre. *Les allures naturelles.* Paris: P.O.L., 1991.

———. *Natural Gaits.* Trans. Cole Swensen. Los Angeles, CA: Sun and Moon, 1995.

———. *Sentimentale Journée.* Paris: P.O.L., 1997.

Allen, Donald, and Warren Tallman, eds. *The Poetics of the New American Poetry.* New York: Grove Press, 1973.

Aristotle. "Poetics." *The Basic Works of Aristotle.* Ed. Richard McKeon. New York: Random House, 1941.

Armantrout, Rae. *Necromance.* Los Angeles: Sun and Moon, 1991.

Artaud, Antonin. *Oeuvres Complètes,* vol. 1. Paris: Gallimard, 1956.

Ashbery, John, and Kenneth Koch. *A Conversation*. New York: Interview Press, n.d. [1965].

Auster, Paul. "A Few Words in Praise of George Oppen." *Paideuma* 10, No. 1 (spring 1981).

———. *Why Write?* Providence, RI: Burning Deck, 1996.

Bachelard, Gaston. *La Poétique de l'espace*. Paris: Presses Universitaires de France, 1957.

Baker, Deborah. *In Extremis: The Life of Laura Riding*. London: Hamish Hamilton, 1993.

Barnes, Djuna. *Nightwood*. 1937. New York: New Directions, 1946.

Barthes, Roland. *Roland Barthes par Roland Barthes*. Paris: Seuil, 1975.

———. *Image-Music-Text*. Trans. Stephen Heath. New York: Hill and Wang, 1977.

Bataille, Georges. "La part maudite." *Oeuvres Complètes,* vol. 7. Paris: Gallimard, 1976.

———. "La littérature et le mal." *Oeuvres Complètes,* vol. 9. Paris: Gallimard, 1979.

———. *The Accursed Share*. Trans. Robert Hurley. New York: Zone Books, 1988.

Baudelaire, Charles. *Oeuvres Complètes*. Ed. Y.-G. Le Dantec. Paris: Gallimard, 1954.

Beckett, Samuel. *The Unnamable*. New York: Grove Press, 1958.

Beebe, Maurice. "Reflective and Reflexive Trends in Modern Fiction." *Bucknell Review* 22, No. 2 (1976).

Benjamin, Walter. *Illuminations*. Ed. Hannah Arendt. Trans. Harry Zohn. 1968. New York: Schocken Books, 1986.

———. *Reflections: Essays, Aphorisms, Autobiographical Writings*. Ed. Peter Demetz. Trans. Edmund Jephcott. New York: Harcourt Brace Jovanovich, 1978.

Benn, Gottfried. "Der Ptolemäer." *Prosa und Szenen. Gesammelte Werke,* vol. 2. Ed. Dieter Wellershoff. Wiesbaden: Limes, 1958.

———. *Gedichte. Gesammelte Werke,* vol. 3. Wiesbaden: Limes, 1960.

———. "Antwort and die literarischen Emigranten" [Answer to the Literary Emigrants]. *Autobiographische und vermischte Schriften. Gesammelte Werke,* vol. 4. Wiesbaden: Limes, 1961.

———. *Primal Vision*. Ed. E. B. Ashton. New York: New Directions, [1960].

Bense, Max. *Programmierung des Schönen*. Baden-Baden: Agis, 1960.

Bernstein, Charles. *Poetic Justice*. Baltimore, MD: Pod Books, 1979.

Berssenbrugge, Mei-mei. *The Heat Bird*. Providence, RI: Burning Deck, 1983.

———. *Empathy*. Barrytown, NY: Station Hill Press, 1989.

Beyer, Renate. "Innovation oder traditioneller Rekurs." *Text und Kritik* 30 (April 1971).

Blanchot, Maurice. *L'entretien infini*. Paris: Gallimard, 1969.

Bloomer, Kent C., and Charles W. Moore. *Body, Memory, and Architecture*. New Haven, CT: Yale UP, 1977.

Boissevain, Ethel. *The Narragansett People*. Phoenix, AZ: Indian Tribal Series, 1975.

Boslough, John. *Masters of Time: Cosmology at the End of Innocence*. London: J. M. Dent, 1992.

Brecht, Bertold. *Gedichte*, vol. 7. Frankfurt: Suhrkamp, 1964.

———. *Schriften zur Literatur und Kunst*, vol. 2. Frankfurt: Suhrkamp, 1967.

Breton, André. *Les vases communicantes. Oeuvres complètes*, vol. 2. Ed. Marguerite Bonnet. Paris: Gallimard, 1992.

Brower, Reuben A., ed. *On Translation*. Cambridge: Harvard, 1959.

Burke, Carolyn. "Translation Modified." *Engaging with Irigaray: Feminist Philosophy and Modern European Thought*. Eds. Carolyn Burke, Naomi Schor, Margaret Whitford. New York: Columbia UP, 1994.

Byrd, Don. "The Possibility of Measure in Olson's Maximus." *Boundary2* 2, No. 1/2 (1973–1974).

Cadiot, Olivier. *Red, Green & Black*. Trans. Charles Bernstein. Elmwood, CT: Potes & Poets, 1990.

———. *Future, ancien, figitif*. Paris. P.O.L., 1993.

———. *Future, Former, Fugitive*. Trans. Cole Swensen. New York: Roof Books, 1991.

Cage, John. *Silence*. Middletown, CT: Wesleyan UP, 1961.

Campos, Augusto de, Décio Pignatari, Haroldo de Campos. "Pilot Plan for Concrete Poetry." *Concrete Poetry*. Ed. Mary Ellen Solt. *Artes Hispanicas* 1, No. 3/4 (1968).

Campos, Haroldo de. "Transluciferation." *Ex* 4 (1985).

Carabelli, Giancarlo. "L'esperienza della scrittura." *Tempo Presente* (June 1964).

Celan, Paul. *Eingedunkelt: und Gedichte aus dem Umkreis von Eingedunkelt*. Frankfurt: Suhrkamp, 1991.

Cixous, Hélène. *Three Steps on the Ladder of Writing*. Trans. Sarah Cornell and Susan Sellers. New York: Columbia UP, 1993.

Cohen, Marcel. "Notes." *Le Travail de l'art* 2 (1998).

Cole, Norma. *Mars*. Berkeley, CA: Listening Chamber, 1994.

Colie, Rosalie. *Paradoxia Epidemica: The Renaissance Tradition of Paradox*. Princeton, NJ: Princeton UP, 1966.

Coolidge, Clark. "From Notebooks, 1976–82." *Code of Signals: Recent Writings in Poetics*. Ed. Michael Palmer. Berkeley, CA: North Atlantic Books, 1983.

Creeley, Robert. *Pieces*. New York: Scribner's, 1969.

———. *A Quick Graph: Collected Notes and Essays*. San Francisco: Four Seasons Foundation, 1970.

———. *The Collected Essays*. Berkeley: U of California P, 1989.

———. *Prefaces and Other Writings*. Quoted in *Postmodern American Poetry: A Norton Anthology*. Ed. Paul Hoover. New York: Norton, 1994.

Dahlhaus, Carl. *Ludwig van Beethoven*. Trans. Mary Whittall. Oxford: Clarendon Press, 1991.

Damaslo, Antonio. *Descartes' Error: Emotion, Reason, and the Human Brain*. New York: Avon Books, 1994.

Davey, Frank. "Six Readings of Olson's Maximus." *Boundary2* 2, No. 1/2 (1973–1974), 291–323.

Derrida, Jacques. *L'Écriture et la différance*. Paris: Editions du Seuil, 1967.

Dickinson, Emily. "Letter to Susan Gilbert Dickinson." *The Letters of Emily Dickinson*. Ed. Thomas H. Johnson. Cambridge: Harvard UP, 1958.

Dolin, Sharon. "Broken English." *AWP Chronicle* (December 1996).

D[oolittle], H[ilda]. *Hermetic Definition*. New York: New Directions, 1972.

Duncan, Robert. *The Opening of the Field*. New York: Grove Press, 1960.

———. "Ideas of the Meaning of Form." *Kulchur* 4 (1961).

———. *The Truth and Life of Myth: An Essay in Essential Autobiography*. Fremont, MI: Sumac Press, 1968.

———. "Towards an Open Universe." *The Poetics of the New American Poetry*. Ed. Donald Allen and Warren Tallman. New York: Grove Press, 1973.

———. "The Delirium of Meaning." *The Sin of the Book, Edmond Jabès*. Ed. Eric Gould. Lincoln: U of Nebraska P, 1985.

———. *Selected Prose*. Ed. Robert J. Bertholf. New York: New Directions, 1995.

Edson, Russell. "Commentary on 'The Tunnel.'" *The Prose Poem* 7 (1998).

Eliot, T. S. *Selected Prose*. Ed. Frank Kermode. New York: Farrar, Straus and Giroux, 1975.

Finlay, Ian Hamilton. *The Blue and the Brown Poems*. New York: Jargon, 1968.

Ford, Mark. "John Ashbery's *Flow Chart*." *Times Literary Supplement* (December 27, 1991).

Forster, Leonard. "Translation: An Introduction." *Aspects of Translation*. Ed. A. H. Smith. London: Secker and Warburg, 1958.

Foster, Edward. *The Space between Her Bed and Clock*. San Francisco: Norton Coker, 1993.

Fourcade, Dominique. *Rose-déclic*. Paris: P.O.L., 1984.

———. *Click-Rose*. Trans. Keith Waldrop. Los Angeles: Sun and Moon, 1996.

———. *IL*. Paris: P.O.L., 1994.

———. *Le sujet monotype*. Paris: P.O.L., 1997.

Freed, Donald. "Peter Weiss and the Theatre of the Future." *Drama Survey* 6 (fall 1967).

Frémon, Jean. *L'île des morts*. Paris: P.O.L., 1994.

Gadamer, Hans-Georg. *Philosophical Hermeneutics*. Trans. David E. Linge. Berkeley: U of California P, 1976.

Galilei, Galileo. *Dialogue Concerning the Two Chief World Systems, Ptolemaic and Copernican*. Trans. Stillman Drake. Berkeley: U of California P, 1953.

Genette, Gérard. *Figures*, vol. III. Paris: Editions du Seuil, 1972.

Gibson, James Jerome. *The Senses Considered as Perceptual Systems*. Boston, MA: Houghton Mifflin, 1966.

Gizzi, Peter, ed. *Exact Change Yearbook* 1 (1995).

Goethe, J. W. v. "West-Östlicher Divan: Noten und Abhandlungen." *Werke: Hamburger Ausgabe*, vol. 2. Ed. Erich Trunz. Hamburg: Christian Wegner, 1949.

———. *Faust, Werke.* Hamburger Ausgabe, vol. 3. Hamburg: Christian Wegner, 1949.

———. "Von deutscher Baukunst." *Werke: Hamburger Ausgabe*, vol. 12. Hamburg: Christian Wegner, 1953.

Gomringer, Eugen. *Worte sind Schatten: Die Konstellationen, 1951–1968*. Hamburg: Rowohlt, 1969.

Gould, Eric, ed. *The Sin of the Book*. Lincoln: U of Nebraska P, 1985.

Grangaud, Michelle. *Poèmes fondus*. Paris: P.O.L., 1997.

Guest, Barbara. *The Countess from Minneapolis*. Providence, RI: Burning Deck, 1976.

———. *Stripped Tales*. Berkeley, CA: Kelsey St. Press, 1995.

———. *Rocks on a Platter: Notes on Literature*. Middletown, CT: Wesleyan UP, 1999.

———. *Miniatures and Other Poems*. Middletown, CT: Wesleyan UP, 2002.

Guglielmi, Joseph. "Edmond Jabès et la fascination du désert." *Critique* 296 (January 1972).

Hallberg, Robert von. "Olson, Whitehead, and the Objectivists." *Boundary2* 2, No. 1/2 (1973–1974).

Harryman, Carla. *Under the Bridge*. San Francisco: This, 1980.

H. D. See D[oolittle], H[ilda].

Heelan, Patrick A. *Space-Perception and the Philosophy of Science*. Berkeley: U of California P, 1983.

Heissenbüttel, Helmut. *Über Literatur*. Olten: Walter, 1966.

———. *Textbücher 1–6*. Stuttgart: Klett-Cotta, 1980.

Hejinian, Lyn. *Gesualdo*. Berkeley, CA: Tuumba, 1978.

———. *My Life*. Providence, RI: Burning Deck, 1980.

———. *The Guard*. Berkeley, CA: Tuumba, 1984.

———. "The Rejection of Closure." *Poetics Journal* 4 (May 1984).

———. "Two Stein Talks: Language and Realism; Grammar and Landscape." *Temblor* 3 (1986), 128–40.

———. "The Person." *Temblor* 4 (1986).

———. *The Cell*. Los Angeles: Sun and Moon, 1992.

Hocquard, Emmanuel. "Prenez-le vivant." *Critique* 347 (April 1976).

———. *Un privé à Tanger*. Paris: P.O.L., 1987.

——. *Thèorie des tables.* Paris: P.O.L., 1992.

——. *Theory of Tables.* Trans. Michael Palmer. Providence, RI: Oblëk Editions, 1994.

——. "Blank Spots." Trans. Stacy Doris. *Boundary2* 26, No. 1 (spring 1999).

Hölderlin, Friedrich. "Anmerkungen zum Oedipus." *Sämtliche Werke,* vol. 5. Ed. Friedrich Beissner. Stuttgart: Kohlhammer, 1954.

Hoover, Paul, ed. *Postmodern American Poetry: A Norton Anthology.* New York: W. W. Norton, 1994.

Howe, Susan. *The Western Borders.* Berkeley, CA: Tuumba, 1976.

——. *Singularities.* Middletown, CT: Wesleyan UP, 1990.

Humboldt, Wilhelm von. "Aeschylos Agamemnon metrisch übersetzt." Trans. Sharon Sloan. *Theories of Translation: An Anthology of Essays from Dryden to Derrida.* Ed. Rainer Schulte and John Biguenet. Chicago: U of Chicago P, 1992.

Jabès, Edmond. *Le Livre des Questions,* 7 vols. Paris: Gallimard, 1963–1974.

——. *The Book of Questions: Vol. I* [The Book of Questions, The Book of Yukel, Return to the Book]. Trans. Rosmarie Waldrop. Middletown, CT: Wesleyan UP, 1991.

——. *The Book of Questions: Vol. II* [Yaël, Elya, Aely, El, or the Last Book]. Trans. Rosmarie Waldrop. Middletown, CT: Wesleyan UP, 1991.

——. *The Book of Dialogue.* Trans. Rosmarie Waldrop. Middletown, CT: Wesleyan UP, 1987.

——. *The Book of Shares.* Trans. Rosmarie Waldrop. Chicago: U of Chicago P, 1989.

——. "Repondre à repondre pour." Trans. Rosmarie Waldrop. *Acts* 10, 1989.

——. *The Book of Resemblances.* Trans. Rosmarie Waldrop. Middletown, CT: Wesleyan UP, 1990.

——. *Intimations, The Desert.* Trans. Rosmarie Waldrop. Middletown, CT: Wesleyan UP, 1991.

——. *Le Livre de l'Hospitalité.* Paris: Gallimard, 1991.

——. *The Ineffaceable The Unperceived.* Middletown, CT: Wesleyan UP, 1992.

——. *The Book of Margins.* Trans. Rosmarie Waldrop. Chicago: U of Chicago P, 1993.

——. *A Foreigner Carrying in the Crook of His Arm a Tiny Book.* Trans. Rosmarie Waldrop. Middletown, CT: Wesleyan UP, 1993.

——. *The Little Book of Unsuspected Subversion.* Trans. Rosmarie Waldrop. Stanford, CA: Stanford UP, 1996.

Jaeggi, Urs. *Literatur und Politik.* Frankfurt: Suhrkamp, 1972.

Jakobson, Roman. "Linguistics and Poetics." *Style in Language.* Ed. Thomas A. Sebeok. Cambridge, MA: MIT Press, 1960.

Jakobson, Roman, and Morris Halle. *Fundamentals of Language.* The Hague: Mouton, 1956.

Jandl, Ernst. *Sprechblasen*. Neuwied: Luchterhand, 1968.

Joron, Andrew. *The Emergency of Poetry*. Berkeley, CA: Velocities Chapbooks, 2002.

Judt, Tony. "Americans and the War." *New York Review of Books* (November 15, 2001).

Juliet, Charles. *Recontres avec Samuel Beckett*. Montpellier: Fata Morgana, 1986.

Kafka, Franz. *Description of a Struggle*. Trans. Tania and James Stern. New York: Schocken Books, 1958.

Kellerer, Christoph. *Object trouvé Surrealisme Zen*. Köln: DuMont, 1982.

Klemperer, Victor. *Die unbewältigte Sprache*. München: dtv, 1969.

Krauss, Rosalind. *The Optical Unconscious*. Cambridge, MA: MIT Press, 1993.

Kristeva, Julia. *La révolution du langage poétique*. Paris: Editions du Seuil, 1974.

Langer, Susanne. *Philosophy in a New Key: A Study in the Symbolism of Reason, Rite, and Art*. New York: Mentor Books, 1948.

Laroque, Françoise de. "La langue et l'équarrisseur." *Action Poétique* 87 (1982).

Lattimore, Richmond. "Practical Notes on Translating Greek Poetry." *On Translation*. Ed. Reuben A. Brower. New York: Oxford UP, 1966.

Leiris, Michel. "Le Caput mortuum ou la femme de l'alchimiste." *Les Cahiers du double: Constat* 1 (fall 1977).

Leroi-Gourhan, André. *L'homme et la matière*. Paris: Albin Michel, 1943 and 1971.

Levin, Samuel R. *Linguistic Structures in Poetry*. The Hague: Mouton, 1969.

Lindberg, David C. *Theories of Vision from al-Kindi to Kepler*. Chicago: U of Chicago P, 1976.

Linhartová, Vera. *Mehrstimmige Zerstreuung*. Trans. Dorothea Neumärker. München: Deutscher Taschenbuch Verlag, 1971.

Lispector, Clarice. *Agua Viva*. Trans. R. H. de Oliveira Machado. Paris: Des Femmes, 1981.

Mac Low, Jackson. *4 Trains*. Providence, RI: Burning Deck, 1974.

Malraux, André. *Les Noyers de l'Altenburg*. Paris: Gallimard, 1948.

Mandelstam, Osip. *Selected Poems*. Trans. Clarence Brown and W. S. Merwin. New York: Atheneum, 1974.

McCaffery, Steve. *North of Intention: Critical Writings, 1973–1986*. New York: Roof Books, 1986.

Merleau-Ponty, Maurice. *Phénoménologie de la perception*. Paris: Gallimard, 1945.

Miller, Perry. *Roger Williams: His Contribution to the American Tradition*. New York: Atheneum, 1966.

Mon, Franz. *Texte über Texte*. Neuwied: Luchterhand, 1970.

Monroe, Jonathan. "Untranslatable Communities, Productive Translation, and Public Transport." *We Who Love to Be Astonished: Experimental Women's Writing and Performance Poetics*. Ed. Laura Hinton and Cynthia Hogue. Tuscaloosa: U of Alabama P, 2002.

Mottram, Eric. *Selected Poems*. Twickenham: North & South, 1989.

Musil, Robert. *Der Mann ohne Eigenschaften*. Ed. Adolf Frise Reinbeck.: Towohlt, 1952.

Nida, Eugene A. *Toward a Science of Translating*. Leiden: E. J. Brill, 1964.

Niedecker, Lorine. *The Granite Pail: Selected Poems*. Ed. Cid Corman. San Francisco: North Point Press, 1985.

Novalis, "Blütenstaub," *Schriften,* vol. 2. Ed. Richard Samuel. Darmstadt: Wissenschaftliche Buchgesellschaft, 1965.

O'Brien, Justin. "From French to English." *On Translation*. Ed. Reuben A. Brower. Cambridge, MA: Harvard UP, 1959.

Olson, Charles. *The Maximus Poems*. New York: Jargon/Corinth Books, 1960.

———. *Call Me Ishmael*. [1947]. San Francisco: City Lights, 1966.

———. *Human Universe and Other Essays*. Ed. Donald Allen. New York: Grove Press, 1967.

———. *Maximus IV, V, VI*. London: Cape Goliard Press, 1968.

———. *Causal Mythology*. San Francisco: Four Seasons Foundation, 1969.

———. *The Special View of History*. Berkeley, CA: Oyez, 1970.

Oppen, George. *Collected Poems*. New York: New Directions, 1975.

———. "Notes on Prosody?" Quoted in Paul Auster, "A Few Words in Praise of George Oppen." *Paideuma* 10, No. 1 (spring 1981).

Palmer, Michael. *First Figure*. San Francisco: North Point Press, 1984.

———. *At Passages*. New York: New Directions, 1995.

———. Interview with Peter Gizzi. *Exact Change Yearbook* 1 (1995).

Palmer, Michael, ed. *Code of Signals: Recent Writings in Poetics*. Berkeley, CA: North Atlantic Books, 1983.

Pearlman, Daniel D. *The Barb of Time: On the Unity of Ezra Pound's Cantos*. New York: Oxford UP, 1969.

Perloff, Marjorie, ed. *Postmodern Genres*. Norman: U of Oklahoma P, 1989.

Poggioli, Renato. "The Added Artificer." *On Translation*. Ed. Reuben A. Brower. New York: Oxford UP, 1966.

Portugal, Anne. *Le plus simple appareil*. Paris: P.O.L., 1992.

———. *Nude*. Trans. Norma Cole. Berkeley, CA: Kelsey St. Press, 2001.

Pound, Ezra. *The Literary Essays of Ezra Pound*. Ed. T. S. Eliot. Norfolk, CT: New Directions. 1954.

Proust, Marcel. *Contre Sainte-Beuve*. Ed. Pierre Clarac. Paris: Gallimard, 1971.

Prynne, J. H. *Kitchen Poems*. London: Cape Goliard, 1968.

Quine, Willard Van Orman. *From a Logical Point of View*. New York: Harper, 1961.

Ratcliffe, Stephen. "Two Hejinian Talks." *Temblor* 6 (1987).

Retallack, Joan. "Post-Scriptum—High-Modern." *Postmodern Genres*. Ed Marjorie Perloff. Norman: U of Oklahoma P, 1989.

———. "Blue Notes on the Know Ledge." *Poetics Journal* 10 (1998).

Reznikoff, Charles. *Testimony I: The United States, 1885–1890: Recitative.* Santa Barbara, CA: Black Sparrow, 1978.

Ricoeur, Paul. *La métaphore vive.* Paris: Editions du Seuil, 1975.

Riffaterre, Michael. *Semiotics of Poetry.* Bloomington: Indiana UP, 1978.

Rilke, Rainer Maria. *Sämtliche Werke,* vol. 1. Ed. Ernst Zinn. Frankfurt/Main: Insel, 1955.

Roubaud, Jacques. *Some Thing Black.* Trans. Rosmarie Waldrop. 1986. Elmwood Park, IL: Dalkey Archive Press, 1990.

———. *Le grand incendie de Londres.* Paris: Le Seuil, 1989.

———. *The Great Fire of London.* Trans. Dominic Di Bernardi. Elmwood Park, IL: Dalkey Archive, 1991.

———. *The Plurality of Worlds of Lewis.* Trans. Rosmarie Waldrop. 1991. Elmwood Park, IL: Dalkey Archive Press, 1995.

———. *L'Invention du fils de Leoprepes.* Saulxures: Editions Circé, 1993.

———. *Poésie, etcetera: ménage.* Paris: Stock, 1995.

———. "Hypothèse du compact." *Revue de littérature générale* 1 (1995).

———. *Mathématiques.* Paris: Le Seuil, 1997.

Royet-Journoud, Claude. *Le renversement.* Paris: Gallimard, 1972.

———. *Reversal.* Trans. Keith Waldrop. Providence, RI: Hellcoal, 1973.

———. Interview with Mathieu Bénézet. *France Nouvelle* (November 27, 1978).

———. *La notion d'obstacle.* Paris: Gallimard, 1978.

———. *Lettre de Symi.* Montpellier: Fata Morgana, 1980.

———. *Les objets contiennent l'infini.* Paris: Gallimard, 1983.

———. Interview with Natacha Michel. *Le Perroquet* 35 (February 13, 1984).

———. *The Notion of Obstacle.* Trans. Keith Waldrop. Windsor, VT: Awede Press, 1985.

———. Interview with Keith and Rosmarie Waldrop. *Lingo* 4 (1995).

———. *Les natures indivisibles.* Paris: Gallimard, 1997.

Royet-Journoud, Claude, and Emmanuel Hocquard. "Conversation Dated 2/8/1982." Trans. G. Young. *Code of Signals.* Ed. Michael Palmer. Berkeley, CA: North Atlantic, 1983.

Rühm, Gerhard. *Gesammelte Gedichte und visuelle Texte.* Hamburg: Rowohlt, 1970.

Salisbury, Neal. *Manitou and Providence: Indians, Europeans, and the Making of New England, 1500–1643.* New York: Oxford UP, 1982.

Sartre, Jean-Paul. "What Is Literature?" *Situations,* vol. 2. Paris: Gallimard, 1948.

Saussure, Ferdinand de. *Cours de linguistique générale.* Paris: Payot, 1949.

Scalapino, Leslie. *Considering How Exaggerated Music Is.* San Francisco: North Point Press, 1982.

———. *The Front Matter, Dead Souls.* Middletown, CT: Wesleyan UP, 1996.

———. *New Time.* Middletown, CT: Wesleyan UP, 1999.

Schlegel, Friedrich. "Athenaeums-Fragmente." *Kritische Schriften.* Ed. Wolf-dietrich Rasch. München: Carl Hanser, 1956.

Schleiermacher, Friedrich. "Über die verschiedenen Methoden des Über-setzens." Trans. Waltraud Bartscht. *Theories of Translation.* Eds. Rainer Schulte and John Biguenet. Chicago: U of Chicago P, 1992.

Schmidt, Siegfried. *Ästhetische Prozesse.* Köln: Kiepenheuer and Witsch, 1971.

Scholem, Gershom G. *Major Trends in Jewish Mysticism.* New York: Schocken, 1961.

Scholes, Robert. *Structuralism in Literature.* New Haven, CT: Yale UP, 1974.

Schulte, Rainer, and John Biguenet, eds. *Theories of Translation.* Chicago: U of Chicago P, 1992.

Sebald, Winfried G. *Schwindel, Gefühle.* Frankfurt: Eichborn, 1990.

Shklovsky, Viktor. *Theory of Prose.* Trans. Benjamin Sher. Elmwood Park, IL: Dalkey Archive Press, 1990.

Silliman, Ron. *Paradise.* Providence: Burning Deck, 1985.

Smith, A. H., ed. *Aspects of Translation.* London: Secker and Warburg, 1958.

Snodgrass, W. D. *Six Troubadour Songs.* Providence, RI: Burning Deck, 1977.

Solt, Mary Ellen, ed. *Concrete Poetry. Artes Hispanicas* 1, No. 3/4 (1968).

Spire, André. *Plaisir poétique et plaisir musculaire.* New York: Vanni, 1949.

Stein, Gertrude. *Selected Writings.* Ed. Carl van Vechten. New York: Modern Library, 1962.

Steiner, Wendy. *The Scandal of Pleasure: Art in an Age of Fundamentalism.* Chicago: U of Chicago P, 1995.

Sternberger, Dolf, Gerhard Storz, and Wilhelm E. Suskind. *Aus dem Wörter-buch des Unmenschen.* Hamburg: Claassen, 1957.

Stramm, August. *Das Werk.* Wiesbaden: Limes, 1963.

Straus, Erwin W. *Vom Sinn der Sinne.* Berlin: J. Springer, 1956.

——. *Phenomenological Psychology.* New York: Basic Books, 1966.

Taggart, John. "Were You." *Code of Signals.* Ed. Michael Palmer. Berkeley, CA: North Atlantic Books, 1983.

Teunissen, John J., and Evelyn J. Hinz, eds. *Roger Williams: A Key into the Lan-guage of America.* Detroit: Wayne State UP, 1973.

Tzara, Tristan. "7 Manifestes Dada," *Oeuvres,* vol. 1. Paris: Flammarion, 1975.

Underhill, Evelyn. *Mysticism: A Study in the Nature and Development of Man's Spiritual Consciousness.* New York: Noonday Press, 1955.

Valéry, Paul. "Introduction à la méthode de Léonard de Vinci" and "Varia-tions sur les Bucoliques." *Oeuvres.* Ed. Jean Hytier. Vol. 1. Paris: Gallimard, 1957.

——. "Monsieur Teste." *Oeuvres,* vol. 2, 1960.

——. *Aesthetics.* Trans. Ralph Manheim. Bollingen Series, vol. 13. New York: Pantheon Books, 1964.

Venuti, Lawrence. *The Translator's Invisibility: A History of Translation.* London: Routledge, 1995.

Vygotsky, L. S. *Thought and Language*. Ed. and trans. Eugenia Hanfmann and Gertrude Vakar. Cambridge, Mass.: MIT Press, 1962.

Waldrop, Keith. *The Quest for Mount Misery*. Isla Vista, CA: Turkey Press, 1983.

———. *A Ceremony Somewhere Else*. Windsor, VT: Awede Press, 1984.

———. Interview with Peter Gizzi. Part 2. *The Germ* 5 (summer 2001).

Waldrop, Rosmarie. *Against Language?* The Hague: Mouton, 1971.

———. *The Aggressive Ways of the Casual Stranger*. New York: Random House, 1972.

———. Edmond Jabès and the Impossible Circle." *Sub-Stance* 5/6 (spring 1973).

———. *The Road Is Everywhere or Stop This Body*. Columbia, MO: Open Places, 1978.

———. *When They Have Senses*. Providence, RI: Burning Deck, 1980.

———. *Differences for Four Hands*. Philadelphia: Singing Horse Press, 1984.

———. *Streets Enough to Welcome Snow*. Barrytown, NY: Station Hill Press, 1986.

———. *The Hanky of Pippin's Daughter*. Barrytown, NY: Station Hill Press, 1987.

———. *The Reproduction of Profiles*. New York: New Directions, 1987.

———. *A Form/Of Taking/It All*. Barrytown, NY: Station Hill Press, 1990.

———. *Lawn of Excluded Middle*. New York: Tender Buttons, 1993.

———. *A Key into the Language of America*. New York: New Directions, 1994.

———. *Split Infinites*. Philadelphia: Singing Horse Press, 1998.

———. *Reluctant Gravities*. New York: New Directions, 1999.

Weiss, Peter. *Die Verfolgung und Ermordung Jean Paul Marats dargestellt durch die Schauspielgruppe des Hopizes zu Charenton unter Anleitung des Herrn de Sade*. Frankfurt: Suhrkamp, 1965.

———. "Interview." *New York Times* (December 26, 1965).

———. *Materialien zu Peter Weiss' Marat/Sade*. Ed. Karlheinz Braun. Frankfurt: Suhrkamp, 1967.

Whitehead, Alfred North. *Modes of Thought*. New York: Free Press, 1968.

Whiteman, Michael. *Philosophy of Space and Time*. London: Allen and Unwin, 1967.

Williams, Emmet, ed. *Anthology of Concrete Poetry*. New York: Something Else Press, 1967.

Williams, William Carlos. *In the American Grain*. New York: New Directions, 1966.

———. *Selected Essays*. New York: New Directions, 1969.

———. *Paterson,* Book IV. Ed. Christopher MacGowan. New York: New Directions, 1992.

Willis, Elizabeth. *The Human Abstract*. New York: Penguin, 1995.

Wittgenstein, Ludwig. *Philosophical Investigations*. Trans. G. E. M. Anscombe. Oxford: Basil Blackwell, 1968.

———. *On Certainty*. Trans. Denis Paul and G. E. M. Anscombe. New York: Harper, 1969.

———. *Zettel*. Trans. G. E. M. Anscombe. Berkeley: U of California P, 1970.

Worringer, Wilhelm. *Abstraction and Empathy*. Trans. Michael Bullock. New York: International Universities Press, 1953.

Yeats, W. B. *A Vision*. [1937]. New York: Collier Books, 1966.

Zukofsky, Celia, and Louis. *Catullus*. London: Cape Goliard, 1969.

Zukofsky, Louis. *Prepositions: The Collected Critical Essays of Louis Zukofsky*. New York: Horizon Press, 1967.

———. "A." [1959]. Berkeley: U of California P, 1978.

———. *Le Style Apollinaire: The Writing of Guillaume Apollinaire*. Ed. Serge Gavronsky. Middletown, CT: Wesleyan UP, 2004.

Index